STOP THE Press!

An Inside Story of the Tabloids in Ireland

An Inside Story of the Tabloids in Ireland

John Kierans

MERLIN

PUBLISHING

First published in 2009 by
Merlin Publishing
Newmarket Hall, Cork Street,
Dublin 8, Ireland
Tel: +353 1 4535866
Fax: +353 1 4535930
publishing@merlin.ie
www.merlinwolfhound.com

Text © 2009 John Kierans

Editing, Design and Layout © 2009 Merlin Publishing
Except
Photographs © of individuals or institutions listed underneath each
image in the plate sections

ISBN 978 1907162 022

A CIP catalogue record for this book is available from the British
Library.

10 9 8 7 6 5 4 3 2 1

Typeset by Artwerk Limited
Cover Design by Fairways Design
Front Cover image courtesy of www.istockphoto.com © Roger Lecuyer
Back Cover Image courtesy of www.imagefile.ie
Printed and bound in Denmark, by Norhaven A/S

Dedicated to Karen, Katie and JP

Acknowledgements

There is a saying in newspapers that you are only as good as your last story. But equally you are also only as good as the people who helped you along the way. I've been talking for years about writing a book but early this year my wife Karen and my two kids, Katie and JP, pushed me into it. They never once complained when I was writing for hours on end at the weekends.

I'd like to thank all my colleagues in the *Daily Mirror* family who encouraged me and gave me all their support, especially my boss London Editor Richard Wallace, the Deputy Editor Conor Hanna, Managing Editor Eugene Duffy and our General Manager in Ireland Joanne McGreevy. Also our Deputy Editor in Ireland, Kevan Furbank, Northern Irish Editor, Gerry Millar, the Editor of the *Irish Sunday Mirror* Chris McCashin, our news desk in Dublin, Niall Moonan and James McNamara, and our senior reporter, fellow Drogheda man Pat Flanagan, plus the wonderful Maeve Quigley, Aine Hegarty and Mr Showbiz himself Paul Martin.

I have to thank Michelle Treacy for all her research and without whom this book would not be possible, Nicola Doonan and Jenny Murray for wrecking their heads from time to time, and our Marketing Manager Joanne Friel.

I have to thank many of my former colleagues for their help and advice along the way, especially Sean Boyne, Neil Leslie, Nicola Tallant, Paul Williams, Cathal O'Shea, John Donlon, Hugh Jordan and Jim McDowell, all of the *Sunday World*. Big Jim incidentally came up with the name for this book over a pint in the Duke of York bar in Belfast.

One of my great heroes is Paddy Clancy, the country's veteran tabloid hack and the founder of *The Irish Sun*, and a man whose friendship I have enjoyed throughout my career. Paddy was always there for me whenever I needed a few wise words and was of great assistance during my research.

I would also never have got to where I am now without having soldiered on the road with the best photographers in the country, Charlie Collins, Alan Lewis, and my great old pal John McAvinney, all of whom put manners on me and kept me focussed from time to time.

I'd also like to give a special word of mention to Joe Gorrod in our Belfast office for his wonderful humour, Craig Mackenzie, Piers Morgan, Diarmuid McDermot, Miriam Lord, the late Tom McPhail of the Ireland International News Agency in Dublin, and the late great Ted Oliver for guiding me through the bright lights of London.

I also want to salute Brian Hitchen for giving me my break in London and men like Bill Akass, Nick Parker, Phil Hannaford, Ramsey Smith, Gordon Hay, Don Mackay, Ian McKerron, and the late Tommy Merrin and Ron Ricketts who all helped me on the road across the globe. I will always cherish each of their friendships.

I have to thank all the Kierans family, my parents Johnny and Carmel and my brothers and sisters Geraldine, Marie, Betty, Padraig, Peter and Carmel – I love you all to bits. There will always be a special place in my heart to my sister-in-law Rosemary, her late husband Mark and their two beautiful children Emma and Lucy Mullen, who are like sisters to my kids.

I must also thank the Managing Director of Merlin Publishing Chenile Keogh for all her help, support and encouragement on this project and Paul Feldstein of the Feldstein Agency who did all the sub-editing. I hope I wasn't too difficult to deal with.

I have to personally thank the people of Drogheda for putting up with me for all these years and if I upset any of them with my stories I apologise. Everyone in Drogheda knows I never forgot where I came from.

And last but not least I have to thank my close friends Kieran and Mary Carr, Sandra and Declan Finnegan, Karen and Sylvio Vechionni, Mattie and Jackie Rice, Tony Dillon, Mick Doyle, Declan Hoey, and Martin Kelly for always being there for us over the years through thick and thin.

I hope you all enjoy this book.

Contents

Glossary of Newspaper Terms

Big hit	A story that gets a lot of space
Copy tasting	Going through the day's stories to decide what is put in the newspaper and what goes where
Doorstep	Go to a subject's house or premises, uninvited, to try and question them about a story
Fill-in	Provide the details of a story
Fixer	A freelancer used on a story to facilitate details, usually someone with local connections
Flyer	A story that could be true, but has not been verified
Front up	Confront a subject over a story
Leader	Editorial comments or opinions from the newspaper's editors
Off stone	A newspaper's deadline for going to pr.ess
PR	A public relations person
Snatch shot	A photograph taken from a distance without the subject's knowledge
Splash	Page 1 lead story
Stand up	Prove or verify a story
Wipeout	A story taking up all of page 1.

Introduction

It is often said that newspapers are in the blood and they are certainly in mine. My father Johnny was a compositor on our local paper, the *Drogheda Independent*, and he used to cover sport at the weekends to earn extra money to help rear his seven kids. From when I was three years of age I was brought around the county to GAA matches, coursing meetings and greyhound racing in Navan and Dundalk, where my elderly granny Agnes, who loved a flutter, would regularly take the bookies to the cleaners!

Every Sunday night my dad would sit for hours on end typing up his reports and occasionally sending the odd piece to the nationals. It was fun, it was exciting and it was what I wanted to do.

When I was eight years old I got a part time job taking the hot metal picture plates that were used in the edition off the wooden blocks. This would take two hours a week and occasionally I would cut my hand with the screw driver trying to separate the block and the plate.

By the time I was 13 years old I was asked to be a runner at the local elections. Local radio was in its infancy and I had to telephone the results in from the counting hall to the editor back at the office, who would then put them up on big posters in the front window of the *Drogheda Independent* offices in Shop Street, Drogheda. Hundreds of people would gather to see what the latest news was.

Working with great local hacks like Jim McCullen, Tom Corr, Anne Kane and Brian Conyngham, I soon got the bug. I felt really important and never had as much fun in my life.

The following year I got a job in the Boyne Valley Honey factory thanks to owner Malachy McCloskey, and my job for eight hours a day was to put the empty glass honey jars on the assembly line. The money was good but it was boring, and no disrespect to Mr McCloskey, I hated every minute of it. Putting on one glass jar after another all day long drove me around the twist but there was no escape; there was no walking away.

My father's view was if you don't study that's what you'll be doing for the rest of your life. Working in a factory like that was bloody hard. In fact to an energetic teenager like me, it was soul destroying. But it made me appreciate that every day millions of people right across the globe do jobs they detest because they have to feed their families. I was determined that I would not be one of them.

After I finished my Leaving Certificate exam in June 1980 I landed a job as a trainee accountant with Olan Allen but I found numbers so boring that I lasted only six months. I was paid £14 a week and gave half of it to my mother. But I got my lucky break before the end of the year.

A job for a cub reporter came up on the *Drogheda Independent* or the *DI,* as we affectionately called it, and by some fluke I got it. Jobs in the eighties in Ireland were very scarce and over 400 hopefuls applied for this one. My dad put a word in for me, but there was no guarantee I'd get it. The applicants were narrowed down to six candidates for the interview.

I remember going in to Editor Kevin Mulligan and being scared out of my wits. I knew I had the nose for a story but I wasn't the world's greatest writer. Kevin, thankfully, was only interested in stories and he wanted someone who knew everyone in the town and was prepared to put himself about. All the years coming in and out of the *DI* offices stood to me.

I started in the *Drogheda Independent* on January 7, 1981 on £50 a week, which was fantastic. I was 18 years of age. On the same day a young reporter called Miriam Lord started her career in journalism at the *DI,* and now has a highly successful column in the *Irish Times*.

I remember my first job, which was the opening of a new Irish speaking primary school Scoil Aonghusa. Our local Bishop James Lennon was there and all the members of Drogheda Corporation including my good old friend Alderman Frank Godfrey, who for years was the proud source of many a good story. I went home to my Mam for my dinner at lunch time and I recall her asking me how I was getting on. I told her it was great, there were tea and sandwiches and the most amazing buns. It certainly beat working in a honey factory. A reporter's job was the bee's knees.

I spent three happy years on the *Drogheda Independent,* where the deputy editor Jim McCullen religiously made me buy the *Daily Mirror* every day to learn how to write tabloid. All I ever heard was write one sentence paragraphs. One sentence paragraphs – that was the *Mirror's* style. Little did I realise that one day I'd end up working on one of the world's greatest newspapers.

Jim also had a great news sense and he had no qualms about passing the tricks of the trade on to me. Tom Corr and Anne Kane taught me how to cover the courts and the council meetings. They put tremendous time, effort and patience into this student and it was training I'll never forget. Then Brian Conyngham, one of the tightest sub-editors I've ever met, and

Kevin Mulligan kicked my ass into shape. Kevin once made me rewrite a story 14 times until it was right, and to this day I thank him for it.

Newspapers are the most exciting place in the world to work. Every day is different and you just don't know what is going to happen next. And to be quite honest, that is what gives each and every one of us the buzz.

I often joke that it is not a real job; that the loyal readers who pay our wages day in day out are the ones doing the real work out there, in the factories and on the building sites across the nation.

Newspapers are exciting and challenging places to be but most important of all they are great fun. I hope this book gives you an insight into the great and rewarding times I've had along the way.

Sunday World
1985-1988

CHAPTER 1

She was old enough to be my mother. The big busty blonde had her hair in a pony tail, yellow teeth and a real working class, northside Dublin accent. "Come in love, it's freezing out there," she said as I was let into the seedy massage parlour. The basement flat of a rundown Georgian building in the city's Mountjoy Square was the secret location of one of the capital's busiest brothels, and we were about to expose it.

I was anxious and nervous as I walked down the steps to press the intercom buzzer. The Madame had a red top on and a short black skirt halfway up her ass. She looked at me suspiciously, probably wondering what a 22 year old young lad was doing in her house of sin, a place normally the preserve of dirty old men. I asked her if I could have a massage; I'd hurt me back playing football and needed a rubdown.

She asked me twice was I sure I was in the right place! I said I was and paid the £10 charge, and was ushered into a small room with a bed pushed up against the wall. It was dimly lit by a lamp on a small table in the corner, which also had a bottle of baby oil and talcum powder appropriately placed there. The woman, who was easily in her late fifties, threw me a towel, asked me to strip off, said she was just "finishing off a client", and she'd be with me in a few minutes.

My heart was thumping like mad as I lay there naked wondering what in the name of God had I got myself into. I'd worked for five years on the local papers in Drogheda, Co

Louth, covering the corporation meetings, the courts, writing up obituaries — all the mundane bread and butter issues of small town life, and here I was going undercover for Ireland's biggest tabloid newspaper, the *Sunday World*, and my trousers were on the floor.

Sex was its bread and butter, and the punters loved hard-hitting stories about the hookers in the capital. By the mid-1980s there were at least 40 brothels operating under the guise of massage parlours, and they all advertised their business in underground magazines sold in bars and nightclubs. We'd come across this one after a tip-off from the Garda Vice Squad, and the word was that it was a popular haunt with some politicians, a judge, and a number of our top legal eagles. We'd heard a few names on the grapevine, but we'd no pictures of them coming in or out, and little proof. The cops couldn't be bothered raiding most of these places, as they were up to their eyes fighting the heroin tide flooding the country at the time. As long as the girls didn't peddle smack they didn't really care.

The Madame returned, removed the towel and started rubbing my back. Would I like oil or powder? I didn't mind either way, but she advised that if I was married I'd better avoid the oil in case my wife smelled it when I got home. I told her I was alright, I was single, and I'd go with the powder. Before I knew it she'd offered to strip off, claiming she wanted to get me "warmed up". I told her to keep her clothes on, and asked if we could just talk for a while.

We got chatting and since I was half her age she seemed to like me. I asked what her name was and she said to call her whatever I liked. I explained I'd never been to a place like this before and didn't know what to expect. She said she'd give me a full body massage and then I could have "extras" if I wanted.

Her price list was very clear – £15 for hand relief, £30 for Swedish (oral sex) and £50 for full blown intercourse for half an hour.

I kept her talking and started quizzing her on what sort of people her clients were. She admitted to having two TDs and a Senator, and that one of them loved a bit of bondage. She'd often get him to bend over and give him a good spanking! It was all a bit of fun, no one got hurt, and most of the clients were married men who were no longer having sex with their wives.

As pleasant as she was, the Madame didn't do anything for me. I was under strict instructions not to sample the goods on offer or I would jeopardise the investigation, so I very politely made my excuses and left. I ran up the steps at a hundred miles an hour, anxious to get the hell away from the place and relieved I had my first brothel bust under my belt.

Within minutes I was on the phone to my news desk, where they were directing operations like military commanders in a battlefield. They had a team of reporters hitting several sex dens as they lined up the big scoop for the weekend. Every time the *Sunday World* needed to boost sales, a brothel exposé would do the trick, especially since its catchphrase "Are you getting it every Sunday" was known the length and breadth of the country.

The paper wrote about so many whorehouses in those days that the standard joke in the newspaper business was that its journalists would slide off a leather couch they'd so much baby oil on their bodies.

* * *

The *Sunday World* was started by Gerry McGuinness, the cinema usher turned advertising guru who, along with his initial partner, Hugh McLaughlin, saw the British press barons making a mint sending their kiss and tell scandal sheets into Ireland every Sunday, and decided that there was a gap in the market and room for a full blown Irish tabloid.

The *Sunday People,* the *News of the World,* and the *Sunday Express* were a must for the people of Ireland in the repressive years of the late Sixties, in a society where sex was taboo, contraception was banned, living in sin abhorred and children born out of wedlock treated as bastards. The country was crying out for its own down-market rag with Irish girls in bikinis on page one, randy priests replacing dirty three-in-a-bed vicars, and home grown stars of the showband era like Dickie Rock and Joe Dolan spilling the beans on their fame and fortune.

McGuinness hadn't a bottomless pit of cash but saw his opportunity. In March 1973 he remortgaged his house in Castleknock and borrowed to get his dream off the ground. He was part owner of the Creation Group, which published a number of magazines from their print plant in Drumcondra.

Gerry was a natural born publisher who had earned his bread and butter in ad agencies around the city, but he was gifted just like Rupert Murdoch, with an eye for a story and a great nose for what ordinary people wanted. He would have made a brilliant journalist himself.

He recruited a fine editor in Joe Kennedy, who gave up the top job at the *Evening Herald* to join him, a hungry pack of young reporters from around the country, a genius of a columnist in Kevin Marron, and Ireland's first colour paper was born.

Nobody expected Gerry to succeed, but from a sales point of view the paper was an instant success. Circulation soared with the weekly diet of gossip, TV, sex, showbiz and exposés, yet advertising was slow. The advertising industry, aligned to the old guard of the *Sunday Independent* and the *Sunday Press,* were reluctant to support the paper, but eventually they couldn't ignore market forces, primarily the numbers, and the *Sunday World* became a runaway success.

The Creation Group went under, McGuinness and McLaughlin went their separate ways and Gerry held on to his baby. He subsequently made millions when he sold the *Sunday World* to Tony O'Reilly's Independent Newspapers, staying on as Executive Chairman and continuing to run the business on a day to day basis with Financial Director Derek Perkins. By the time I arrived in 1985, the paper was the biggest selling in the country, with a glorious sale under the then Editor Colin McClelland of 381,000 copies – 300,000 in the Republic and 81,000 in the North.

* * *

I got my first job as a cub reporter at the *Drogheda Independent* in 1981, at the tender age of 18. I worked in the local market until 1985, when I caught the eye of an editor at the *Sunday World*. Coming as I did from working as a staff reporter for local newspapers, the *Sunday World* hired me as a freelance news reporter, which meant I would be paid for anything that got into the paper, plus my expenses. As it turned out, that would yield me a reasonable income and, more importantly, give me the opportunity to show them what I could do!

You never know what to expect when you join a new paper. The *Sunday World* might have been "Ireland's Number One", but life there was anything but glamorous. Situated in Terenure on the south side of Dublin, in a big old grey building with offices at the front and a press hall at the back, it was the last place you'd expect to find the voice of working class Ireland.

I was expecting to find a big posh newsroom when I drove up to start as a full time freelancer. Instead I was shocked to discover the newsroom was in a grubby old prefab building at the side of the car park, just like those used in secondary schools across the country that were short of classrooms. It was green and ugly on the outside, but bursting with energy on the inside.

There were about 14 desks with ugly old typewriters, phones ringing non-stop and stacks of old newspapers everywhere. Some days there were ten reporters in the office, other days there could be three, depending on who was in and who was out on the road on stories.

The newsroom was at the bottom of the building while the sub-editors and production people were in a room up at the top near the editor's office. Friday and Saturdays were always the busiest and generally, as a rule, all major decisions on what stories were running in the paper were made by Friday night. Saturday was a day for reacting to breaking stories, but we largely ignored them unless they were earth-shattering.

Colin McClelland was an extremely pleasant, smartly dressed Northern Prod who knew boobs, sport and shagging was what mattered. He didn't booze with the thirsty troops and had an open door to McGuinness, socializing with him and the money men of Dublin society. He was a very fair and reasonable boss, who loved giving new talent a chance, and gave you a great slap on the back if you brought in a shit-hot story. "Gerry loved it, well done, keep it up."

One of Colin's most important jobs was picking the page one pin-up of the week. This entailed examining hundreds of bikini-clad shots photographed at a studio in England, and changing the caption to Ailish from Ballina or the like. He knew his readers inside out. A country girl was a bigger hit with the natives than a city girl. The size of her breasts was of huge importance to the punters coming out of church after morning mass. An erect nipple was essential in the cold chill of an Irish winter. This work could take up a whole afternoon. It was a tough job but somebody had to do it! There were very few Irish glamour models in those days. The girls didn't take their clothes off and it was nearly impossible to get them into a bikini.

If Colin had the eye for the girls then Sean Boyne, the diligent, razor sharp News Editor, had an eye for a story. With his red hair, beard and glasses he looked like a professor from Trinity College, and would be the last person you'd expect to be giving the people scandal on a Sunday. He was blessed with a wonderful temperament, very rarely got angry and could guide his reporters through a story like a conductor with an orchestra. He also had an amazing memory, and would remember stories and names going back years. This amazing attention to detail is what made him so good. Perhaps his greatest gift was his patience – he would never pressurise a journalist to write a story until he or she had it in the bag.

An out and out Dub, Boyne had cut his teeth as a reporter with the Irish Press Group, covering the early days of the Troubles in the North, before being sent to the prestigious London office. He was with the *Sunday World* from day one and became News Editor after the management fell out with civil rights activist Eamon McCann, when they disagreed with his left wing opinions.

The name of the game was get good stories but don't cost

McGuinness a pile of money. The boss didn't mind paying for a scoop – he just hated forking out the punts to a bunch of greedy lawyers out to make a quick buck. Sean had an eye for young talent and was renowned for giving kids a chance.

I first came across him a few years earlier when I worked on the local papers in Drogheda. I was sitting in the district court on a Friday afternoon when right out of the blue a cracking case came up. A man called Gerry Campbell admitted to having a shebeen at the back of his council house in the St Finian's Park estate in the town. He had built it with his bare hands because the nearest pub, The Thatch, was half a mile away. He had a bar, a telly, a pool table, a dart board and rings. He made his own home-made brew and sold it at 50p a pint – great value in the hard, recessionary days of the 1980s. Gerry's pub was naturally packed seven nights a week and business was booming until, unfortunately, the Gardaí got wind of it. Gerry put his hands up, was fined £50, and agreed to close down his little business.

I got hold of Gerry after the case and he agreed to bring me up to the Shebeen. Proud as punch, he happily posed for pictures behind the bar. I rang Sean and told him I had a cracking story. That Sunday I had my first splash in the *Sunday World*. At the time I was being paid £50 a week at the *Drogheda Independent*. Sean paid me £300; I had hit the jackpot. From then on I was constantly looking out for stories for Ireland's Sunday best until Sean decided to bring me to Dublin.

Competition in the newsroom was hot. Eddie Rowley, one of the gentlemen of the business, had landed the job as the showbiz reporter, right out of the sticks in South Meath. An unknown hack by the name of Paul Williams was given a junior reporter's job along with a beautiful bubbly girl, Cathy

Kelly. Little did we know that they would become two of the most famous writers in Ireland over the next two decades.

Williams was as hungry then as he is now. He was obsessed with the guards, and was continually badgering the news desk to let him have a look at crime stories. One night we all got so pissed we played *Starsky and Hutch* down Grafton Street, pretending to be cops hunting the hoods. We had been boozing around the town with a couple of lads, and Williams decided we'd run from one door to the other using our fingers as weapons. I'd cover him and he'd cover me. It was fun and games running down the street, but people walking by must have thought we were idiots.

The *Sunday World's* watering hole was Brady's pub across the road from the office. From 5 p.m. onwards more stories were hatched there every night. The Deputy News Editor Dave Mullins was as mad as a March hare. A self-confessed alcoholic, he fought a constant battle with the bottle and eventually won, and thankfully has been on the dry for years. He was a fabulous tabloid writer and could make shit shine. He idolised Cathy, a charming girl and a great writer. Mullins smoked like a chimney. He would wear dark glasses because of a problem with one of his eyes. He looked every inch the tabloid hack and didn't let the side down.

When he was off the desk he was on the road. He had great contacts with the hookers in Dublin who gave him all the sleazy stories the paper needed. Dave was constantly on the lookout for a kiss and tell and the call girls would ring him up and, for a few hundred quid, would give him wonderful tales of lesbian three in the bed romps, and even animal sex. The girl spilling the beans would of course be photographed in her undies, but her face wouldn't be identified.

The newspaper's biggest fear was that one of the team

would sample the goods on a brothel special and ruin the whole story from a legal point of view. A journalist having sex with a prostitute meant we'd broken the law, and it only ever happened once.

We were doing a nationwide exposé of the massage parlours and hired a couple of guys around the country to help out. On the eve of publication the editor did a check to ensure nobody had sampled the goods. The news desk later got a call from a certain hack to inform him that he'd done his duty for the *Sunday World*, but that the girl was so irresistible he returned later that night on his own time and had sex with her. The bosses went ballistic. The whole piece had to be reworked with the person concerned, who happened to be a bachelor, getting a serious bollocking.

In every newsroom anywhere there is always one person everybody is terrified of. In the *Sunday World* the man concerned was Bill Stuart, the Deputy Editor. He was a straight up, no-nonsense guy who didn't suffer fools gladly. If he disliked you, he'd kill you journalistically. If the legendary Editor of *The Sun*, Kelvin Mackenzie, put the fear of God into people in Fleet Street, then Bill played the same role for Colin McClelland, and nobody fucked with him.

Bill knew the market inside out, and the one thing he appreciated was hard work. He would call you aside if you were doing well, give you little words of encouragement, and he liked people who were driven and had a pair of balls. All newspapers run on ideas and Bill knew this, but he also had a tremendous handle on rural Ireland, and knew exactly how the readers would react to various stories, and headlines. He had the highest personal respect for Boyne and the two of them worked extremely closely together. If Sean fancied a story as a page one splash, then Bill would nearly always back him.

The greatest character in the whole building was the "swashbuckling" Andy Devereaux, a down table sub-editor who looked after the stories at the back of the paper, like top RTÉ presenter Gay Byrne's [of the *Late Late Show*] weekly column and celebrity priest Fr Brian Darcy's *Little Bit of Religion* column, which still runs today. Andy was also the paper's colourful rock and roll king.

A likeable rogue, Andy had a foul mouth from early morning til late at night. Dressed in his trademark leather jacket, jeans and cowboy boots, he would roar into the car park every morning in his Ford Granada with the fag stuck in his mouth, scaring the living daylights out of the security men, roaring and swearing.

Andy lived with his mother in a pretty house overlooking Dublin Bay, in Sutton. He was a bachelor boy through and through.

The arrival of the satellite dish transformed Andy's world forever. He was one of the first in the country to have one and it meant he could watch music channels from Holland, to Italy and Germany. He had a friend who could tune them all in!

His favourite drink was a "napper" – a brandy and 7up – and boy could he drink them. He would sit in the corner of the bar in Brady's holding court, regaling us with stories about everybody and anyone.

One of his most important jobs was looking after the "Chairman's" page for Bill. This entailed getting pictures and plugs into the *World* for every Tom, Dick and Harry who spent money with the paper. The ad agency guys loved reading their names or seeing their picture in the paper at this golf day, a fun run or whatever charity event they supported around the country. It also gave Andy the chance to look after various nightclub bosses who looked after him.

One of our regular haunts was Annabel's, in the Burlington Hotel, which was managed by Aidan Doyle, one of Andy's good buddies. We would head down on a Wednesday or Thursday night and get in for nothing. Aidan would give us the lowdown on every woman in the place; who was single and who was married. All the posh southside girls went there, and as far as we were concerned the posher the better!

A drunken Andy in a nightclub was hilarious. He'd chat them up one minute and insult them the next. The woman wouldn't know how to take him. His attitude was never poisonous, just fun. He loved the banter and the craic.

Apart from his mother the only other woman Andy adored was…Tina Turner. She was the sexiest woman and greatest singer on the planet to him. There was nothing he liked more than criss-crossing the globe to see her live. He would catch up with her in London, Amsterdam, Tokyo and Los Angeles, on many occasions out of his own pocket. He would write up a spectacular spread, accompanied by free close-up pictures he took himself. Tina was the woman of Andy's dreams, and every time he interviewed her there was no living with him. It was Tina this, Tina that for weeks on end.

He would also make an official state visit to the United States once a year. In those days it was very rare that reporters got a foreign trip because of the huge cost involved. Andy would plan his assignment meticulously. He would go for three weeks and come back with five or six spreads, from the inside story of the strippers in LA to hanging out with the big Hollywood stars. There would be the obligatory picture of the big name with our man Andy, and the punters loved it.

One of the great stories about Andy related to his mother's funeral. He loved the ground she walked on and was devastated when she passed away. They had a big easy-going dog named Rosco. The great and the good went to the funeral in Sutton church. Andy pulled up like a film star in a black limo dressed in a black suit, and holding Rosco by his lead. Andy wore sunglasses while the dog had a big black bow around his neck. On the eve of the funeral the local priest asked Andy if he intended to bring the dog to the church. Andy said he did but the priest expressed serious reservations about it, and said he'd be unhappy with an animal in the church. But Andy took no nonsense and firmly turned around to the clergyman and said: "Hey Padre, no Rosco no gig." He made it clear that if Rosco couldn't go to the Requiem Mass neither would he, and the priest relented. The Mass went ahead as planned and Rosco got to say his goodbyes to Mrs Devereaux.

Andy cultivated an image in the paper as a legend and he really was one. But behind that big mouth of his was a character with a heart of gold who we all loved and adored. There wasn't a single bad bone in his body. He was great fun and a pleasure to hang out with.

* * *

The biggest story I did during my time on the *World* came on October 10, 1987. Martin Cahill, the notorious General, was running amok, and the country was horrified. He and his gang, in a 20 year crime spree, were responsible for over £40 million worth of robberies, and the authorities couldn't lay a finger on him.

The heat was really on after the infamous Beit art robbery in May the previous year, when Cahill and his crew nicked 11 paintings, in what was then the second biggest art theft in the world. He had also personally masterminded the Thomas O'Connor jewellery heist in Harold's Cross, Dublin, in 1983,

after a number of unsuccessful attempts by the paramilitaries
to do the same. Cahill was consistently making the headlines
in the papers as "the General", but nobody had the balls to
publicly name him. Sean Boyne was obsessed with Cahill,
and knew the public would be too. If the Gardaí couldn't nail
him we certainly would.

An old school friend of mine had been assigned to a
special 24 hour Garda surveillance unit who were watching
Cahill morning, noon and night. The 70 member squad was
set up by Chief Supt John Murphy, the then head of the
Central Detective Unit in Harcourt Terrace, as the state
authorities decided to go after the General once and for all. I
had also managed to establish a very good contact at
Rathmines Garda Station, and between my two sources we
had a great in on the Cahill story.

The General had a Corporation house at Swan Grove in
Rathmines, but he had also purchased a plush four bedroom
house in leafy Cowper Downs, just down the road. How could
a man living on social welfare afford such a luxurious pad?
Everyone knew he was living on the proceeds of crime, but
no one could prove it. I went down and doorstepped him on
several occasions after tip-offs from my detective pal.

Sean was anxious that I talk to Cahill. To be perfectly
honest, the first time I called to the house I was shitting
myself. I pulled up in the car outside and didn't know what
to expect. I had this fear of the General coming out ranting
and raving with a gun in his hand, or sending some of his
cowboys after me. I consoled myself that he'd hardly shoot
me in public, he was too clever for that, so the worst that
could happen was we'd have a fist fight, and if it was just me
against him I'd have a good chance of protecting myself since
I'm a big lad. I could just see the headlines... "Our Man Goes
Three Rounds with the General, Rocky Kierans, How Are

You!"

I calmly walked up to the front door and rang the bell. For about two minutes there was no answer, and I just kept pressing the button like the pushy journalist I am. Eventually this woman, who I later discovered was his wife, Frances Lawless, answered through the letterbox. I introduced myself, said I was from the *Sunday World,* and asked if I could speak to Martin Cahill. She was polite and said she didn't know the person I was looking for and could I leave them alone. For a whole week we tried to get talking to Cahill but to no avail. On the last occasion they set a guard dog on us but luckily no one was hurt.

The heat was starting to rattle the General. The Gardaí and the press were right on his tail, and it was driving him round the twist. The neighbours in Cowper Downs were afraid for their lives and despised Cahill with a vengeance. None of them, however, would go on the record for fear of reprisal. The last thing they needed was to fall out with Dublin's godfather of crime.

Up in the Corpo flats it was a different story. The ordinary people trapped in a life of poverty loved him. They saw the General as a "Robin Hood" figure, who robbed the rich and looked after the poor. They also hated the cops and protected him at all costs. You couldn't get anyone to say a bad word about Martin. No matter who you asked they all sang from the same hymn sheet – he was a good old-fashioned criminal who didn't do drugs and looked after the old people.

Cahill was terrified we might get a picture of him. Everyone knew of this mafia-style crime figure, but no one knew who he was or what he looked like. We had a team of photographers led by Liam O'Connor and his nephew Mitchell outside the house, but they couldn't get a shot of him. Martin was like the Scarlet Pimpernel – he would only ever come and go after dark with his face covered, and normally it was through the back door and via the neighbours' gardens. We were getting as frustrated as the Gardaí – he was almost impossible to pin down.

Slowly but surely we started to compile a whole dossier of information on Cahill. The cops gave us everything they had. We discovered that he was collecting the Dole, yet he had paid £85,000 for the Cowper Downs house, which was in the name of his sister-in-law Tina Lawless. We got details of his criminal record plus the crimes he was suspected of carrying out, so we were nearly ready to rock and roll. Boyne decided he had had enough messing about on the story and we'd write it.

On the Saturday we were due to go to press, Boyne went into a long conclave with McClelland and the lawyer Paul Gill. Sean passionately believed there was a way of getting Martin Cahill's name out in the public domain, without leaving us at the mercy of the libel courts. A simple strategy was devised. We'd name the Cahill family as the country's number one crime family, we'd give every last detail of Martin and his brothers based on their criminal records, we'd publish a picture of the house in Cowper Downs, but we'd avoid any references to Cahill as the General or linking him to all the crimes the General was suspected of committing. Boyne and McClelland showed great courage. Many other editors would have run a mile, but they were determined to have Martin Cahill's name out there in the open. The readers weren't stupid, they'd read between the lines.

The page one banner headline under the by-line of *Sunday World* reporters read "Gardaí Name No 1 Crime Family". We said Gardaí had identified the Cahills as the most notorious family in the Irish underworld, and potentially the most dangerous family to hit the Dublin crime scene since the

Dunnes, who ran the heroin trade across the inner city. By 5 p.m. page one was done and it looked fantastic. The first edition would be out on the streets of Dublin by 8 p.m. We all adjourned to Brady's to celebrate our great coup. Sean was over the moon and the whole team were cock-a-hoop. But when Cahill saw the paper he went nuts. By midnight he sent a team up to the *Sunday World* car park and they slashed every tyre in the place.

For some strange reason I'd moved my car over to the pub car park earlier in the evening. I'd done most of the Cahill story and I'd missed his retaliation. It was the start of the tabloid war with the General which would end with his execution by the IRA seven years later on August 18, 1994. The public naming and shaming was Boyne's opening shot; he had the bit between his teeth and was going to write about him all the way. The reaction to the story was phenomenal. The paper sold out and the cops were thrilled that the Cahill's name was out there.

We then moved on to his family arrangements. We discovered he was married to one woman but sleeping with two of them. His wife shared him with her sister Tina Lawless, and the bizarre love triangle became the talk of the nation. No one sold papers like Cahill and every paper in the country would soon discover this.

* * *

If crime was a vital organ of the tabloids, sex was the heartbeat of the industry. My home town of Drogheda was historically known for two events, Cromwell's slaughter of the natives and the Battle of the Boyne, when King Billy beat King James. A bristling industrial town only 28 miles from Dublin, it was the last place you'd expect to find a sex scandal.

But I soon discovered we had one right on our doorstep.

Drogheda traditionally split into two parishes, St Mary's on the south side of the Boyne in the Diocese of Meath, and St Peter's on the north side, which is part of the Armagh Diocese. In the mid-eighties Thomas O'Fiach was the Cardinal based in Armagh, and the Primate of Ireland. Our local parish priest was Fr James Lennon, a long time family friend, who regularly visited our house in the Brookville Park estate. Because of the Cardinal's increasing workload, he was promoted to Bishop, a wonderful personal achievement for him and the people of the town. The Bishop was an honest-to-god decent man who cycled around Drogheda, constantly visiting the sick and looking after his parishioners. He rarely spoke out from the pulpit but when he did people listened. It wasn't too long before the *Sunday World* and I felt the full force of his anger.

One Saturday night I was out for a drink in Drogheda's top hot-spot, the Weavers pub, owned by Eamonn Duffy, a brother of multi-millionaire Gavin of *Dragon's Den* fame. A friend of mine approached me and asked me if I had heard about the "sheet parties" going on in a housing estate in the town. Apparently it was a full blown orgy with 10 to 15 people taking part. I genuinely hadn't heard a whisper, and was fascinated by what he had to say.

He explained how a workmate of his was invited and went for the craic. His friend was totally shocked by the antics and so was he! Six to seven couples attended and got pissed out of their brains. The girls then put a sheet right across the sitting room, with a hole for each man at waist level. The men then put their privates through the hole but the girls couldn't see which person was on the other side. After drawing lots they picked their partner and went off with them to have full sex. My contact said it wasn't a set up and swore the story was true. The next Tuesday I told the news desk about the story and they were very keen on it. I got my contact to introduce me to his pal so we could get every last detail. My contact's friend agreed to go to another party and I asked him to try and get pictures but, unfortunately, he bottled it.

This time the sheet party was held on a Saturday night in the Moneymore council estate. Our friend went in, got drunk and the sheet went up. This time he was too embarrassed to take part but five other couples did. Yet again they stripped off and were picked by the girls. Some of the women involved were married and in their late twenties and early thirties. Their husbands took part and had no inhibitions about themselves or their wives swinging.

The *World* splashed the story and the fallout was spectacular. Ireland was still in a dark sexual age, and we lived in a society where there was a black market in condoms, no divorce, and couples for the most part stayed together, even if they hated each others guts, for the sake of their children. The sheet parties in Drogheda story was sensational stuff.

We deliberately didn't name the estate at the time in case it would give people living there a bad name. Instead we used the phrase "a house in the Boyne Valley" which was a big mistake. You see, the Boyne Valley Hotel on the Dublin road in Drogheda was the posh hotel in the town, and right beside it was an up-market private housing estate called Stameen. Everyone wrongly assumed the parties were there.

The people in Stameen went on the warpath, and we were accused of trying to destroy their good reputation. I couldn't walk down the main street of Drogheda without Stameen residents having a go at me. The whole scandal was the talk of the place for a week. When the Bishop got wind of it he was furious. The following Sunday he gave a sermon from

the pulpit, condemning everyone involved in the sheet parties
for their low morals, and the paper for running the story. He
was enraged such despicable behaviour was going on, and on
his doorstep. I was also subsequently accused of bringing
Drogheda into disrepute. Everywhere I went people were
asking me: "Any chance of getting us into a sheet party
tonight?"

Within a month the entire episode became one big joke.
The Bishop had a right go at me when I met him several days
later walking down the town. He asked if I had any idea the
trouble I had caused. I said I was only doing my job and it
wasn't my fault people were having orgies in their homes. We
were to soon discover that swinging in Irish society was the
least of the Catholic Church's problems, compared to the
monsters in collars who sexually abused hundreds of
Ireland's children. But the double standards were there at the
top – blame the press for heterosexual orgies, but cover up for
your own perverts.

In fairness to Bishop Lennon, it never did get personal.
But a great divide was starting to open up between the church
and the media. There would be many more battles to come.

* * *

I was soon to have my first real education about the Troubles
in the North. Coming from Republican Co Louth, the people
always had close ties with the beleaguered Catholics across
the border. Drogheda and Dundalk were traditionally great
places to hide men on the run, and our IRA and INLA links
would give me some stories over the years.

The Irish National Liberation Organisation (INLA) was
always a maverick group, dominated by a handful of
individuals who behaved more like dictators than freedom
fighters. They ruled by fear and the law of the gun and God

help anyone who got in their way. The INLA was the military wing of the Irish Republican Socialist Party, run by "Bap" McQuillan from an office that looked like Fort Knox, on the Falls Road in Belfast.

Dominic "Mad Dog" McGlinchey was the leader of INLA, and his name became synonymous with murder and mayhem. When I started freelancing for the *Sunday World* he was the most wanted man in the country, believed to have been personally involved in over 30 killings. The INLA carried out the murder of Tory MP Airey Neave in a House of Commons car bomb in 1979, an attack that shocked the Callaghan Government. He masterminded the Dropping Well pub bombing in Ballykelly, Co Derry, in which 11 off duty British army soldiers and six civilians were slaughtered in 1983. He was also suspected of being involved during the same year in the murder of three church elders in Darkley, Co Armagh, a shooting which caused outrage among the Protestant community in the North.

For three years McGlinchey was on the run and ran riot all over the country, as the police on both sides of the border tried to catch him. He was eventually captured by the Garda Special Branch after a shootout in Newmarket-on-Fergus, Co Clare on St Patrick's Day, 1984.

Mad Dog made legal history when he became the first Republican to be extradited from the South to the six counties for terrorist offenses. He was handed over at Killeen, on the main Dundalk to Newry road, in a blaze of publicity, with the world's press watching. He was convicted and sentenced to life imprisonment for the murder of 63 year old postmistress Esther McMullan. But the sentence was quashed in 1985 on appeal and McGlinchey was then handed back across the border, where he was jailed for 10 years for possessing firearms.

Mad Dog's arrest and jailing was to leave a huge vacuum in the INLA, and within three years the whole organization descended into civil war. I first came across the INLA when Thomas Power and John Gerard O'Reilly were shot when they went to a meeting arranged at the Rossnaree Hotel, two miles outside Drogheda. Another lunatic, Gerard Steenson, nicknamed "Dr Death", pulled the trigger. I did a series of stories for Sean Boyne on the feud.

McGlinchey's wife Mary, who was also a committed Republican, was living in Dundalk. Weeks later she was murdered as she bathed her young children Dominic and Declan. The brutality of her execution caused deep shock and anger, and led to a spate of tit-for-tat killings that left several INLA terrorists, including Steenson, who had started it all, dead.

I made contact with one of the top guys in INLA, Jimmy Brown, and arranged to meet him in the back room of a pub in Belfast city centre. It was my first trip to the city and I didn't really know where to go. I knew the different factions of INLA were annoyed at some of our coverage, and I was praying to God I didn't end up with a hood over my head, being taken for a spin. The one thing I was very aware of was that these guys were in their own personal war and had no respect for life. Boyne had warned me to take no chances.

Jimmy Brown was an official spokesman for one faction of the terror group, and he was up to his eyes in the feud. He knew all the players and was completely ruthless. He was so blinded by the Republican-Socialist cause that there was absolutely no sense of realism. He was very cold, nervous, and constantly watching over his shoulder. He asked me a thousand and one questions before agreeing to speak to me.

Was I followed? Did I have a photographer with me? I asked him was he carrying a gun, and he said he wasn't. He was literally a child of the Troubles, but this man was living on a different planet than the rest of us. His loyalty to the cause was unquestioned but his hatred of the enemy was frightening. He was nevertheless intelligent, articulate, and had very direct views. It was my first face to face meeting with a terrorist and he had a cold, unforgiving attitude I would never forget. Our meeting lasted two hours; I got what I wanted and we stayed in touch.

He talked about the war; growing up in the North; how his childhood was ruined by British soldiers on the streets; being constantly stopped and searched; being questioned about everything you do; being branded a "fenian bastard"; the lack of civil rights; how there was one law for the Protestants and a different one for Catholics. If he hated the army he absolutely despised the Royal Ulster Constabulary, as well as the Protestant part-time soldiers of the UDR, the Ulster Defence Regiment. Jimmy told me he wouldn't lose a night's sleep about shooting any of them, he was so committed to his cause. I knew he meant every word of it – such was the pure hatred.

Jimmy gave me the OK to call him any time, and he would always ring me back on a public payphone. He was one of the founding members of another breakaway group of the INLA, the Irish People's Liberation Organisation, the IPLO, and soon became its leader. We built up a good relationship but events were to overtake both of us. Brown was involved in a very public war of attrition with the Loyalist DUP firebrand, George Seawright, an outspoken councillor from the Shankill Road. Seawright's public hatred of Catholics was legendary. He was making headlines in the Northern Ireland edition of

the *Sunday World* every other week, and it wasn't too long
before he was assassinated by the IPLO in a gun attack on the
Shankill Road.

His murder really put Brown in the firing line, but in the
end he got the bullet himself from one of his own men in
August 1992, as the IPLO descended into chaos, becoming a
bunch of drug dealers fighting over money. It was another life
wasted in the never-ending cycle of murder in the North. I
actually felt sad when Jimmy died. In my view he hadn't died
for Ireland, he'd died for nothing. He would be one of many
to lose their lives, brainwashed by the cause. Bobby Sands,
the hunger striker, would turn in his grave, if he knew the deal
the IRA settled for. Yet Gerry Adams and Martin McGuinness
were right to do what they did, engaging in the peace process.
Sands, like many hard line Republicans, was blinded by
idealism.

Over the next several years I regularly got word from
Portlaoise prison that Dominic McGlinchey was extremely
annoyed about some of the stuff we'd written about him and
his family. Unlike some of his cohorts in the INLA, he was
driven by the Republican-Socialist cause, a 32 COUNTY
Ireland and he hated being referred to as "Mad Dog" and a
terrorist. In his absence the organization descended into a
cover group for drug dealers and criminals, collectively
driven by one goal – money.

I couldn't believe it in March 1993 when McGlinchey was
eventually freed from prison and moved to Drogheda. Worse
still, he actually rented a house in Brookville, where I grew
up, and only five minutes away from my own home. I drove
over one day to have a look and saw him outside fixing his
car. I didn't stop for a chat. Within days I got a call from the
local Gardaí telling me to watch my back. They'd heard on

the grapevine that McGlinchey was out to get me, and asked if I wanted 24 hour protection.

Our house was in a small cul-de-sac and easy to watch. I asked the cops if they could keep a discreet eye on our home. We also had an alarm system and I would make sure that, if I was away at night on a job, my wife Karen wouldn't be left on her own. I never told Karen about the McGlinchey threats because I didn't want her spooked. And as seriously as we had to take them, I didn't think in my heart of hearts that "Mad Dog" was going to risk his newfound freedom to get back at a hack. The Gardaí, and particularly one of my neighbours, the late Garda Tom Connolly, kept an eye on our place for two months. McGlinchey got on with his life and we with ours. He had far more important business to take care of than me.

During his time in Drogheda McGlinchey became friends with Tommy Coyle, a distant cousin of mine, who was regarded by the authorities as the local Godfather of crime. Tommy was one of those untouchables who had widespread contacts in the criminal underworld, but no one could lay a finger on him. If you stole something Tommy was the man to get rid of it. He was extremely close to Martin Cahill, and regularly shifted stolen goods for the General's gang. For a man who never worked, Coyle, like Cahill, had no shortage of money. He too saw himself as a "Robin Hood" figure, and was well known for giving cash to the poor. He also knew a lot of people around Newry and South Armagh.

Tommy made the headlines when he was arrested in London over the theft of bonds worth a couple of hundred million in the City. I was working in Fleet Street at the time, and was put on the story only to discover a fellow Drogheda man was in the frame. Coyle knew no one in England and

called me a handful of times in the newsroom from jail. He
spent a year behind bars awaiting trial but was released after
the case collapsed.

Tommy was the link between Martin Cahill and the
notorious loyalist killer Billy Wright, otherwise known as
"King Rat", boss of the Portadown based Loyalist Volunteer
Force, the LVF. Coyle set up dialogue between Cahill and
Wright to try and get the LVF to sell on some of the Beit
paintings the General had nicked, for a cut of the action.
Cahill wasn't in any way political, and didn't give a damn
about Wright's religion or terror links. To him business was
business; it was all about getting the money for his pictures.
But news of the deal leaked in the underworld and the IRA,
whom Cahill also didn't give a damn about, went ballistic.
The idea of the General dealing with a lowlife hood like
Wright caused fury among members of the Provos' army
council. Cahill was a marked man after that, and it wasn't
long before the IRA would get him.

Coyle would hang out in The Pheasant pub in Duleek
Street, Drogheda, right across the road from his house, and
McGlinchey would visit him regularly. McGlinchey got
involved with Coyle in the transport and distribution of pirate
videos, resulting in a feud with a rival Newry based
smuggling gang. The INLA boss was also suspected of
carrying out a couple of armed robberies. McGlinchey
however, was busy telling anyone willing to listen that his life
of crime was over. He was very good to his new neighbours.

In his last interview, 12 days before his death, he admitted
the biggest threat to his life was from inside the INLA. He
claimed one particular family from Monaghan were out to get
him. This family, he said, had wrongly blamed him for the
torture and murder of their son, an alleged informer, a decade

previously. They had killed his wife Mary in revenge and had paid a hit man to get him. He said he was extremely worried that his children would be left fatherless at such a young age. He knew hired hit men were stalking him.

But there was talk on the street of him starting up his own new terror group, and his enemies were waiting in the wings. A couple of months after his release they tried to kill him in Ardee, Co Louth. Two gunmen pulled up and shot him twice as he walked into a friend's house, but he managed to flee. McGlinchey himself claimed he recognized one of the gunmen as Billy Wright, yet ironically, "King Rat" was doing business with his new found friend, Tommy Coyle. The next time they went after him there would be no escape.

On the night of February 10, 1994 I got a phone call from a detective Garda friend of mine telling me: "You've nothing to worry about anymore – Dominic McGlinchey has just been shot dead five minutes ago at a phone box in Hardman's Gardens." The scene was only two minutes from my house, and I arrived to find McGlinchey's body slumped at the phone box. The Gardaí had the area sealed off and were waiting for an ambulance to arrive. One of the first people I met was Tommy Coyle, who had tears in his eyes and said Dominic had been with him only 20 minutes earlier.

It appeared the killers had tailed McGlinchey from Coyle's house and then got their chance when he stopped at the phone box to make a call. His son Dominic, who had already witnessed his mother being shot dead as a child, was sitting in his father's Vauxhall Cavalier car across the road when three masked men jumped out of a Northern registered red Mazda that pulled up, and opened fire. Carrying 9mm handguns, they shot him in each knee, the stomach, the chest, then in the neck and head before making their getaway.

The terrified child ran into local man Paddy Black's nearby house screaming: "Help me, help me, the bastards have shot my father". Mr Black and his wife Margaret ran up the street and found McGlinchey slumped on the ground. Margaret recalled: "It was the most horrible thing I've ever seen. I knelt down beside him and felt a weak pulse in his neck. I knew he was on the way out. He then said to me 'Jesus help me Mary' and then he died." Fr Sean Larkin, who lived at Our Lady of Lourdes Church nearby, gave him the last rites. Young Dominic, who was hysterical, was taken to a doctor.

Dominic McGlinchey's funeral in Bellaghy, Co Derry was a massive public affair which over 1,000 mourners attended. Everyone who was anyone within the IRA and INLA was there. I ended up sitting next to Martin McGuinness, then Chief of Staff of the Provos, who carried the coffin along with nationalist firebrand Bernadette McAlliskey. She also gave the oration in the graveyard, hailing her late friend as a fearless champion of Republicanism, claiming he was the bravest Republican she had ever known.

There are many who say that those who live by the sword deserve to die by the sword. And I'm sure the families of McGlinchey's victims would not have shed a tear at his death. I did, however, feel extremely sorry for his two sons, who were left without their mother and father as a result of the mayhem in the North. I had one prayer at the funeral – that they would go on and live normal lives despite the immense pain and suffering they endured, and I think they have. My one regret was not meeting McGlinchey, especially after all the stories I wrote about him, but I had been strictly warned to stay away from him.

For a long time Tommy Coyle was suspected of setting McGlinchey up. Nobody really knows the truth. He later died of cancer, but he spent his last few years looking over his shoulder everywhere he went. The ghosts of Cahill, McGlinchey and Billy Wright would haunt him to the end.

* * *

My work at *Sunday World* would lead to my first staff reporter job at a national paper, when *The Irish Star* came calling in 1988.

The Irish Star
1988-1989

CHAPTER 2

In the days before cheap flights abroad the Rose of Tralee Festival was one of the highlights of the summer calendar. Thousands would invade the Co Kerry town for a week long party, with live music every night, culminating in the crowning of the Rose in a giant tent before an audience of 2,000 people and over a million watching live on television. The veteran broadcaster Gay Byrne presented the beauty pageant over two consecutive nights, with the contestants flying in from Irish communities across the globe. Unlike Miss World, it wasn't about who had the sexiest body. Instead, the whole emphasis was placed on personality and entertainment. Each girl had to sing, dance or recite a poem as they chatted about their families and roots. The Rose was one of the hottest programmes on RTÉ and Editor Vic Mayhew had it in his sights.

Photographer Jim Walpole and I were sent down to the festival to see if we could come up with some juicy angles. The editor wanted to find the real Rose of Tralee. He had a very strong view that, if we looked hard enough, we'd very quickly find people living on the breadline, while millions of pounds were being splashed out all around Tralee at one great booze-up. Vic wasn't being a party pooper – he just wanted to open the nation's eyes to the suffering that was going on out there and to prove that the Charles Haughey led Government needed to start helping many sections of our society.

The whole decade had been a nightmare with soaring unemployment, mass emigration, sky high interest rates, and little or no confidence in the country. There was serious poverty on the streets and you didn't have to look far to find it.

Coverage of the Rose of Tralee Festival up until then had always been very soft from a news point of view. The papers would write about the lovely girls, the genius of Gaybo, his wife Kathleen Watkins, the occasional drunken fight in the town — all lightweight stuff. The Festival was a good gig for the hacks. It involved long boozy lunches every day, the Tralee races, and a few dinners thrown in. Journalists were treated like royalty by the festival committee, who were very conscious of the need for good public relations. They also had a paid PR guru down from Dublin, Michael Dennehy, to ensure the coverage ran smoothly and was favourable.

We started looking for our Rose of Tralee. Jim and I agreed we needed to find a pretty little kid and to tell her and her family's story. We drove around housing estates chatting to parents to see if we could find anyone before we hit the jackpot in a council estate just a couple of hundred yards down the road from the big dome, where the show was being broadcast. We spotted this beautiful little red headed girl on the street, and as we later learned, she was seven years old. We soon found her mum and explained how we wanted to do a story on the real Tralee, the hardship and the suffering the people endured when the Festival was over and the visitors gone home. There was widespread unemployment in the town and many families found it extremely tough to make ends meet from one end of the year to the other.

As it turned out the girl was the youngest of eleven children. Her parents lived in an estate called Mitchell's Crescent, which at the time was known locally as Dead End Street, and was just around the corner from the Festival headquarters. Her mum and dad opened their hearts and told us how difficult they found it to feed and clothe their family every day in such a tough economic environment. Their small house was falling to bits and neither the local council nor the then Minister for the Environment, Padraig Flynn, would do anything about it. There were about 100 families living in similar harsh conditions, and unemployment in the estate was running at 80 percent. Many of the homes were rat infested and four other children had, in the previous fortnight, been taken to hospital suffering from lead poisoning, and nobody seemed to give a damn. Their children's playground was a wasteland. The whole community was angry and outraged at their living conditions. The Tralee Council had given £5,000 to provide water and a campsite at the festival but not a penny towards these people's rundown toilets.

For a campaigning tabloid newspaper the story was right up our street. We bought the girl a new dress and got a crown for her head, photographed her with her parents' approval, and made her our Rose of Tralee. The tradition in Tralee is that the Rose is announced shortly before midnight on the Wednesday night, and then she parades through the town on the back of a lorry and is greeted by the drunken masses in the early hours of the morning.

Vic was raving about the story of our little Rose. He splashed it and did a page one wipeout with the headline, "The Real Rose of Tralee". When Jim and I bought the paper the next morning we were over the moon with our piece and the coverage. The Festival organisers went ballistic. The PR man confronted me in the press room and called me every name under the sun. He accused me of being a disgrace to my profession, saying that I had undermined the Festival, and that *The Irish Star*'s front page was a cheap shot. Some of my

colleagues in the other papers gave me the cold shoulder and
one of them argued we had exploited a child just to be
sensationalist, a charge Jim and I totally rejected. The truth
was we had touched a nerve.

The page one was just classic old-fashioned tabloid
journalism. This was one of the first times the establishment
in Ireland had seen it in action, and they didn't like it. Before
this nobody had dared question the Rose of Tralee, but we had
the courage to ask the questions. For all the state's money
being thrown at the festival there was still a lot of poverty in
Tralee that had to be faced up to and we'd highlighted it. Vic
Mayhew was thrilled, and many of the local radio stations
across the country followed up on our story. For years
afterwards there was an urban myth in Tralee that we'd picked
up the child off the street, put dirt on her face and took the
picture without her family's permission, all of which is totally
untrue.

* * *

Gerry McGuinness decided that if the people of Ireland were
getting it every Sunday then maybe they'd also like the
opportunity to get it seven days a week. And out of the bosom
of the *Sunday World*, a *Star* was born! The boss flew to
London and did a deal with Lord David Stevens of Ludgate,
Owner and Chairman of Express Newspapers, which
published the *Daily Star*, the *Daily Express* and the *Sunday
Express* in Britain. They agreed to bring out an Irish edition
of the Fleet Street red top since it only had a small presence
on the Irish market. But Gerry was nobody's fool, he knew
sport sold tabloids, and by linking up with the powerful and
influential Express Group, he was getting immediate access

to English soccer, racing, showbiz stories and celebrity pictures for peanuts, saving him a potential fortune in editorial costs.

He set up Independent Star Ltd. and split the company 50/50 with Express Newspapers. The first person he hired to run the show and make his dream come true was John Thompson, a brilliant marketing guru, who had known McGuinness from the early days of the Creation Group. JT, as he was affectionately known, was a visionary, who worked his ass off and was blessed with balls of steel. He also had huge respect within the industry after a very successful spell at the *Irish Farmer's Journal*, a tabloid more renowned for its cows than birds.

The new *Irish Star* would be full of colour, with a topless girl on page three, and the catch line under the front page masthead screaming *Ireland's Brightest Daily*. Gerry asked Colin McClelland to leave the *World* for three months and move over to launch the country's new daily. In January 1988 Colin called me in and asked if I fancied a permanent staff job on the new paper, with a much bigger salary than I was earning. I had the biggest smile in Dublin when I signed my contract and I felt like a footballer who'd just signed for Manchester United.

Colin wanted a small young team of hungry hacks who were ready to roam the land to sniff out scandal, and the staff read like a "Who's Who" of the Irish tabloids today. Mick McNiffe, now Editor of *The Irish Sun*, was brought up from the *Limerick Post*; Joanne McElgunn, now *The Sun* Crime Editor, came over from the *World*; Lorraine Smith came from college and went on to anchor the *Nine O'Clock News* on RTÉ; Cathal Dervan left the *Sunderland Echo* and is currently Chief Sports Writer with *The Irish Star on Sunday* after a long career on the daily; Roy Curtis came from the *Sunday World* where he still writes a brilliant weekly column; Sam Smyth, the *Irish Independent* Political Commentator; photographers Jim Walpole and Noel Gavin; while Tom Ryan, *The Irish Star's* veteran Night Editor was the first sub along with Liz Ryan.

We also had, in advertising, Gerry Lennon, now the Managing Director of the *Sunday World*, his sister Siobhan, now News International's Commercial Manager, and her husband Darragh Meaney, now RTÉ's Head of Advertising, along with a young accountant, Paul Cooke, *The Irish Star's* current Managing Director from Waterford.

Thanks to Paul Williams and Sean Boyne, Colin also got his hands on a super news editor from the *Longford News*, John Donlon, who years later replaced Boyne as News Editor of the *Sunday World*, and another great reporter, Eugene Masterson, the Gossip Columnist with the *Sunday World* today. The *World's* Astrologer, John Little, would also write about the stars every day.

We had about eight weeks to the launch in March, 1988 on what would be a whirlwind of fun and games. Within days I was to get my first introduction to the wily ways of the British red tops.

The English *Daily Star* was based in Manchester in the old Express building on Great Ancoats Street. They also had an office for their London reporters in Fleet Street. It was the only national paper left with its full editorial production in the north of England.

The News Editor, Geoff McGowan, was sent over to do a tour of the country and to help set up the whole Irish news operation. McGowan dressed like a Lord but he was an out and out ruthless tabloid hack. He could see a story from a million miles away, sometimes when it wasn't even there! Dressed in his pinstripe suit, waist jacket, and flower in his button hole, he would have given Louis Copeland a good run for his money in the fashion stakes. He was accompanied by the Picture Editor, Scotsman Jimmy Sutherland, a close friend and confidante of the powerful London Editor Brian Hitchen.

I gave Geoff the names of various freelance journalists across the land, most of whom were working on local papers, and he met each one of them personally for a chat and a drink, offering them big money for stories. He wanted human interest, off-beat tales, pictures of giant potholes, good sexy court copy, and anything that would give people a laugh. People in England have always loved their dogs and cats, while the only animal we Irish ever cared about was horses. Reflecting that public infatuation, British newspapers were forever publishing animal stories and particularly, highlighting cases of cruelty. We Irish on the other hand, with our history of famine, were always more concerned about feeding ourselves and weren't really all that bothered about animals.

Geoff also wanted slick, free flowing copy where the words were extremely well written and sang like a hymn sheet. Stories were rewritten and rewritten until we got it right. He was a good old fashioned pro, who would pontificate about forward planning and things like a news editor's futures file, a diary of upcoming events. He'd get extremely irritated if the team didn't come in with fresh ideas all the time.

It soon became clear with days to go to our first edition that the Brits didn't trust the Paddies, and the feeling was mutual. John Donlon was thrown in at the deep end but rolled up his sleeves and got on with it. Moving from a weekly to a daily newspaper was a gigantic step – in fact it was a huge learning curve for all of us.

Our newsroom was also based in Terenure, just around the corner from the *World*. It was full of excitement, energy and passion. A number of dummies were produced, which gave us an idea of what the new paper would look like. John Thompson took them around to the ad agencies touting for business. We were soon all learning the marketing man's language, with non-stop references to the product and the brand.

The daily conference was hilarious, with McGowan and Sutherland, who had over 50 years experience in the industry between them, giving Colin McClelland their ideas as to how stories should be handled. They would each come in with a news and picture list detailing their top 15 stories of day, and we would all sit around the table going through each story one by one. McGowan would explain what every story was about and how he thought it should be presented, and everybody would pitch in with possible headlines.

A plan would be devised as to how the edition would run from page one to the back of the paper, in order of importance, but mixing hard news with light stories, show business and features. The idea was to keep the reader amused, entertained and interested as he or she turned every page.

Geoff and Jimmy just adored good news pictures. Two snappers, Tony Fisher and Bob Aylott, were sent over to help, along with Dick Durham, one of the paper's best news reporters, plus the chief English Sports Writer Bryan Cooney, now Sports Editor of the *Daily Mail*. Fisher got a great picture of Mick McNiffe washing a baby doll in a giant pothole in Cavan, while Durham and Aylott did a feature about a Viking ghost ship haunting Dublin Bay, producing a picture of a mysterious figure aboard the vessel!

The lads were staying in the Burlington Hotel and it was mayhem. The days were long and the nights were short but there was no end to the partying. They worked hard and played hard and we were given a crash course in the other great Fleet Street pastime – drinking. Jimmy could handle his beer but Dickie was a bad drunk. On a number of occasions he even ended up fighting with himself! Bryan was a teetotaller, extremely charming and enjoyed a joke. He was also blessed with a wonderful writing gift and the great and the good in the world of sport loved talking to him.

Jimmy Sutherland and I were to become very good friends. I soon learned one of the number one rules of newspapers: a picture tells a thousand words. He had worked for a number of years on the *National Enquirer* in America and knew the USA inside out. His contacts across the world were phenomenal, and if you were hungry and wanted to learn he was the man to teach you a few tricks of the trade. Colin might have been Gerry McGuinness's man but Jimmy was London's eyes and ears. If the Irish team needed any help from our colleagues across the water Jimmy made sure it happened. He also had huge admiration and respect for John Thompson.

We needed a big story for our first edition and we were all under big pressure to deliver. At the time, Donegal artist Kevin Sharkey was a big TV star, and we discovered he was adopted. He decided to go public and wrote a heart-warming letter appealing for his natural mum to contact him. I did the full interview and we got all the pics. After a long debate between Colin and the powers that be they decided to splash it.

The first night of publication, February 29, 1988, was absolute chaos. Nearly everything was written in advance. John Thompson decided to have a big launch party that day in the Powerscourt Centre off Grafton Street. There was bunting and balloons, every model we could get our hands on and Gay Byrne, who was given a column in the new paper, was thrown in just for fun. Doing a dummy is one thing but going live is a whole different ball game. We had a few glasses of champagne and all headed back to the newsroom. We covered the live stories of the day and managed to get the baby off stone on time.

We all went over to the *Sunday World* print hall to watch the paper coming off the press, under the watchful eye of the then Plant Manager, the late Paul Feeney. When we saw the first copies and had them in our hands we were all proud as punch. I was over the moon to have my name on the first *Irish Star* splash and we all headed over to Brady's pub to celebrate. JT was the happiest man in the country and thanked us all individually for our efforts. The kids had come up trumps. We all signed the first ever copy of *The Irish Star* and it remains on the wall in Brady's pub to this day.

Twelve days later Kevin's mum got in touch after reading the story and eventually rang him. We splashed with the headline billed as a world exclusive, "I've Found My Mum", and Kevin was reunited with her. We were all over the moon and claimed a big public relations coup.

Over the years I was to subsequently cringe at that splash, and I don't mean any disrespect to Kevin Sharkey, a very nice fella. How in the name of God we launched a newspaper with a crap story about a Z-list celebrity is beyond me. It just proved at that time how little we knew about the market we were in, and things were soon to go from bad to worse.

The English *Daily Star* was selling around 15,000 copies in Ireland prior to the launch of the Irish edition. The plan was to sell 50,000 copies of *The Irish Star* within a year, a good base for a profitable business. The new paper was a hybrid, mixing the best of the Irish and English content in news and sport. Initially some of the sub-editing was done in Manchester, leading to all sorts of mistakes with names and places being spelt incorrectly.

At one stage Cathal Dervan was sent over on a Saturday night to help police the sports subs so there would be no fuck-ups in Monday's big sports edition, after they referred to Croke Park as Choke Park. You had to educate the English subs about the intricacies of Gaelic football, hurling and geography. Nothing offends readers more than if the name of their town or village is spelt incorrectly or placed in the wrong county.

There was tension with our English colleagues every time a British soldier was murdered in the North. They wanted to go hell for leather in the reporting of each tragic incident, praising the courage of "their boys" and focusing on the evil cowardice of the IRA. Although the loss of any life was regrettable, we on the other hand wanted to play it straight down the middle, fearful of offending nationalist readers.

John Donlon was determined that the paper wouldn't be seen as a mouthpiece for either the British Army, the British Government or the IRA, and he called it absolutely right. Maggie Thatcher was Prime Minister across the water and the people of Ireland hated her guts. We couldn't be seen to be siding with her in any way. There was also no love for the British Army in the Republic as a result of Bloody Sunday, when paratroopers killed 13 innocent Catholics on a civil rights march in Derry.

The paper in London was extremely right wing, and deplored the Provos, Sinn Féin and everything they represented. Dublin and London would publish two different versions of the same story in their respective editions, each with their own spin on it. We deliberately always played it straight down the middle, told the reader the facts and let them make up their own mind.

The one thing I learned very quickly was that every time we put the IRA on page one, the sales went down. The Troubles in the North were a turn-off to the people down south, and the vast majority didn't want to know about it.

It soon became very clear that Colin McClelland wasn't really a daily newspaper man and was itching to return to the *Sunday World*. *The Irish Star* was struggling and wasn't the instant success everyone had envisaged, so changes would have to be made. Enter one Mr Vic Mayhew, the silver fox, as he'd call himself, who was brought over from England to run the show.

Vic, who was in his mid fifties, had made his name as Northern Editor of the *Daily Mirror*, a very powerful job up until the 1980s, and was Assistant Editor of the *Daily Star* in Manchester. The first time Cathal Dervan ever met him he was asleep with his feet up on the desk. There was a big sign on the wall of his office which said: "We call him Vic because he gets up our nose!" At least we knew he had a sense of humour.

Mayhew, or Mayhem, as we so often affectionately called him, was your typical old-style tabloid editor, full of energy, ideas, confidence and bravado. He was also prone to the occasional long lunch and enjoyed his drink.

The Irish job was a great chance for Vic to rejuvenate his career, and he totally embraced it. He moved over to Dublin and was hoping to stay til the end of his career. He started reading up on Irish history and went to night school once a week to learn the Irish language. There was nothing he'd like more than to throw a cúpla focal of Gaelic to the lads to show how committed he was to Ireland.

Vic would always say that the paper was our own train set and if we could get the sale up to fifty thousand, it would run forever. He adored the Irish countryside and fell in love with the people. There was nothing he liked more than heading off at the weekend to remote corners of rural Ireland on his motorbike to see for himself what the country was really like.

Vic soon formed a great friendship with the late Jim Dunne, or JD as he was nicknamed. Jim had covered Ireland for the *Sunday Mirror* for over two decades and was made redundant during the Bob Maxwell era, when the eccentric tycoon owned the whole of Mirror Group, before getting into financial trouble and falling off his yacht to his death in the Mediterranean. Jim lived out in a beautiful house on the hill of Howth overlooking Dublin Bay with his gorgeous wife Trish, and had great connections around Dublin. He was on first name terms with every RTÉ star. Gay Byrne was a neighbour and he knew every public relations man or woman in the city. He also had bags of experience and contacts which the paper, with its very young team, badly needed. If something needed to be done Jim would literally fix it.

He was also extremely dapper, and would arrive into work dressed to the nines with his tiepin, cufflinks and a handkerchief in his suit pocket, putting the rest of us to shame. Jim would forever tell young reporters how he was once sent home to change at lunchtime at the *Daily Mirror* in London because he came into the paper wearing a sports jacket, when he should have been wearing a suit. Jim and Vic would entertain each other for hours on end about the glory days of Fleet Street, laughing and joking through the day. It came as no surprise to the rest of us when Vic promoted Jim to the post of Assistant Editor within weeks of him coming into the office to freelance.

One of the great difficulties for Vic and the whole team was that we were effectively bringing out the paper blind. Those were the days before the arrival of the internet and all newspapers were heavily dependent on wire services such as the Press Association, Reuters News Agency, and the Associated Press for information about what was going on around the world. Unfortunately, due to a lack of money, we didn't have any of these services in our Dublin office, so it was extremely difficult for us to keep up with the opposition. We were heavily dependent on teletext, so we would be scouting RTÉ, the BBC and ITV for information. And if it were not for the guys on the local papers around the country flogging us stories, we would have found it extremely hard to come up with enough good material to fill the paper.

* * *

The Lockerbie bombing was one of the first big stories to help make *The Irish Star*. Pan Am flight 103 from London to New York was blown out of the sky by a Libyan bomb, killing all 258 passengers and crew on board, as it flew over the Scottish town on the night of Wednesday, December 21, 1988. A further 11 people, including four children, lost their lives on the ground, as the wreckage demolished forty houses.

Our colleagues in London were out at their Christmas party when word of the atrocity broke. The news desk hired a private jet and a team of reporters and photographers were sent to Scotland, working around the clock for 48 hours.

Many had a few drinks in them before heading for the airport, but they soon sobered up. The golden rule of tabloid newspapers is that the story comes first, no matter what; you work hard and play hard.

We did a wipeout, one subject symbolic page one with a picture of the cockpit on the ground with the headline "Jumbo Tomb", which had a huge visual impact. We also had pictures of a large number of the victims and interviews with their heartbroken families. The story travelled around the world and caused deep anger and sadness. It led to improved security at international airports all over Europe, but sadly, America didn't follow suit, and it left them wide open to attack on 9/11.

Watching Vic Mayhew draw the page ones was like witnessing an artist at work. He was extremely creative, a fantastic headline writer, and once he had the picture he'd map out his front page on a layout sheet, and it would be drawn to a tee on the computer by the night editor. If he dared to divert from it, there'd be war.

Vic also had a short fuse, especially when stories or pictures didn't materialise. One day he was out for lunch with Jim Dunne for his birthday; the lads had sunk a couple of bottles of wine and returned for the afternoon conference at 4.30 p.m. The Cork freelance Ann Mooney had a lovely story about a one legged hockey referee, not the greatest story on the planet but a nice human interest page lead for us. A photographer was asked to go out to the ref's house and get a picture. He did and sent us up a head shot, just a plain picture of his head and shoulders and no shot of the ref's body, the whole point of the story. Vic went ballistic. He kicked the bin in his office around the newsroom ranting and raving as the rest of us dived for cover. The poor Picture Editor Martin

Maher got the greatest bollocking of all. Vic wanted to know
– was the photographer just plain stupid or was he taking the
mick. If the editor had got hold of the photographer he would
have rung his neck. The snapper was sent back out to retake
the picture and this time he got the right shot. The new pics
were sent up by train the next day, and everyone was happy.
Peace returned to the newsroom.

* * *

The Irish Army in the late eighties was in dire straits. Our
soldiers were understaffed, underpaid, badly equipped and
morale was rock bottom. For a new tabloid newspaper this
was our market. The *Daily Mirror* and *The Sun* in England
were forever competing on stories about "our boys" and we
would learn from them. The Irish security forces were very
stretched because of the Troubles in the North, and the
soldiers were constantly required for border duties,
accompanying the Gardaí on patrols and at checkpoints and
also protecting cash deliveries all over the state in case they
were stolen by paramilitaries or Dublin gangsters. While the
Gardaí got overtime for all this work, the soldiers didn't; they
were paid paltry allowances and it led to deep resentment
throughout the force.

In fact, the Irish Army was held in such low esteem that
they became the butt of jokes everywhere. They had also been
called in when the bin men went on strike in the early 1980s,
causing friction with the unions. The only real chance the
troops got to earn hard cash was to go on a six month tour of
peacekeeping duty with the United Nations in Lebanon,
where they would put their lives on the line on a daily basis
as a buffer between the feuding Arabs and Jews.

We got a tip off in a telephone call that Irish soldiers were
selling their weapons and ammunition on the black market to

help make ends meet. The source was a soldier himself, who felt we needed to be aware of what was going on because it was a serious security risk to the state. He told us how most troops had little or no money so they couldn't feed their families and were desperate for cash. He told how the IRA and criminal gangs were constantly offering cash for arms, and most of the soldiers were extremely vulnerable. He felt that neither the Government nor the Gardaí had a clue about what was going on, but the issue had to be highlighted in the public interest.

He claimed it was very easy to smuggle weaponry out of an army barracks and he would prove it. Jim Dunne and myself were assigned to the story, and the news editor John Donlon was very excited as was Vic. Over a series of phone calls Jim had built up a degree of trust with the source, and told him that we needed to get our hands on guns or ammo to stand up the story. My role was purely one of backup and to ensure Jim wasn't being set up. We asked for a gun, army uniforms, and bullets.

After much negotiation the informant told us that he had the gear and would leave it at a drop off point near a park in Rathfarnham, in the foothills of the Dublin Mountains. It was arranged for a time late at night.

Vic pondered over the story but the lawyers started getting nervous. Effectively, our contact was going to steal the gear from a quartermaster's armoury and then give it to us. We were leaving ourselves wide open to prosecution if we had possession of a stolen gun. The lawyers demanded we leave the guns out of it, but if we had the uniform and bullets, it was enough to prove that Irish Army equipment and weapons were being sold on the black market.

The contact was due to call before we left the office for the pick up. Jim told him not to bring guns but that we would take the rest of the stuff. He gave us clear instructions as to where to go and the goods were to be left in a hole in a wall at a precise place for pick up. Jim was smoking like a trooper as we drove around following our instructions. He was nervous but excited at the thought of cracking a big story, while I felt we were like Woodward and Bernstein in a scene from *All the President's Men*, on the way to meet Deep Throat, the source who brought down Nixon and exposed the Watergate scandal in Washington. I was wondering if anyone would resign over this one. The idea of underpaid Irish troops selling their guns to make a few quid would be seriously embarrassing to the Government.

Jim collected the package from the hole in the wall and we rushed back to the office where Vic and the team were all anxiously waiting. We opened up the box and there were uniforms, boots and a box of bullets. They all felt it was enough to stand up the story. We didn't have a gun but we had bullets taken from the barracks, and that proved that there were arms for sale.

The next morning, because we were dealing with stolen army equipment and ammunition, we decided to cover ourselves legally, so Jim made a phone call to the Gardaí in Terenure. He informed them we were now in possession of items belonging to the army, we were doing a story on the issue, and we were willing to turn them over to the authorities.

Vic decided to do the first five pages on the story. I was photographed on page one in the army uniform which I struggled to fit into. The boss wrote the headline "Irish Army Guns for Sale".

The defence forces officially denied any troops were selling guns. Two detectives were sent up to interview Jim Dunne. We both had to make full detailed statements outlining exactly what happened. The cops claimed we had broken the law and Jim could be charged with possession of stolen bullets. They were trying to play hardball but Jim, like the experienced pro that he was, didn't blink, and insisted that they hadn't a case against him or the paper. Vic thought it was quite hilarious that they were trying to make such a big issue about a few stolen bullets, when they should be more concerned about the bigger picture, and the potential exposure to blackmail of our soldiers because they were so poorly paid.

The army top brass were, of course, livid with rage. The story showed they had very little control over their men, and that there were huge fundamental issues simmering beneath the surface with the rank and file soldiers. They were mad to know the source of the story but Jim wouldn't give them an inch. At one stage the Gardaí were talking about going to court to get an order giving them permission to check the records of every phone in the office to see whether they could pinpoint precisely who we'd been speaking to. The whole stupid exercise would have taken months.

The page one went down brilliantly with the punters and the troops. Numerous soldiers called *The Irish Star* congratulating the paper for highlighting their pay plight. Vic and Donlon were thrilled as they both knew we had touched a raw nerve. The Government was embarrassed but did everything in its power to play down the scandal. The Gardaí huffed and puffed about sending a file on Jim Dunne to the Director of Public Prosecutions, but in the end common sense prevailed and the whole episode blew over. Jim was never charged and the army got their bullets back. There was also a big crackdown in the protection of state guns and ammunition afterwards.

The whole issue of army pay was later to prove a big sales driver for us. We ran a whole campaign on it, day in and day out, and soon army wives were protesting outside barracks across the country, demanding their loved ones got a fair deal. Eventually the soldiers got their own union, PDFORRA, and received decent money for the wonderful job they've always done protecting the institutions and the people of the Republic of Ireland. They weren't second class citizens anymore and rightly so.

* * *

Although the paper had difficulties from a financial point of view, the early days of *The Irish Star* showed the power of real tabloid journalism in Ireland. Nobody on the daily market could present stories like we could. We were beginning to shout and roar on the bread and butter issues which affected our readers and, slowly but surely, politics became a very important part of the agenda.

The News Editor John Donlon decided I was to start spending some time down in Dáil Éireann, the Irish parliament, to hunt out some stories. We'd didn't have an official Political Editor, so I was to fill the role.

I'd met the Taoiseach, Charlie Haughey, on a number of previous occasions and had interviewed him for the local papers in Drogheda. Alan Dukes, the Fine Gael leader, was leader of the opposition, while the young Dick Spring was busy rebuilding the Labour party, along with his brilliant right hand man Fergus Finlay, after losing the 1987 general election.

Although we all know now that Haughey was a crook, there was deep suspicion even at that stage regarding how Charlie got his money and lived such a lavish lifestyle, with his mansion in Kinsealy, North Dublin, and his own private island Inishvickillaun, one of the Blasket islands off the coast of Dingle, Co Kerry. The Haugheys were like the royal family in Ireland and it was hip to be seen out and about around town with his sons, Conor, Ciarán and Seán. They also had their own yacht, the Celtic Mist, a helicopter and racehorses, in what seemed a dream lifestyle which the rest of the country envied.

The people were fascinated by the Haugheys. And while Charlie famously went on RTÉ television and told us all to tighten our belts, it never once caused him personally to curtail his appetite for riches. Stories and pictures of the Haughey clan sold newspapers, and whether journalists liked it or not, the ordinary people had a soft spot for Charlie, forever praising him for giving free travel to the old age pensioners and for increasing the pension.

I knew his short fuse was legendary but I found Charlie to be intelligent and sharp, but most important of all, extremely charming. He also had great time for young people and loved being photographed with his kids and their friends, whether it was on their boat or out horse riding.

The Dáil in those days was a real old boy's club. There was a snob's attitude within the parliamentary lobby, where the political editors were briefed daily by the Government Press Officer PJ Mara. Like his boss, PJ was a man of the people, brought in by Charlie to help rebuild the party when they lost power in 1982 to the Garret Fitzgerald led Fine Gael-Labour coalition. PJ had a wonderful sense of humour, was totally matter of fact and didn't tolerate fools gladly. He would have a daily battle with the political correspondents, led by Chris Glennon of the *Irish Independent*, Sean Duignam and Donal Kelly of RTÉ, Liam O'Neill of the *Irish Examiner*, Dick Walsh of *The Irish Times* and Emily O'Reilly of the *Irish Press*. PJ could spin before the word was even invented, giving the Government's opinion on this, that or the other, with or without Haughey's blessing.

I wanted to get into the lobby but I was refused. Chris Glennon, a first class reporter, who was chairman of the Dáil Press Gallery, claimed I wasn't a bona fide political editor, so therefore I couldn't get in. Neither was I allowed to share the same office as them, and I was ordered by the Oireachtas Press Committee to use a chair and phone in the foreign press room at the back of the chamber in Leinster House. Glennon felt that I was entitled access to parliament to cover whatever was said in the Dáil Chamber, but under no circumstances was I to be allowed into the lobby for the Government briefings. It was a real put down which clearly questioned the Irishness of *The Irish Star*. But there was a bigger game going on. The other papers clearly didn't want *The Irish Star* getting in on political stories, so they were doing everything to block us. I was absolutely furious but didn't let it get to me. I knew I was out of the loop, but if they wouldn't work with me I'd work around them.

PJ played ball and started giving me separate briefings by phone to make sure I didn't miss a line the political correspondents were getting. I knew what they were doing but they hadn't a clue what I was at, and it suited me perfectly. Soon numerous backbenchers were queuing up to give me stories about their constituents, stuff they could never get into the broadsheet papers.

What the Dáil Press committee did was a clear case of victimisation. It would never happen today. They didn't want to give *The Irish Star* credibility in any shape or form. Nowadays, Governments are more concerned about their image in the tabloids than the broadsheets. How times have changed!

I only ever crossed swords with PJ Mara once, and that

was while I was having a few drinks in the Dáil bar. We wrote a story that was negative on Haughey and the Taoiseach clearly got the hump. PJ stormed in and, in a four letter rant which left little to the imagination, he told me in no uncertain terms what he thought of me and the paper before marching back to his office. I didn't think any more of it and got on with my job. Later that evening he returned to the bar, pulled me aside and apologised. Charlie had given him a right going over, so unfortunately I received some of the pain. It was typical PJ but we laughed and joked and very quickly moved on. He had plenty of fish to fry and I was the least of his worries.

Around the same time rumours were sweeping Leinster House about Charlie's relationship with the *Sunday Independent* gossip columnist Terry Keane. The dogs in the street knew they were having an affair but no one could prove it. I started sniffing around the Dáil about their secret romance but didn't get very far. Nearly every TD and Senator was aware of it but no one wanted to talk about it for fear of destroying their political future. At one stage I was actually warned off in the Dáil bar by another Government official and told in no uncertain terms to mind my own "fucking business". I also don't think the powers that be at *The Irish Star* wanted a spat with Charlie at that time, since the paper was anxious to secure Government advertising to help keep it afloat.

Terry however, was very brash and daring and repeatedly referred to the Taoiseach in her column by the pet name "Sweetie". The only way we could stand it up was to put a team on them around the clock, but we didn't have the resources to do it. We needed pictures of the two of them kissing together for starters.

There was an unwritten rule in the Dáil that the press didn't write about the private lives of the politicians, and whatever went on in Leinster House stayed there. Indeed there were a number of other marriages on the rocks, right across party lines, but they were kept below the radar. They were, in fairness, far more discreet than Haughey, and neither did they play happy families, being publicly photographed with their wives and kids all over the place.

One incident during a debate on the divorce referendum in the 1980s involved a TD giving a passionate speech against the new divorce laws, deploring the affect it would have on family life in Ireland, while his mistress sat in the visitor's gallery, listening to him! It was a classic case of hypocrisy, but he was just playing to his electorate and didn't give a damn about his own moral compass.

It was several years later on May 14, 1999, after Haughey had resigned as Taoiseach, when Terry Keane decided to go public on their affair. A number of newspapers were about to spill the beans in advance of her autobiography, which was due to be published later that year. In a classic kiss and tell and the first ever of its type in Ireland, she decided to sell excerpts from the book for a six figure sum to *The Sunday Times*. On the Friday before publication she poured her heart out to Gay Byrne on the *Late Late Show*, in what was to be one of the most gripping Irish television programmes of all time.

Terry and Charlie had been secret lovers for 27 years and everyone in politics and business appeared to know about it except the public. She revealed how they fell in love after meeting at a dance, and began an affair that lasted right throughout Haughey's political career. She claimed that Charlie's wife Maureen, a daughter of former Taoiseach Sean Leamass, knew about the relationship, as did Terry's ex-husband Mr Justice Ronan Keane and the rest of her family. She told how neither she nor Charlie considered ending their respective marriages or running away together. She loved him to this very day and he loved her.

She recalled: "We never talked about each other's spouses. Charlie was an old-fashioned man and he thought splitting from our partners would be beyond the bounds of decency. But of course Maureen knew about it and my husband and family knew. It really was love and yes people did get hurt but you can't help who you fall in love with. I am sorry that my family and his family got hurt. People think affairs are about sex but sex is a very small part of an affair. Affairs are about trust and friendship and looking after each other, the good times and the bad. He was not Taoiseach at the beginning but it made it more exciting when he was. He would discuss the affairs of state with me, and he would often listen to me and maybe change his mind."

The couple use to regularly meet for sex in hotels and houses around Dublin, all arranged by Mr Haughey's various friends. They would also dine regularly in different restaurants, almost always in the company of small groups of people. Terry, however, was never discreet about it, and anytime she was out with her fellow hacks having a few drinks, when the subject of Charlie came up, she would openly boast about her close personal relationship with the Taoiseach and left little to the imagination.

How Charlie could get away with it for so long, in both his financial and personal lives, is a damning indictment of Ireland at the time. It would never happen in the current climate. Politicians in Ireland up until the early nineties wielded great power and influence, and even if editors wanted to go after them, they were never allowed to do so.

Even now our political leaders want to return to the bad old days, by bringing in a new privacy law which would prevent the press from exposing the double standards which Charlie Haughey so openly displayed. The basic argument is over what is private and what is not. The rich and famous would use the law to hide behind and to stop the public knowing what they are really at. Our Government, as usual, is doing their bidding. And no matter what anyone says, the public interest, the public's right to know, far outweighs any individual's right to privacy. Such a negative law would protect the privileged from the fourth estate – the media – and that is not good for democracy.

One man who we had a great relationship with was Albert Reynolds, who became Charlie's Minister for Finance in 1988 after Ray McSharry, and then replaced him as Taoiseach when Charlie quit in January 1992. A no-nonsense Longford man, Albert was extremely friendly with John Donlan, our News Editor, a friendship that lasts to this day. John gave me the Minister's home number, and I would often call him, looking for a story or to get our card marked about the thinking in Government on a variety of issues. Albert always played with a straight bat, and wouldn't fill you with bullshit. It was a trait that later helped him persuade Sinn Féin and the IRA to give up the armed struggle and to call a ceasefire, a remarkable personal achievement.

Albert Reynolds was the type of man you'd trust. He'd made his money running ballrooms of romance in the west of Ireland, and later opened his own pet food factory in Longford. One of our first big stories came from Albert's budget. I'd received a tip that the Government were going to cut the rate of tax and I needed to stand it up. I rang Albert at home and I put it to him straight. Albert confirmed the story was true and that they were cutting the top rate by a penny. It might not have seemed much at the time, but it was the first time in living memory an Irish Government was cutting taxes. Donlon was delighted. Having a leak on the budget gave us great credibility, and we were indebted to Albert for the break. You'd find it very hard to get the home number of a minister today, especially when they spend most of their time surrounded by spin doctors and living in cuckoo land.

* * *

Ireland has always been a very hard place to get a drink on Good Friday, so when the opportunity came along it was very hard to turn down. Traditionally, the bars close for the day, but I got a tip off that Ronnie Drew and the Dubliners were filming a new video in O'Donoghue's pub in Merrion Row just off Dublin's St Stephen's Green. The group were managed by the late Jim Hand, a fellow Drogheda man, who also looked after the Furey Brothers and Johnny Logan in his time, before they fell out. Jim had a keen interest in politics, was Fianna Fáil mad, and extremely pally with Charlie Haughey.

The whole film crew took over the pub and myself and Mick McNiffe, on Jim's invitation, headed down for the craic. Ronnie Drew, John Sheahan and Eamon Campbell were in flying form, sipping pints of Guinness and singing songs. O'Donoghue's has a worldwide reputation for promoting traditional music and ballads and is always a famous port of call for American and English tourists. Donlon loved the idea of doing a piece about the only place in Ireland where you could get a Good Friday pint, and the Dubliners loved the publicity. The group even had special dispensation from the Gardaí to go into the bar for the day. We got a lovely story and some great pictures but worst of all we got the hangover from hell. Vic thought the story was hilarious and he gave it a big hit. The great man had a wonderful news sense but unfortunately he only lasted a year at *The Irish Star*.

Tony O'Reilly became concerned that the paper was losing so much money and decided it needed to become a full blown Irish product and required investment. He was bang on the money, but if he was putting more money in he needed his own man there, so Michael Brophy became the third Editor of *The Irish Star* in 12 months, and was to become one of it's most successful. I was only to work with him for a couple of weeks, because London had come calling, and soon I would realise my dream of working in Fleet Street.

Fleet Street - The Daily Star
1989-1992

Part 1

CHAPTER 3

My first taste of the national newspaper scene in Britain came in late 1988 and it ended in a bust-up with one of the most obnoxious people I've ever met, the former world snooker champ and son of Belfast, Alex "Hurricane" Higgins.

I persuaded Geoff McGowan to let me go over to Manchester for a week in a straight swap with one of the *Daily Star's* reporters, John Mahoney. The *Daily Star* sold just under a million copies a day, and the newsroom was based at the Express Newspapers building in Great Ancoats Street.

I can still remember the smell of ink as you walked by the huge printing presses and up the back stairs into the newsroom, where the old metal typewriters sang like the chorus of a choir as the stories were hammered out one after the other. Everything was written in the house style of one sentence paragraphs and sent from the reporters to the news desk, and then to the sub-editors.

The hub of the paper was the back bench, a large desk at the top of the newsroom where the night editor sat with his deputy and the chief sub-editor, and ruled the room with an iron fist. This was the engine room of the paper – the place where the headlines were written and all the major decisions taken. The other senior executives, the Editor, Deputy Editor and Associate Editor sat in offices behind the back bench.

Higgins had been in the wars yet again and had fallen out with his ex-wife Lynn following a booze-up. McGowan, the News Editor, sent me off to find him. I knew this was my first big test, and if I wanted to end up at the home of the London national newspapers, Fleet Street, I was going to have to deliver the goods.

The older reporters on the *Daily Star*, Tony Brooks and Frank Curran, were a breath of fresh air and a wonderful help. They came up with contacts and telephone numbers of people who knew Higgins and within two days I tracked him down to a housing estate on the outskirts of the city.

I walked up and knocked on the door and he came out ranting and raving like a lunatic who'd just been freed from the asylum. I asked politely whether we could speak about the bust up with his wife, but he was having none of it. Eventually a black taxi arrived for Higgins and he made a run for it.

I tried to speak to him a second time but he started throwing punches at me and swearing and cursing. I wasn't taking any of his bullshit and I hit the Hurricane a couple of thumps in the smacker. He went even more ballistic but I didn't care – he was getting a taste of his own medicine and I warned him if he punched me again I'd put him six feet under. Higgins backed off like a little lamb and cowered in the back seat hissing and mumbling to himself. He could give it but he sure couldn't take it.

I wouldn't mind but I had always been a fan of the Hurricane. I admired the way he played snooker at a hundred miles an hour, giving the fans great entertainment. I, like so many people, was thrilled when he became world champion for the first time, in that historic seesaw match with Steve Davis at the Crucible in Sheffield. We all shed a tear when he cried like a baby in Lynn's arms when he sank the black for victory.

But the Higgins I met was a shadow of his former self. He

was cursed by drink and self importance, and truly believed that as a superstar he could do whatever he liked, was above the law, and could even beat his wife if he wanted to.

The *Daily Star* loved my story and it got a page seven lead in the paper. McGowan was thrilled at the way I tackled Higgins and soon word reached the boss, the Editor Brian Hitchen that he had a hot young Irish kid on his hands who was keen to move over. And move over I did in 1989.

* * *

Brian Hitchen was already a legend in Fleet Street. He made his name as a reporter and then News Editor of the *Daily Express,* and then became Deputy Editor of the *Sunday Express*.

There was a great story about Brian when he was News Editor of the *Daily Express* in the mid 1970s. A famous gangster had died in the East End and a reporter and photographer were assigned to cover the funeral. Brian told them no matter what they were not to leave the cemetery until 30 minutes after the widow and children had left.

Right on cue and out of the blue this beautiful woman appeared in the graveyard dressed in black from head to toe, and carrying a single red rose. She walked over to the gangster's grave, knelt down to pay her last respects, and wiped away a tear. The photographer couldn't believe his luck and got some fantastic exclusive pictures. The reporter nosed his story on who was the woman in the graveyard, and was she the gangster's secret lover?

The *Express* gave it a big hit, but it took until a few months later before the real story unravelled. The mysterious beauty was in fact the wife of one of Brian's best mates, and he had asked her to go to the funeral as a favour to cause a stir.

Brian said: "In those days we had very little money compared to the other papers, and if you wanted to be different you had to think outside the box. The girl in question was Joanne Hawke, she was Latvian and extremely beautiful. Her husband John was the leader of the Red Arrows, the RAF aerobatics team, and a very good friend of mine. I came up with the idea of sending her to the funeral. I asked her to put the widow's net over her face and to carry a single rose. Nobody except me had a clue who she was. The story ran in the tabloids for days. It was all a bit of harmless fun."

Brian was your typical bulldog Brit, and he lived up to the stereotype. He was small, bald, well built and extremely passionate about the newspaper business. The other good thing for me was that he was married to an Irish woman, Nellie Purfield, from Co Kildare. Her brother John, a big potato farmer in Co Meath, and a long serving director of our local racecourse, Bellewstown, knew my father.

Talking about a small world, on top of that, a North London businessman, the late Paul Corrigan, who left Kildare when he was 14 years old, and went on with his brother Frank to own seven butcher shops and a meat factory in the English capital, was also friendly with Brian. Paul was dating my best friend's sister Sabina Carr, in London at the time, and they later married. If there were any stories about British sausages Paul would give them to Brian.

So when I first met Hitchen we had plenty to talk about and we hit it off straight away. He offered me a job on £10,000 more than I was on in Ireland to move over, plus I was paid in Sterling. The other big part of the deal was I also got a brand new Ford Sierra company car, which I loved.

The *Daily Star* in England was entering a new era. It was closing down its production operation in Manchester and moving it all down to London, to shiny new offices just around the corner from Fleet Street at Blackfriars Bridge. I had first walked down Fleet Street when I was 14 years of age and told my father I was going to work there someday. I didn't quite make it but I was only 500 yards around the corner.

Rupert Murdoch had started the great exodus from the street when he broke the all-powerful print unions and moved *The Sun*, *The London Times* and *News of the World* to his new plant and newsrooms at Wapping in January, 1986. Now the Express Group, the *Daily Star* and the *Daily Express* were following suit, and soon after that the *Daily Telegraph* and the Press Association departed, leading to the effective demise of the old Fleet Street. The pubs were still there though; The Old Bell, The Tipperary, El Vinos and The Poppintree, but very little else.

Lord Stevens actually opened a bar on the group floor of our building called the New Poppintree, so none of us would miss the old one. It was a very busy place, and many a good night was had in it as we waited for big stories to break.

I moved over to London after the Irish general election in June, 1989 and stayed for the first couple of months with Paul and Sabina, in a house over one of their shops in Camden Town. It was very near the tube station and easy to get into the office on the Northern Line.

On my first day on the *Daily Star* in London I was as nervous as hell. I was walking into a big newsroom not knowing anyone, and having nearly no contacts to bring stories in. The big difference between London and Dublin was the news desk operation. They had an army of people, while at home we just had a one man show, John Donlon.

Hitchen had brought in a new News Editor, Graham Jones from the *Daily Telegraph*, to replace Geoff McGowan. Geoff had no interest in moving down south to the big smoke so he took the money and ran. Graham was a real dour Yorkshireman who was more broadsheet than tabloid. He was highly intelligent and very academic, two traits Brian loved in him. He also enjoyed his two pints of bitter at lunch time, which in our world meant at least he was normal. He would stand at the window at one o'clock every day and listen intently to the BBC Radio 4 news headlines. I was the first hack hired under the Jones regime and we hit it off straight away, even though many of the other reporters, especially the girls, despised him.

Our Deputy News Editor was Hugh Whittow, a wonderful Welsh man. Stuart Wintour was the Assistant News Editor, while Rab Anderson, a Scotsman, was number four on the desk, and Gordon Gregor and Joe Clancy were the Night News Editors. Gordon had worked with Brian Hitchen on the *National Enquirer*, the gossip bible of the United States – he was a brilliant journalist with a wonderful nose for a story.

Hugh had become embroiled in one of the most controversial Fleet Street stories, the saga of Blackie the Donkey. It made the front page of all the tabloids and led the BBC nightly news at the height of the summer silly season back in 1986.

The Pero Palo festival was traditionally held in Villanueva de la Vera, a village halfway between Madrid and Granada in Spain, to commemorate the capture of a rapist many years previously, who was paraded through the streets on a donkey before being executed. The donkey, however, was subjected to a grotesque ritual where the fattest people in the village would jump on its back, alcohol was put down its throat, and the poor animal left badly injured, lame or crushed to death.

There had been a public outcry in Britain the previous year when a donkey was killed during the Fiesta, and animal rights campaigners, led by Englishwoman Vicky Moore, vowed to stop it happening again. Brian Hitchen got the *Sunday Express* to do a big feature on it, and then the race was on between the *Daily Star* and *The Sun* to save Blackie, as that year's donkey was affectionately named.

The village, set high in the mountains, only had one hotel, the Parador, with just two phone lines and six bedrooms. Within days Fleet Street's finest descended on Spain to save the donkey and bring him back to Britain in triumph.

The notorious *Sun* Editor Kelvin MacKenzie, who had a mouth like a lion and was as hard as nails, sent Hugh, who worked for the *Sun* back then, over to rescue Blackie. The *Daily Star's* editor Lloyd Turner dispatched veteran hack and wily Scotsman Don Mackey.

On the eve of the festival Mackey got in first and did a deal with a local farmer to buy the donkey and he had a bill of sale to prove it. Whittow made a counter offer of £10,000 as negotiations ran through the night. Unknown to Hugh, Mackey had Blackie picked up and hid him in a barn below the hotel at the back of the local chapel. He was able to watch all night so that no one could nick him. Hugh in turn claimed he owned the donkey, had bought it for *The Sun,* and Mackey had taken it from him.

The whole episode descended into a bun fight between the papers, and even the rival editors were on television slagging each other off and claiming that Blackie belonged to them. Kelvin was obsessed with the donkey and went ballistic when he heard the *Daily Star* had got him. Whittow was told no matter what to get him back his "fucking donkey". Hugh in turn felt he had been shafted and the *Daily Star* had no right to take Blackie. The whole story caught the imagination of the public, but better still, the war between the tabloids made great TV viewing and was hilarious.

Mackey persuaded a donkey sanctuary down in Devon to take ownership of Blackie and to look after him on their return. But first of all he had to get him away from the rest of the pack and put him into quarantine at a "safe field" in Spain before someone else discovered him. He reached agreement with the Spanish to put him in quarantine for three weeks and then ship him to England. He then hired a jeep and horsebox to bring Blackie home to Plymouth to a fanfare of publicity.

Don even got a big banner made up: "Blackie Rescued by The Daily Star" in case Kelvin and *The Sun* tried to highjack Blackie's homecoming. Brian Hitchen reckons they were fighting over the wrong donkey anyway. He says: "We did the story first and Blackie had a special mark on his kneecap – the donkey brought home didn't have that mark. The real Blackie was roaming the hills of Spain for years and nobody knew any different. The main thing was that the festival was cruel and was stopped as a result of all the publicity. Which paper saved Blackie was irrelevant. Years later, when I became editor of the *Daily Star,* I was getting bills of £1,000 a go for Blackie's straw."

Publicly though, the *Daily Star* was the victor, and the paper revelled in it. Lloyd Turner told Don Mackey his great work had saved his editor's job for another six months. Vicki Moore, of course, claimed both papers had saved Blackie. The donkey lived happily in the sanctuary in Sidmouth, Devon until he died in May 1993. He was one of the few donkeys to be buried in the sanctuary, and was actually given his own gravestone, he was so special!

Whittow had to face the music on his return, and Kelvin's

wrath. He eventually left *The Sun* as his face didn't fit anymore, and ironically, the paper which had cost him so much trouble, the *Daily Star*, gave his career a new lease of life. Hugh had a great sense of humour about most things, but you wouldn't dare mention Blackie to him. He and Mackey never got on after the whole controversy. Hugh is now Deputy Editor of the *Daily Express*.

* * *

One of the first people I met in London was Ted Oliver, a *Daily Mirror* reporter who immediately took me under his wing. When I arrived I knew no one, and yet within weeks I had met many people in the business thanks to Ted. A native of Belfast, Edward Samuel Oliver, to give him his full name, was educated at Trinity College, Dublin and had cut his teeth on the Troubles in the North before landing a job on the *Daily Mail* and then later switching over to the *Mirror*.

In the summer of 1989 the *Daily Mirror* was owned by tycoon Robert Maxwell and situated in a great building at Holborn Circus, just round the court from the Old Bailey, the scene of so many criminal trials in the UK. The journalists had two favourite watering holes, The White Swan, or the "Stab in the Back", as it was more commonly known because so many journalists got shafted in it, and Vagabones, a private gentleman's club inhabited by scoundrels and run by John Mullaly, a former sergeant in the City of London Police Fraud Squad. Originally from Co Fermanagh, Mullaly and I hit it off straight away, and he was to be the source of many stories for me.

Vagabones was full of cops, lawyers, and journalists. Editors like Hitchen and Richard Stott of the *Mirror* regularly drank there or dined with contacts in the restaurant. It was a place where you'd always meet someone in the know and it became my new local. The club would open from midday until four or five the following morning. No matter what hour of the day you would always find somebody important there.

Friday night was a must. The hacks would come from every other paper for a great big piss-up and a sing song on the karaoke machine. On one occasion, a female reporter got so drunk she ended up having sex with three different hacks one after the other downstairs in the basement. She was an out and out nymphomaniac who deliberately targeted each of her men and didn't give a damn. Mullaly was aware of what was going on but turned a blind eye. If she wanted to have sex that was her own business.

I soon met one of my teenage heroes, Frank Thorne of the *Mirror*. Frankie had made his name on the *Sunday People* and I used to read his big investigations and exposés every weekend, as my mother Carmel loved the *People* when we were growing up in the seventies.

Richard Stott loved Frank and brought him to every paper he edited. Thorne would work on a story for months on end if necessary, an opportunity we rarely got on the *Daily Star* because we were so short of staff compared to the bigger papers.

Frank and Ted spent 18 months travelling all over Britain, after a tip-off that Colonel Gaddafi and Libya were bank rolling Arthur Scargill and the National Union of Miners. They stood it up and the story won Scoop of the Year at the British Press Awards. Maxwell personally bankrolled the story, as he couldn't stand Scargill. Ordinary people couldn't believe the Miner's Union would take cash from the country and its dictator, internationally blamed for the Lockerbie bombing in which so many innocent people lost their lives.

Vagabones opened so many doors for me it was unbelievable. I also became friendly with a group of Scots; Ramsey Smith and Gordon Hay of the *Mirror* and Ian McKerron of the *Daily Express*. They all worked in Glasgow together and then all got jobs within a year of each other in London. They were all great reporters and you crossed them at your peril. McKerron, or "The Molecatcher" as he was nicknamed, had a fantastic ability to get people to speak to him.

* * *

There is a golden rule in Fleet Street that you don't stitch up your colleagues. Generally, when a big story breaks, reporters have to decide if they are in the "pack" and willing to share information with their opponents from other papers, or do they work alone looking for that elusive exclusive. What you can't do is receive information from your colleagues and then not give anything back if you have a story in return. The last thing a reporter needs is to be getting angry phone calls from their news desk when the first edition drops at 10.30 p.m., wondering why they haven't got this line when another paper has it. The majority of editors prefer their reporters to work alone, but go mental if their journalists miss out for not being in the "pack".

There was a big story in Germany in which the wife of a British Army officer had killed his mistress in a bizarre love triangle, in what became known as the "case of the galloping major". Major Tony Dryland and his wife Christine where living with their two sons, aged 16 and 3, at an army base in Soltau, near Hanover, but the Major shared a love of horses and riding with his young German lover.

He first met Marika Sparfeldt, age 34, in August 1990. He was an expert horseman who owned two magnificent black Hanoverian horses which required expensive stabling. She was a riding instructor at the stables and an equestrian journalist. They quickly became close friends and were soon lovers. The Major was dispatched to the first Gulf War in Saudi Arabia and Iraq with the Seventh Armoured Brigade, and wrote no less than 47 passionate love letters to Marika while he was away. He also made the fatal decision that he was going to divorce his wife of 24 years and marry his lover.

Initially, Mrs Dryland took it calmly and headed off with her children to stay with her parents in Australia while her divorce was being finalised. Marika left her German partner of five years to move in with the Major. However, while she was away, Christine became angry and extremely resentful. She developed a bitter hatred for her husband and his lover.

On her return she visited the stables several times and verbally abused Marika. On the day of the Major's 46th birthday it all ended in tragedy. Mrs Dryland had been drinking a bottle of whiskey while her husband spent the day with his lover. Christine got into her green Saab 9000 car and drove the short distance over to the stables, where she rammed the Major's Mercedes. When he and Marika came running out of the clubhouse to see what was happening, she deliberately put her foot down on the accelerator and drove her car at her hated rival. The car hit Marika's legs, throwing her over the bonnet, and she smashed her head on the windscreen before falling to the concrete. Christine then reversed the car over Marika's injured body as she lay helpless on the ground. The German girl was rushed to hospital but died hours later from massive internal injuries.

Mrs Dryland was tried before a military court, where she

tearfully pleaded not guilty to murder but guilty of manslaughter, by reason of diminished responsibility. The jury heard that she had a history of depression that had turned into murderous rage, leading her to become bent on revenge. Much to the fury of her victim's family, she was sentenced to a year in a psychiatric hospital for treatment.

The whole scandal made page one headlines and we all spent a couple of weeks on and off in Germany working on the story, from the time it happened to the trial. There was also much public sympathy back in Britain for the betrayed wife. There was a mad dash to get photos of Christine and Marika, and we all worked together to get them.

Everyone in the Army had seemed to know about the affair except Mrs Dryland. Throughout the whole story one particular female hack had really annoyed McKerron and would not play ball with any of us. She kept getting different lines on the story and every night she would rub our noses in it back at the hotel bar. The situation wasn't helped by news desks continually calling and wondering why we hadn't got what she had on the story.

By the end of the trial, on a Friday night, Graham Jones, the news editor, was about to pull us back to London. But Ian called me and a few of the lads aside and told us that under no circumstances were we to leave as we'd be missing out on a massive Sunday for Monday story.

Unknown to the rest of us, McKerron had made contact with the Major, had done an interview with him, and he had agreed to pose for a picture putting flowers on Marika's grave, a page one picture if ever there was one. I persuaded the news desk to trust me and let me stay on. Ian gave me a full fill-in on the Saturday night and we all ran with it on Monday morning.

I was eternally grateful to McKerron, who could have turned us all over but he didn't. He even gave the reporter who annoyed him a fill-in at the eleventh hour because he was friendly with her boyfriend. Ian's view was that we had all covered the story together so we would finish it all together. He still is one of the great gentlemen of our business.

* * *

I always regarded the English as a very tolerant people. They had allowed immigrants from all over the globe into their country, different races and different cultures, the fallout from the empire; all of whom were welcomed with open arms by the majority of her citizens. Equally, when the IRA were killing and maiming on mainland Britain through the 1980's with their evil bombing campaign, the people of London could always differentiate between the genuine law abiding Irish people living and working in Britain, and the Provo killers responsible for the atrocities.

I don't think we Irish would be as understanding if the same thing had been happening to us. We'd have lynched the first Englishman we got our hands on if an English terror group were setting off bombs and killing innocent people in Dublin. We wouldn't care who they were.

One of the worst acts of murder during my time in England was the slaughter of ten Royal Marine bandsmen in Deal, Kent on September 22, 1989. I'd witnessed a lot during the Troubles at home, but nothing compared to this. As military targets go, this was a really soft one. These soldiers were only kids — teenagers learning to play their instruments at the Royal Marine School of Music. None of them would have seen any military action, never mind have done a tour of duty in Northern Ireland

Andy Devereaux, the swashbuckling veteran journalist and rock and roll king of the *Sunday World*. © *Sunday World*

Top criminal Martin Cahill, who was forced to unmask as The General by the *Sunday World*.
© *Collins, Dublin*

The secret romance
between the late
Charlie Haughey &
Terry Keane was
hidden from the
public for 27 years –
the worst kept
secret in the
business!
© Collins, Dublin

Former Taoisigh Albert Reynolds and Bertie Ahern swap a few stories.

Their remarkable role in bringing peace to Ireland will go down in history.
© *Collins, Dublin*

Albert was always part of the country & western wing of Fianna Fáil. Bertie became a late member when he succeeded him. © *Collins, Dublin*

Bishop Eamon Casey being confronted by Gordon Thomas about his secret romance and love child with Annie Murphy, while in hiding in South America. © *Collins, Dublin*

The singing priest Fr Michael Cleary with his son Ross and his "wife" Phyllis Mitchell. © *Collins, Dublin*

Veteran *Mirror* reporter, the late and great Ted Oliver, shows his facial wounds minutes after being bitten on the nose by footballer Vinnie Jones.
© *Collins, Dublin*

The monster of Mountshannon, evil Brendan O'Donnell, who killed Imelda Riney, her son Liam and Fr Joe Walsh with a shot to each of their heads.
© Collins, Dublin

The beautiful Imelda Riney had the misfortune of feeling sorry for O'Donnell and paid the ultimate price with her life.
© Collins, Dublin

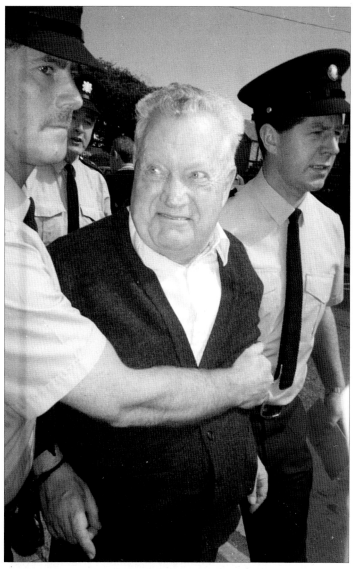

The man who rocked the Catholic Church to its foundations, notorious paedophile Fr Brendan Smyth, who ruthlessly abused children all over the country. © *Collins, Dublin*

The master and his apprentice – tabloid legend Paddy Clancy and myself in Cork covering the Sophie du Plantier murder. © *Collins, Dublin*

Piers Morgan bravely stood up to the Blair government and took a stand against the war in Iraq.
© *Collins, Dublin*

The young men had been out on the parade ground marching around playing their music after 8 a.m. A half an hour later a device exploded in their recreation centre changing room, causing absolute carnage. Apart from the ten who died, a further 22 were maimed or injured. The blast was so loud it could be felt two miles away in the middle of Deal town centre.

I was down in Sussex on another story and my beeper went off, informing me of the explosion and instructing me to go immediately to Deal, which was about an hour away. I got there around 10.45 a.m., and for the first time ever, I felt genuine anger and hatred towards my Irish accent. I started asking questions but received no answers, and if looks could kill, the local people wanted me dead. I was extremely nervous and scared.

To this day I believe none of them accepted I was a reporter and that they suspected that I was one of the bombers. They were angry, bitter, and seeking revenge. They wanted blood for what had happened, and at that stage anyone Irish would do. Very few Irish people were living in Deal, unlike the other bigger towns in the county, Dover and Folkstone, where thousands were residing as they worked on the Channel Tunnel.

One of the first reporters I met that day was the late Tom Merrin of the *Daily Mirror*, who asked me what the hell I was doing in Deal with my accent, and warned me to get out before I was strung up by a mob. Tom had read the mood correctly, and quickly suggested I go to a hotel on the outskirts of Dover and lie low. He would meet me there in a couple of hours and give me a full fill-in on the story, and asked in the meantime if I could ring my security contacts at home and see if I could I come up with anything about the IRA unit that might be involved.

We soon discovered the impact of the IRA bomb was devastating, in addition to the high death toll. Three floors of the army building were destroyed and dozens of houses nearby were severely damaged. One eyewitness, who had spoken to me, 77 year old Doris Lilly, was in her bathroom when the bomb exploded, and the force of the blast blew her 20 ft into her living room. She looked up to see her windows blown out and wallpaper ripped off her walls. She said: "I have a bad heart and the explosion shook me badly. When it went off, I immediately thought 'it's those devils from across the water'." She collapsed into the arms of a milkman who rushed in to rescue her and made her a cup of tea.

Another resident, James Hewitt, 48, who lived in Campbell Road right beside the barracks, was getting into his car when the bomb went off. He said: "You could hear the screams coming from the barracks. It was horrible; we all felt so helpless. I clung onto the car, there was an almighty bang and debris began flying in all directions. It is nothing short of a miracle none of the residents were killed or seriously injured."

The bombing was part of a concerted campaign by the IRA against the British armed forces during the 20th year of the deployment of UK troops in Northern Ireland. In August, 1988 they bombed a North London barracks, and three explosions wrecked the headquarters of the Parachute Regiment in Shropshire seven months later. There were also five attacks on British soldiers based in West Germany.

I never felt any bitterness towards the people of Deal; their hatred was quite understandable. A lot of Irish people in Kent were attacked in the weeks following as the hunt for the IRA gang intensified. I spent several days in Kent on the story but never returned to the town centre. Tom Merrin and my colleagues in the pack kept me completely up to date so I didn't miss a line. It was the start of a great friendship with Merrin, who had spent a lifetime in Fleet Street, and although in his mid-fifties, still had the time and patience for young reporters.

Within weeks he'd signed me up as a member of the Royal Brighton Yacht Club, even though he never sailed on a boat in his life. Tom had a fantastic sense of fun and wonderful humour. He was so talented and is, to this day, the only man I've known who could file a 1,000 word story off the top of his head from his notebook, without writing it, and it would appear word for word in the paper in the best English you could ever dream of. The sub-editors would never have to lay a finger on his copy.

He also had a great nickname for news desks – the grown-ups. It is a phrase I love and every time I hear it, I think of Tom. Merrin unfortunately died of cancer a few years after he retired from the *Daily Mirror*.

* * *

One of my dad's many cousins, Peter Kierans, spent much of his life working on a voluntary basis for Concern, the Irish aid agency. He tipped me off that there was a serious story developing in Uganda – an AIDS epidemic where a whole generation from 20 to 40 years old had died leaving thousands of children orphaned. There was also a second Drogheda connection in the Medical Missionary of Mary nuns, who ran the local Our Lady of Lourdes Hospital, and also had a team of 14 sisters who ran a hospital and school on the ground in southern Uganda.

Brian Hitchen loved foreign stories, and he was particularly proud when his paper was breaking international news. Despite the big cost, he agreed that I would travel to Uganda with photographer Tony Fisher and do a three-part series.

I made contact with the nuns and they agreed to bring us around and show us the pain and suffering when we got to Africa. We flew from London to Nairobi in Kenya, where we stayed for a few nights before getting a connecting flight to Entebbe airport, overlooking beautiful Lake Victoria.

The first two things that struck me on landing were the scenery and the corruption. Uganda is situated right on the equator, and the land is among the most fertile in the world, yet thanks to the dictator Idi Amin, its people lived in dire poverty, when they should have been one of the richest on the continent. Amin ruled Uganda with an iron fist from January 1971 to 1979. He came to power in a military coup, deposing Prime Minister Milton Obote. His regime was scarred by human rights abuses, repression, ethnic persecution and killings.

It is estimated by international observers and human rights groups that between 100,000 and 500,000 people were slaughtered during his reign. He was overthrown after getting embroiled in a war with neighbouring Tanzania over the Kangera province. He fled to Libya before moving to Saudi Arabia, where he lived until he died in 2003, at the age of 78.

We had to pay a five dollar bill to six different people to have our bags removed from the aircraft to the terminal building, and everywhere we went it was the only currency people wanted to know about. There was only one hotel that was safe to stay in, the Sheraton, in Kampala, which was surrounded by a large wire fence and was heavily guarded. My room overlooked the city and there was nothing I enjoyed more than sitting out on the balcony with a vodka and coke in my hand listening to the wonderful sounds of Africa.

I understood very quickly how the English expatriates and other Europeans were attracted to this amazing continent over the previous two centuries. Africa is like your very first love, once you fall for her, you will never forget her.

I walked the old streets of the city where the whites and the Asians lived before Amin and his army ran them out of the country and destroyed Uganda's trade and wealth in the process. You could see row after row of big old colonial houses where they enjoyed a fantastic life of luxury. Now these buildings lay in ruin, surrounded by overgrown gardens and empty swimming pools.

I just imagined the lives they led, but when the Europeans and the Asians left Uganda, tragically for the natives, all the jobs went with them. The only ones who made any money were maverick Amin and his cronies, before he was eventually overthrown and forced to flee. His dictatorship, as the movie *The Last King of Scotland* showed, brought his country to its knees.

We got our directions and headed off to Southern Uganda to see the impact of AIDS. I will never forget a little painted sign at the side of the road, which simply said Equator. What we came across was a series of shanty towns, and people wandering around in bare feet and threadbare clothing. After driving for several hours we reached our destination and met up with the nuns.

Tony Fisher was not a particularly religious man and he found it highly amusing that we were going to stay in a convent for a couple of days with all these nuns. But his opinion soon changed, for what we found was a dedicated team of women who were so determined and driven by what they did that they put us to shame. One was a surgeon, another

was an anaesthetist and a third was a dentist, and there were
nurses, teachers, and a chef; everything the community
needed the nuns could do.

Their small hospital, built by the bare hands of the local
community, served a hinterland of over half a million people.
Their school was full of fantastic children with big smiles,
eager to learn. Many walked up to six miles to and from
school every day without batting an eyelid. The work the
nuns were doing on the ground was quite phenomenal.

Nothing however prepared me for the terrible human
tragedy I witnessed the next day. Uganda in the late eighties
was just like Ireland during the famine. Everyone lived on a
half acre of land and the staple diet in Uganda was the
banana, compared to the potato at home. At every house we
called in to, the mother and father were dead, victims of
AIDS. At farm after farm we came across grandparents who
were rearing the children of their own sons and daughters
killed by the epidemic.

One man we met was feeding 11 grandchildren; all his
own sons and daughters had perished. We soon met young
mothers with only days and weeks to live, many holding
children a year or two old who were also HIV positive. The
nuns and the Ugandan authorities gave us statistics showing
that a whole generation was in the process of being
eliminated, and thousands upon thousands of children were
being left to the grandparents to bring up.

The problem was simply that there was little or no
contraception in Uganda. Neither the men nor the women
believed in it, and the virus was spreading like wildfire.
Education and the availability of condoms were the keys to
solving the deadly crisis. Even though the nuns were devout
Catholics, they were extremely pragmatic and didn't let

their religious beliefs get in the way of their mission to save lives.

The story was just heartbreaking. It's very rare that I get emotionally involved in a story but I will never forget, for as long as I live, the faces of all those little children whose mums and dads had died. All we could do was highlight the situation and hope the world would give Uganda some help.

The editor was very moved by the story I filed and gave it a massive show in the paper. A couple of weeks later ITN picked up on the story and sent a team out to Uganda. The story made the lead on the *News at Ten*, so our work wasn't in vain. AIDS will always be a problem in Africa, but the situation in Uganda is, thankfully, now nothing like it used to be. Condoms are more freely available and fewer lives are on the line. In all we spent two weeks in Uganda; it was a trip I'll never forget.

* * *

In the autumn of 1990 I was to get my first exposure – excepting the Troubles of course – to the horrors of war.

The Iraqi invasion of Kuwait on August 2, 1990 caused shockwaves around the world. After several months of war mongering, the country's dictator, Saddam Hussein, decided to send his army across the border in a smash and grab raid for oil. Between them Iraq and Kuwait controlled 20 percent of the world's oil revenues. The West and the Israelis in particular were aghast, and Saddam's actions sent the cost of crude oil soaring. There were also fears he would try and take Saudi Arabia next.

By August 9 the Baghdad regime declared Kuwait part of Iraq and closed the borders. There were 4000 Britons and 2500 Americans living and working in Kuwait, and Iraq decided to round them up and hold them as "human shield" hostages, detaining them at key military and strategic locations.

Within days Operation Desert Shield was launched and the United States and her allies began a military build up in the Middle East over the following months, vowing to send the Iraqis back where they came from.

The world and its mother flew to the region trying to get a handle on the story, and the race was on for journalists to get into Iraq and Kuwait city.

Most newspapers and broadcasters decided to base their reporters, photographers and TV crews in Amman, the capital city of Jordan, which also borders Iraq. Initially, our Editor, Brian Hitchen, dispatched Barry Gardiner, one of our most experienced reporters, to the region, but within a month I was ordered out to replace him, and so began my tenure as a war correspondent. The fact I was single meant I had no baggage and wasn't under pressure to get home.

Photographer Frank Barrett and I were based in the five-star Sheraton Hotel in the heart of Amman along with the rest of Fleet Street's finest journalists. There was Nick Parker and Phil Hannaford from *The Sun*, Paul Thompson and Philippa Kennedy from the *Express*, Bob Graham of the *Daily Mail*, Colin Adamson and Stuart Payne from the *London Evening Standard*, Tony Gallagher from *Today*, Jeremy Thompson, then with ITN and Kate Adie of the BBC, to mention but a few.

Jordan was ruled by the charismatic King Hussein, a friend of the West, and the only level-headed and sensible leader in the whole volatile region. Amman itself was a bustling city filled with friendly people, brilliant markets, and most importantly of all, it was a country where you could get a drink. The only downside, if you suffered from a touch of asthma like myself, were the occasional sand storms which left you with a terrible cough and a wheeze in your chest.

We were all basically on a wait and see mission, filing the latest copy daily, filled with the ranting of Saddam from Baghdad, all the diplomatic fallout, plus countless interviews with Kuwaiti refugees who'd managed to cross the border into Jordan and tell us their horror stories. It was exciting and challenging.

We were blessed that the hotel had a Reuters News Agency Middle East newswire on telex, which meant we were getting information from their correspondents in Baghdad three hours ahead of our news desks in London. Our bosses in London had the general Reuters service, which didn't contain as much Middle East news as we were receiving. This was a great help to us in being able to put together reliable, accurate pieces from Iraq even though we weren't in the country. It also gave us a decisive edge, in that we knew more than our bosses and helped justify our expensive existence abroad.

It was a five to six hour drive from Amman to the Iraqi border, all of which was effectively across a desert. Over 100,000 refugees, mostly Arabs and Asians, fled Kuwait and crossed the border into Jordan. Many of the refugees were coming over at night, when Saddam's soldiers couldn't catch them. Most arrived with just the shirts on their back and a suitcase, carrying their passport and most important of all, US dollars, if they were lucky enough to have some.

Kuwait had a population of 1.9 million people. The majority of native Kuwaitis were paid a share of the oil money from the Royal al-Sabah family, which ruled the country. Most citizens lived in big houses with swimming pools and had their own personal staff, made up of poor Pakistani, Sri Lankan, and Bangladeshi workers. And collectively, they all desperately wanted to escape their new hard line rulers.

Some of the horror stories from the refugees were heartbreaking, and many told how their wives and daughters were stripped, raped and robbed by the Iraqi soldiers within days of the invasion. There was a night curfew in Kuwait City, and after dark gangs of Saddam's soldiers would roam the suburbs looking for prey, breaking into houses seeking victims for brutal sex attacks. The troops, who were poorly paid, endeavoured to get their hands on whatever cash or jewellery they could. They plundered all around them and didn't care who they hurt.

Many families could no longer live under this fear and decided to take their chances and risk their lives by crossing the border. A number of tented villages were set up in the Jordanian desert for the refugees, but many others just roamed the streets of Amman, penniless, begging for food. But the men also wanted to fight for their country, and many trained in military units and participated in the Western invasion to reclaim Kuwait a few of months later.

The Iraqis themselves had a large embassy in Amman. Every week we queued up to see whether we could secure an Iraqi visa. Despite the invasion, there were still daily flights between Baghdad and Amman. Some, like my colleague Paul Thompson, got in for a week, but even though I had an Irish passport, which is traditionally very useful in the Middle East, the Iraqis wouldn't let me in.

We also received regular briefings from the Iraqis in Jordan, giving their spin on the invasion. It was all lies and propaganda and we didn't believe a word of it. There was a large international diplomatic presence in Amman as a result of the invasion. We liaised closely with the British and American embassies, who gave us regular briefings on the build-up of the allied forces in neighbouring Saudi Arabia, under the leadership of the colourful American commander General Norman Schwarzkopf, or "Stormin' Norman" as he became affectionately known in tabloid land.

By October 17 there were 200,000 American troops, 15,000 British soldiers and 11,000 French troops in the Gulf. The Allied force was also soon to include soldiers from other Arab League countries, including Egypt, Syria and Morocco. The tension was growing in Amman, as speculation mounted as to when the air and land war would kick off.

Some of the diplomats threw parties to entertain the hacks and to keep us onside, so to speak. One of the funniest moments was at a party thrown by the US Ambassador, whom I had never met. We all lashed into the free drink, and within hours I was full of vodka and coke and singing Irish folk songs. At two in the morning I got cornered by this middle aged American guy in a shirt and jeans, asking me a hundred and one questions about the old Emerald Isle. He told me he was of Irish descent and that his grandparents came from the west coast of Ireland, and that he would love to hear a traditional Gaelic song. I let rip with an old song I learned in the Gaeltacht in Donegal years ago, to a standing ovation from all the diplomats. Eventually, I asked him was he with the CIA or the US Special Forces. He replied: "No, I'm the new American Ambassador in Amman", much to my embarrassment.

He was a sound guy who enjoyed the craic and like most Yanks had absolutely no airs or graces. I later got into a fist-fight with a drunk, obnoxious journalist from a broadsheet newspaper after he called me an Irish wanker. The Ambassador was also offended and helped kick the dickhead out. The same guy had the hots for a girl in the British embassy, but she couldn't stand the sight of him.

One of the nicest people I met was the former British Prime Minister and Conservative party veteran, the late Ted Heath. He flew to Amman and then on to Baghdad on a mercy mission to try and free British hostages being held as human shields. Mr Heath was warm, friendly and extremely charming.

After a couple of days of negotiations he returned to Jordan, accompanied by 33 British hostages, who told of the brutality of the Iraqi regime and the inhumane conditions they were held in. Most were locked up 24 hours a day and just given the barest rations for survival, and their stories made front page headlines. The British Prime Minister Margaret Thatcher didn't approve of Mr Heath's solo run, but I admired his courage and his humanitarian convictions. Every one of the people he freed will thank him to their dying day.

Over the subsequent weeks Saddam used the hostages as pawns in negotiations with the West. The American President George H.W. Bush got the US Congress to approve a resolution sanctioning the use of military force to free Kuwait. An Amnesty International report also revealed that the Iraqis had inflicted terrible brutality on the people of Kuwait.

I got called back to London in mid-November to have a break from the war zone. I was lucky to be going home for the holidays, but I felt for all the soldiers and their families who would not get to spend Christmas together.

Fortunately, not all of the stories we covered were heartbreaking tales of war and suffering – some were just plain hilarious, and some were not even, in the end, stories at all.

* * *

For years there were rumours in the papers in London that the football manager Brian Clough was a chronic alcoholic, but no one could prove it. The man who won the European Cup with Nottingham Forest, and won the old English First Division with Derby County, was a living legend. Our news desk got a tip off from the United States that Clough had been admitted to the Betty Ford Clinic in Palm Springs, California, a couple of hours drive from Los Angeles. The tip came from one of the Editor's old contacts on the *National Enquirer*, and I was sent out on my own to try and stand it up.

The informant had come up with pretty good information on stories in the past, so Graham Jones and the news desk were extremely excited. Cloughie, as he was known, had put on loads of weight, and his whole face had ballooned in recent years. He had the look of a man who was seriously off the wagon.

I drank in Vagabones until about 5 a.m., and then Mullally got one of his drivers to take me to Gatwick airport to catch a Virgin Atlantic 10 a.m. flight to Los Angeles. I was flying club class which meant my seat could turn into a bed with a reclining back and foot-rest. I put a blanket over me after take-off and woke up almost 12 hours later on the West Coast of the States as we were coming in to land. I had drowned that much vodka that I had the best sleep on a plane I ever had.

When I got to LA the contact met me at the airport and we drove down to Palm Springs. His mother was working in the clinic and he was adamant it was Brian Clough. I listened intently but kept an open mind and decided I wasn't writing a line until I had stood up every aspect of the story.

Palm Springs was a beautiful place where the wealthy lived in big houses in glorious California sunshine. The Clinic had been set up and opened in October 1982 by Betty

Ford. Betty herself was a chronic alcoholic and decided to found a centre that would cater for women like her, after she fought her own demons at a US Naval hospital.

Betty Ford was a very outspoken First Lady who never held back with her opinions, and she was regarded at the time as the most active and successful woman in the White House since Eleanor Roosevelt. Her alcohol and drug rehabilitation centre was regularly used by troubled celebrities, and gained a reputation across the US for putting people back on the straight and narrow. Its tough methods are regarded to this day to be extremely successful.

I started doing the checks and speaking to people coming in and out of the clinic. As confidentiality was sacrosanct, with many of the staff it was difficult to get information. On top of this, Graham Jones kept calling me every day asking when we were going to run with the story. I think he thought I was having the time of my life partying with the girls in California.

Eventually, I got to know a nurse who was working there, and asked if there was an Englishman named Brian Clough, who was 54 years old, at the clinic. I wanted another source apart from our contact. The girl came back to me and confirmed that there was an Englishman there by that name and he was around the age I had suggested. By now the adrenalin was flying and I could sense a world exclusive for the *Daily Star*. However, something told me inside my head that if you can't see it, don't believe it.

I needed to get a picture of this Brian Clough, or see him myself, to confirm it was the great man. After an offer of more money the nurse agreed to get a shot for me and thank God she did. It was a Brian Clough alright, but not our football manager. Everything else matched up except his face. She also got me inside the centre just to prove it to myself. I pretended I was a patient and got talking to the bloke. He was delighted to get chatting to someone from back home.

I knew the news desk would go mental if I phoned them up and told them the story was dead after investing thousands on the investigation. I called the Editor, Brian Hitchen, and told him the story wasn't true. He just turned round and said: "Thanks John, you've just saved me a million quid in a libel action. Go and have a few pints."

The lesson was simple – don't believe what you want to believe, and if you can't see it, don't write it. My admiration for Hitchen, a brilliant editor, just grew and grew. All he ever wanted was the truth, irrespective of whether it was good news or bad news. And that's all any good reporter ever had to do.

* * *

I was starting to enjoy the life in California and hated the thought of going home. As luck would have it, we then got another tip-off that Rod Stewart and the New Zealand model Rachel Hunter were getting married in LA the following weekend, on December 15, 1990. I'd never been to Hollywood so I drove up and booked into a five star hotel on Rodeo Drive. Two friends of mine from home, Caroline Brassil and Davie Byrne, were living in LA at the time, so I called them up and asked them if they fancied going to Rod's wedding, and to bring a few friends in case we needed a bit of cover. The plan was to have our own little party in the hotel bar and no one would think we were hacks.

My current boss at the Mirror group, Richard Wallace, was sent over for the *Mirror,* while Andy Coulson, the former

Editor of the *News of the World,* did the wedding for *The Sun*.
The two boys were good company and good fun. They were
both showbiz reporters so they were more tuned in with all
Rod's crowd than I was.

Rachel Hunter was absolutely stunning. She was only 21
when she met randy Rod, who was 24 years older than her.
He spotted her when she modelled for *Sports Illustrated*
magazine in their annual swimsuit special edition. As the
world's biggest admirer of leggy blondes, Rod felt obliged to
get to know her. They met at an LA nightclub, fell in love and
decided to get hitched in a typically Hollywood whirlwind
romance.

The wedding took place at the Beverly Hills Presbyterian
Church in a 30 minute ceremony. About 250 guests attended,
and the star wore a dark grey morning suit and no tie. Rachel
looked stunning in a calf-length ivory lace dress with a floral
head-dress. He escorted his new wife along a red carpet lined
by eight pipers to his waiting Rolls Royce, proudly boasting:
"She is great, she is wonderful and she is beautiful".

Twenty private security guards were hired to keep out
unwanted guests, and sheets were hung around an outside
courtyard to block the view of the photographers. Rod hired
a double decker bus and three coaches to take his guests to the
reception at the exclusive Four Seasons Hotel, where we were
busy boozing unnoticed in the bar. But it is very hard to teach
an old dog new tricks – we didn't have to go far looking for
the story, for the story came to us.

Later in the evening, Rod left the wedding reception and
came into the bar with all his Scottish mates. They were
laughing, joking, singing and having the craic. But after two
hours of Rod missing in action, Rachel stormed in looking for
her husband, and gave him a bollocking before marching him

back to the wedding. I guess for Rod it was a sign of things to come.

We were thrilled to bits as we had a great story – Rod and Rachel rowing on the wedding night. It made the page one splash in all the tabloids the next morning. The news desk were delighted that the wedding had been well worth going to. All my pals also had a great time, and Caroline even got Rod's autograph!

Unfortunately Rod and Rachel's marriage only lasted nine years. The couple had two children, Renee and Liam, but when Rachel turned 29, in 1999, she decided enough was enough and she walked out of the relationship. Rod was completely shell-shocked and publicly complained: "I was faithful to Rachel for nine years, an astounding achievement for me, and then I got a smack in the head for it."

In 2005 Rod filed for divorce and it took over a year to finalise. Rachel had, however, signed a pre-nuptial agreement. She claimed a lump sum plus full financial support for the kids, thought to be in the region of $66 million, on the condition that she continued to live in Los Angeles.

After the New Year I was to head back to the Middle East, as the build up of allied forces in the Gulf indicated that the war was about to begin.

Fleet Street - The Daily Star
1989-1992

Part 2

CHAPTER 4

The word within the British Government was that a ground and air offensive would be launched in January. By December, a massive army of 580,000 allied troops had assembled in the Gulf, the majority in Saudi Arabia, in preparation for the fight against the 540,000 strong Iraqi army. I needed to get back over to the Middle East.

Even though the West was effectively protecting Saudi Arabia from Iraq, it was very difficult to get into Saudi. While the Saudi Royal Family enjoyed a western education and spent their summers relaxing in Marbella in Spain, most of the country was extremely backward, and there was heavy censorship in a state ruled by the religious police.

Our News Editor, Graham Jones, had a contact at the Saudi embassy in London, and after much negotiation he managed to secure two Saudi visas to cover the war. As soon as New Year's was over both Nick Constable, another reporter on the paper and I were called in to Editor Brian Hitchen's office and told we would be covering the war.

Because I was single, I would be based in Dhahran and be at the frontline of the war while Nick, who was married with two kids, would cover all the British and American military briefings at Allied headquarters in the Saudi capital of Riyadh. The company insured both off us for half a million pounds Sterling and I was told to go and make a will. I decided to leave half to my mother Carmel and the rest to my girlfriend Karen, who later became my wife. It was the first time it hit home to me that I could actually get killed out there.

On the day before we flew off Brian took Nick and me out for lunch. He said that in his experience there were two rules of war reporting – don't take stupid chances and put your life on the line and no matter what, make sure you get your copy back. Remember, this was in the early days of mobile phone technology, and you certainly wouldn't be using one in the desert. Some journalists were given satellite phones to file, but typically, the one that Express Newspapers had didn't work!

Brian is an extremely charismatic and emotional man and always wore his heart on his sleeve. He gave both of us hugs as we left the office and he had tears in his eyes. "No matter what lads, come back safe," he said. I made a mental note that if I ever became an editor, I would always treat my reporters with nothing but the utmost respect, and it is a rule I stand by to this very day.

I had to take a ten hour flight to Bahrain via Abu Dhabi with Gulf Air. I was excited but nervous at the thought of covering the war. Karen was extremely upset and worried sick about my safety. I joked with her that she'd be worth a fortune if I got blown up. I kept telling her she had nothing to worry about and that we were all big boys.

The Saudis had built a 14 mile causeway from Bahrain to the Saudi mainland. Bahrain was totally westernised, full of bars, restaurants, hotels and casinos. Although you couldn't get a drink in the Saudi kingdom, many Saudis would cross over to Bahrain at the weekends to party, totally contradicting their devout Muslim religious beliefs.

I got a taxi to the border checkpoint, where my visa was examined and I was quizzed extensively about the purpose of my visit. My bags were also thoroughly searched to ensure I had no pornography or alcohol with me. The driver was let through and I was taken to my hotel, the Meridian, about half an hour away.

The hotel was five-star, big and posh, overlooking the sea. One of the first people I met was Richard Kay, then the *Daily Mail's* much respected Royal Correspondent, who flew in with Prince Charles to see the British troops, and then was ordered to stay. My great friend Bill Akass also arrived in for the *Daily Mirror* with Ramsey Smith.

Bill had been out during the autumn when the *Mirror's* then owner, crooked tycoon Robert Maxwell, phoned him up and demanded he go around the army bases in the desert selling encyclopaedias from one of his companies to the soldiers! Bill flatly refused, and there followed the mother of all rows between Maxwell and the *Mirror's* Editor over Bill's role in the desert. The row was eventually sorted out and Bill continued his career as a hack. He was hoping and praying maverick Maxwell wouldn't be wrecking his head this time.

We were also joined in the hotel by reporter Nick Parker and photographer Phil Hannaford from *The Sun*. Veteran *Mirror* snapper Ken Lennox was also with us along with Mike Moore from *Today* newspaper, with his reporter Ged Evans. A down to earth Brummie, Nick Parker was your out and out tabloid man, a fantastic reporter but also a terrific writer. He also had a great sense of humour. Nick, Bill and I were like the three young guns, while seasoned hack Chris Walker, *The London Times'* Middle East correspondent, regularly joined our company to give us his great guidance and assistance. Walker had seen it all before all over the world; he was like a father figure to us and we all cherished his advice and company.

One of the first things I did was hire a small white Suzuki jeep which I christened "Baby". It was the only one I could get since nearly every four wheel drive in the desert had been snapped up by the military. The other item I got was a shortwave radio so I could listen to the BBC World Service to find out exactly what was going on. The Beeb had an army of people in the desert between television and radio, and they would be my eyes and ears. We also had CNN on the television in the hotel, and since they were the only broadcaster with a camera crew in Baghdad, information from them would turn out to be invaluable.

The biggest fear for us all was that, when war broke out, the Iraqis would use chemical weapons in retaliation. Saddam had been threatening the mother of all battles as the coalition turned the screws on him militarily and through the use of UN sanctions. He had used chemical warheads in the eight year war with neighbouring Iran, leading to the terrifying deaths of thousands of Iranian soldiers. He also wasn't shy about using chemical weapons when he quelled an uprising by Kurdish rebels in Northern Iraq, wiping out thousands of innocent people, including young children. The effect of chemical weapons is devastating and known to give the victims a horrendous, painful death.

We all had to present ourselves to the British Army Press Attaché in Dhahran, a Colonel David McDine, who had previously worked in the British Army press office in Belfast, so he and I had plenty to talk about.

We were all issued with a chemical weapon body suit plus a gas mask to protect ourselves in the event of an attack. But we were also given Anthrax and shown where to inject ourselves, to have a quick and painless death before the chemicals took hold of our bodies.

The training was very frightening and we all realized for the first time that this wasn't a game in the desert sun; it was war and it was very real. Some of the reporters had applied to accompany the British and American troops in the event of a ground invasion. Richard Kay got permission to be embedded with them, but I decided to go it alone and take things one day at a time.

The biggest problem we all had waiting for the war to start was boredom. There was very little to do in Dhahran except go to McDonalds or KFC. We would drive up to the Dhahran airbase and watch plane after plane of fighter jets taking off, doing training exercises

I found the Saudis to be a difficult and very rude people, and I got the sense that they totally despised all these foreigners being in their country, even though the coalition soldiers were there to save them from Saddam and his mob. The Saudis also treated their women as second class citizens. Women were not allowed to sit with men in restaurants, and instead had to go into a family room with the children.

It all came to a head for us one night when we went to dinner with a female reporter from Houston, Texas. She was Jewish, but only we knew that. She was sitting at a table with us when the religious police, who obviously got a tip-off from the owner, came into the restaurant. Four of them came in, in their uniforms and carrying sticks, and attacked her. We ended up in a fist-fight with them. They were ranting and raving and tried to physically pull her out of the restaurant and take her into custody, and God only knows what would have happened to her there. Someone got hold of some American soldiers and the next thing we knew the US military police were in on top of us. The girl explained what happened and after a bitter argument the religious police were warned off.

I have to be honest – I hated their guts. They stood for everything I despised. In our house, you were taught to treat women with respect and to never hit a woman. Our American colleague was extremely upset and distressed by the episode. And when you think about it, why wouldn't she be? Her young countrymen were putting their lives on the line for the Saudis, and yet she wasn't even allowed to sit and eat with her male friends in a restaurant. What happened was a disgrace, and I still get angry when I think about it. It was the first time I witnessed the clash between Western and Muslim cultures, but I would see it many times in the years to come.

* * *

By the middle of January 1991, Iraq had totally ignored the last United Nations warning to leave Kuwait. As we waited in our Dhahran hotel, we were discreetly warned that the war would start any day. The Allied ground forces were encamped in the desert, ready for the order to invade. I was a bit nervous and didn't know what to expect.

On the night of January 16, 1991, exactly 170 days since the invasion of Kuwait, I knew something was up. After dark, wave after wave of fighter jets starting leaving Dhahran airport. This was unusual; there were too many planes in the air for a training exercise. I phoned the office and told them that my gut feeling was it was all going to kick off. I wasn't in Baghdad but Saudi was the next best place to be. Before we knew it, CNN announced that there had been air strikes in Baghdad, and within minutes there were shots of the city's skyline, with anti-aircraft fire going off all over the place. It was difficult to assess the damage, but I knew it would be devastating. I was also acutely aware that it wouldn't be long before the Iraqis hit back. I got my chemical suit and gas mask and laid them out on the bed in my hotel room, so they were right beside me if needed.

I filed over 2,000 words off the top of my head on the hotel phone to the copy taker in London, and proclaimed Operation Desert Storm, as it was known, was under way, describing how America's giant B52 bombers were bombarding Baghdad. The editor had a great laugh in the office when "giant" was incorrectly spelled "joint", as the copy taker misinterpreted my Irish accent. It was to be the first of numerous little misunderstandings over my brogue, which our great sub-editors found hilarious, but sorted out quickly. London was running with the first nine pages, and I was to keep giving them every last cough and spit right through the night, as they were bringing out a special 6 a.m. London War Edition.

As I went back on the phone for a second take the air raid sirens went off in Dhahran. The city had been preparing for weeks beforehand and everyone was to run to their nearest shelter. I put on my chemical suit and gas mask and ran down the stairs to the kitchen in the basement of the hotel, which was our rendezvous point. Being inside the chemical suit was bizarre. I could hardly breathe, never mind walk. We all looked like astronauts on the moon! I was sweating like mad but afraid to take it off in case one of Saddam's scud missiles had chemical weapons and hit us. After about an hour we were given the all clear and came back up for air. It was such a relief to get the bloody mask off my face, it was driving me mad, and my hair was soaking wet with sweat.

The Americans had, thankfully, placed Patriot anti-missile systems in Saudi Arabia. The plan was for these Patriot missiles to blow up the Scuds that Saddam rained down on us.

No one could overestimate the might of the American war machine and I was thankful for it. I was on the phone again and filed a whole piece about the Scud scare in Saudi and the relief among the masses, that so far, chemical weapons had not been used by the Iraqis. The editor was delighted with my fast, accurate copy and was on the phone to congratulate me. Saudi Arabia was three hours ahead of London and I eventually went to sleep at about 8 a.m. By lunchtime I woke up and got to see the first daylight pictures out of Baghdad.

On the first night of the war the Allies had destroyed many of Iraq's air bases and combat aircraft, and their air defence systems. Some of the Iraqi aircraft got off the ground, but of these, most fled to Iran, never to be returned. More importantly, almost all Saddam's chemical and nuclear plants were destroyed, along with his Scud missile sites. Saddam's palace in Baghdad was hit, and divisions of his elite Republic Guard, the Iraqi army's best and most loyal fighters, were also targeted along the Kuwaiti border, damaging their resistance to the eventual ground offensive. Various Iraqi positions in Kuwait were also hit by missiles.

The Iraqis were quite cleverly playing up the civilian casualties to try and get Arab public opinion on their side. Saddam was ranting about how he would destroy the great Satan, America and defend his people to the death. There were few casualties on our side and all the brave fighter pilots in Dhahran had returned to base safely. I thought to myself that these boys had balls of steel. I'd hate to think how they'd be treated if the Iraqis got their hands on them.

That next night the planes started taking off again. Once again I got the chemical suit out ready for action. This time Saddam wasn't going to lie down, and he retaliated. On January 18 there came the first of several Scud missile attacks on the Israeli capital, Tel Aviv. The terrified population ran to air raid shelters in their gas masks. It was a deliberate attempt to provoke retaliation by Israel, but under pressure from the Americans they didn't respond.

Over the next couple of nights Iraq sent Scud missiles into Saudi. They were all taken out by the Patriot missiles and no one was hurt. The worst thing about it was that you heard the siren going off, but you just didn't know where they were going to strike. After about a week we started to relax and stopped putting on the chemical suits and gas masks.

We were all given pooled reports from American and British reporters who were embedded with the pilots and the ground troops. The Yanks couldn't write for peanuts and we'd always find the story in the third to last paragraph on the sixth page. However, we were glad of the information and it was up to us to analyse and dissect it.

We were also starting to get extremely thirsty. None of us had had a drink for weeks and we were anxious to let off steam. Reporters based in Bahrain were having a great old time, while we were working non-stop. We heard that some British expatriates had a bar on the Aramco oil compound. We made contact with them and they invited us in for some homemade brew. They also had their own version of Poitín, which tasted almost like pure alcohol. We all got completely hammered and woke up with the hangovers from hell the next day, but we didn't give a damn, we were just all pleased to get a beer on Saudi soil.

By the middle of February we were all in full-blown war mode. I also knew it wouldn't be long before the ground offensive began, and that I had to be in the right position. Nick Parker and I decided it was time to leave the hotel and drive up to the Saudi-Kuwaiti border, and try and link up with the land forces as they moved into Kuwait. The Iraqis had planted land mines across many parts of the desert so we knew it would be very dangerous.

On February 24, General Norman Schwarzkopf announced the start of the ground war, after the enemy had been softened up by almost six weeks of non-stop air raids.

The night after we left, a Scud missile came into Dhahran and the Patriot missile system failed to take it out. It narrowly missed the wing of the hotel where we had been staying, and hit a gym nearby, which housed US troops, killing 29 and injuring 91. I couldn't bear to think of the carnage we'd left behind but we had been very lucky; it could have been us any night of the week, there were that many Scuds fired at us. I used to joke to the lads, the Scuds a dud! We wouldn't have been smiling this time, with so much death and destruction in the town.

It was a ten hour drive in the jeep up towards the border. We decided to go to a town about 20 miles from Kuwait. I travelled on my own while Nick and photographer Phil Hannaford were in their jeep behind me. The Saudi border with Iraq and then Kuwait runs for hundreds of miles. Looking for an army, even half a million of them, can be like looking for a needle in a haystack, especially since you weren't really supposed to be there in the first place.

We were also very careful not to stray into Iraq, never mind Kuwait, or we could end up being captured by the Iraqis, held hostage or killed. They'd easily suspect we were Special Forces rather than journalists. We spent the night before the ground invasion with Kuwaiti soldiers we'd come across. One of the most amazing things was how you could feel the ground shake beneath your feet from the force of the aerial bombardment and tank blasts up ahead. It felt like you were in the middle of an earthquake, and I kept thinking that I would not like to be on the receiving end of that.

The Kuwaitis were a picture of calm, and all were eager to right a grave wrong and reclaim their country. Unlike our Saudi hosts, they were delighted to see us and to talk. They had no hang-ups about their religion or the West. And each and every one of them was prepared to die for the cause. I was hoping and praying it wouldn't come to that, that the Iraqi army had taken that much shit that they wouldn't have much energy or the will left to fight.

The next morning, on February 27, we soldiered on towards Kuwait. We came across a track beside a minefield before we were stopped and questioned by US soldiers, who wanted to know who we were and what in the name of God we were doing there. We explained that we were journalists, and he decided to bring us to see his commanding officer. He was your typical American cigar smoking Colonel, gung-ho and ready for battle.

He asked me where I was from and I said Ireland. I knew by his facial reaction that he liked the cut of us. He told me he was from Boston and his parents originally came from the west of Ireland. The Colonel said he was on his way to free Kuwait and we were more than welcome to join him. He ordered us to put our jeeps into the convoy between some of his tanks and to follow them through the minefields.

By a complete fluke we had come across the advance force of American soldiers heading for the city, and we were being given a front row seat on the way to history. They say you make your own luck in newspapers. Nick and I had been largely ignored by the so-called broadsheet reporters who looked down their noses at us because we were tabloid men. Now we were going to get into Kuwait ahead of them all.

An advance guard of US engineers had cleared a track about 6 ft wide through the minefields to make way for the advancing forces. There were thousands upon thousands of coalition troops on the march. You could see hundreds of mines planted on each side of this temporary dirt track. I just kept a tight hold on the steering wheel to make sure I didn't slip off the track onto one of the mines. We were crawling along at a couple of miles an hour. But my hands were sweating like mad and I was terrified I'd make a mistake.

It was only 11 a.m. but soon the sky started getting darker and darker, as we got closer to Kuwait. The oil fields were burning and you could smell the fumes in the thick black smoke. By the time we reached the oil fields we were in total darkness. Saddam had ordered his beleaguered army to retreat from Kuwait the previous day, and they had tried to destroy everything in sight along their way. Oil had been the reason for the invasion, and the Iraqis had set the fields ablaze with explosives as they fled. It was the weirdest feeling in the world being in total darkness at midday. But my main concern as I turned on my full headlights was to avoid the minefields.

After about another two hours we got to the outskirts of Kuwait City. We were now under blue skies and it was a wonderful feeling. There was no fighting to be done; Saddam's men had all run home, terrified of the army hunting them. Yet the bloody scars of war were everywhere. On the way into Kuwait City I saw armoured personnel carriers, tanks and troop-carrying lorries incinerated on both sides of the road. The fleeing force were shown no mercy, and rightly so. The Iraqis got a taste off their own brutal medicine.

Suddenly, out of the blue, people started coming out on the streets. There were men, women and children with big smiles on their faces, proudly waving the Kuwaiti flag. In scenes reminiscent of Paris being liberated from the Germans in World War II, they cheered and applauded the coalition soldiers, many shaking their hands and getting their pictures taken with them. Many of the older women were crying with tears running down their cheeks. A sense of relief could be felt in the air. It was a wonderful scene to witness and one I will never forget. We all take our freedom for granted but boy, when you lose it, it is painful. The Kuwaitis had died as a nation and now they were reborn.

We thanked our American hosts for looking after us so well and Nick, Phil and I made our way to the British Embassy. We were among the first of the hacks there and were joined within an hour by the BBC and ITN. They couldn't believe the tabloid boys had beaten them into the city. I was as proud as punch.

I did a tour of the city centre and the celebrations were in full swing. The night sky was lit up with oil fires and tracer bullets being fired off in victory. The Iraqis made sure they burned all the top hotels, and several other main buildings, along with the Emir's palace. There was a two day battle fought near the airport where over 100 Iraqi tanks were destroyed.

It was 5 a.m. when President Bush announced the war to liberate Kuwait was won and all fighting in the Middle East was to stop. He told the world: "Kuwait is liberated, Iraq's army is defeated and our military objectives are met."

A permanent ceasefire depended on Iraq releasing prisoners of war and Kuwaiti detainees, and also helping to identify minefields and booby traps. Saddam was also warned not to fire any Scud missiles on any other country.

President Bush said: "This is not a time of euphoria; this is not a time to gloat. But it is a time of pride. The victory has been quick, decisive and just, but no one country could claim the victory as its own. It was a victory for Kuwait, for the coalition nations, for the United Nations, for all mankind, for what was right. America must look beyond the victory in the war and become a catalyst for peace."

The fighting ended exactly 100 hours after the ground offensive was launched. General Norman Schwarzkopf told how the coalition forces had rendered 29 Iraqi divisions ineffective, three quarters of the enemy's tanks had been destroyed, two thirds of its artillery pieces were gone, and more than 50,000 Iraqi soldiers taken prisoner, plus a "very large number" of Saddam's soldiers were dead.

The name of the game now was to get my copy back. I had no satellite phone, so getting the words back was a problem, since all phone lines in the city were down. By chance I got chatting to Paul McGeogh, an Australian journalist who worked with *The Age* in Melbourne. He knew a member of the Kuwaiti Resistance who might be able to help me out, provided I kept it secret. McGeogh drove me to a house in the suburbs of the city and there, in the cellar, they had a secure line to the Kuwaiti embassy in Geneva. I filed my piece on the computer and they sent it back to Europe. I gave them the number of my editor in London and they faxed the copy to him.

I didn't get speaking to Brian Hitchen until the next day, courtesy of a sat phone provided by the British Embassy, but he had received every last word of my story. He thought the story of how I got my words out was nearly as good as the liberation of Kuwait!

The actual house I was in was the headquarters of the Kuwaiti Resistance and it was the last place you'd expect to find it. The people who owned the residence were extremely brave. If the Iraqis had found it, each and every one of the family would have been shot on sight. McGeogh and I kept this place to ourselves. If we couldn't get our hands on a phone at least we had a plan B.

I managed to grab a bed in one of the remaining hotels left standing in the city. There was no running water but I didn't give a damn. I had a great night's sleep, the war was over and I was in one piece. The next day I went out to the road to Basra, where the Iraqis were obliterated as they fled in what was the biggest tank battle since the Second World War.

Over 500 tanks and armoured vehicles from the US 7th Armoured Corps had been in a fierce fight with up to 300 tanks of a Republican Guard Division that tried to break through an allied cordon to get back to Baghdad. There were hundreds of bodies everywhere, with burned out tanks and lorries. The smell of burning flesh and death was in the air. Many of the Iraqis were incinerated. It was a sight straight out of hell, and brought home to me the reality of war.

The coalition troops wanted to go the whole way to Baghdad to finish off Saddam's regime once and for all, but President Bush, under pressure from his Arab friends, wouldn't allow it. They were only 150 miles from the capital and could easily have done it. He argued that it was one thing liberating a country, but quite a different story invading another. He made it quite clear that America's quarrel was not with the Iraqi people, but with Saddam Hussein's evil regime, and he looked forward to the day when all could work in peace and harmony with the Iraqi nation. This was a decision, as we all know now, which would come back to haunt the Bush family. After September 11, President George W. Bush foolishly decided to invade Iraq, wrongly claiming Saddam had weapons of mass destruction, costing many young Americans their lives and ultimately, forever marring his Presidency.

The Kuwaiti people I met then started telling me their horror stories. Some claimed that the Iraqis had kidnapped members of their families and had taken them to Baghdad, to hold them as human shields against coalition troops. Others said their wives and children had been raped and murdered. One Kuwaiti fighter showed how the letter S was branded on his arm by the invaders so he would never forget Saddam Hussein.

The Kuwaiti authorities said that 4,000 people had been killed and 15,000 taken hostage since the Iraqis took their country. Many of those taken in for questioning and tortured were often brought back to their homes and then shot in front of their families. There were eyewitness accounts of women being hung by wires at a school, and numerous rape allegations. A family of 12 were executed by the Iraqis after they looted their food supplies, while three teenage boys were shot dead for being suspected members of the Kuwaiti Resistance, before their family home was destroyed by a rocket-propelled grenade.

I decided to do a tour of the city morgues to see some of the atrocities for myself. In one morgue, when you went in the door, there was a stack of about 50 bodies of Iraqi troops piled on top of each other against the wall. At first it didn't really bother me, because I didn't know them. Seeing one body, as any doctor will tell you, is the same as the next. However, the more I thought about it, the more I felt I was wrong. They were all men, aged from their twenties to their forties, and they were probably forced to fight for their country by a ruthless regime that wouldn't think twice about punishing their families if they didn't. Each and every one of these men was still somebody's son, somebody's father. They probably had wives and children worried sick at home, who didn't know if they were dead or alive. I knew they were the enemy, but even in death, everybody is entitled to some dignity. Who was going to identify them, and who was going to send them home to their families for burial?

Several minutes later, I was shown the bodies of seven brothers who had all been tortured and shot by the same Iraqi army I was starting to feel sorry for. You could see how each of them had marks on their bodies from electrocution. They also had their fingernails and toenails ripped out. There were cigarette burns on their bodies. One even had the tops of his fingers chopped off. And each one of them had been shot in the back of the head.

I discovered that all seven had been in the Kuwaiti Resistance and were executed for defending their country. I dreaded to think of the torture they endured before their captors took their lives. Death was probably an escape for them, from the pain they had suffered. They were shown absolutely no mercy, which was typical of Saddam's cronies.

But the saddest sight of all was the little children who had died. Many had been caught up in the crossfire, hit by a stray bullet, or been victims of the bombings. When you looked at their innocent faces, with not a mark on them, you wondered how they lost their lives. The truth is there are no winners in war, and whether we like it or not, innocent people are going to pay with their lives.

I spent five days in Kuwait mopping up before getting the call to come home. I'd been away for almost two months, and I'd had my fill of the Middle East. I spent a night in Bahrain for a good night on the lash before flying home. I'd seen a lot of death, a lot of destruction, but I had made friendships that would last a lifetime.

When I got back to London and eventually Drogheda, I

got a hero's welcome. Hitchen told me I'd done a fantastic job, but more importantly, I had been the only Irish reporter on the frontline of the war. *The Irish Star* in Dublin had given massive shows in the paper, and I had got splash after splash from the Gulf, and my Mam kept cuttings of everything I'd written.

A friend of mine, Paddy Clancy, who later went on to set up *The Sun* in Dublin, was the head of news on the new independent national radio station, Century Radio, and throughout out the whole war he had been ringing me up for live updates, and to give listeners a real life feel of what was going on. Unknown to me, it was great publicity for myself and the paper.

Our national broadcaster and Paddy's main rival RTÉ had sent their star reporter Charlie Bird to the Gulf. But unfortunately for Charlie and the station, he was stuck in Amman in Jordan, and couldn't get a visa to get into Saudi. He was effectively reporting the war from hundreds of miles away while I was right in the thick of the action. This gave Paddy a real upper hand in the battle of the airwaves, and he played it day in and day out. Sadly for me, Century had no money and could hardly pay me. But Paddy returned the favour in kind many times over the years and he and I are still great mates. Not long after the war ended Century went bust. The Irish economy was still in the doldrums, and a national independent radio station was just a few years too early.

I also decided to have the Mother of All Battles party back in Drogheda to celebrate the end of the war. I invited Nick and Bill Akass to come over from London, and we had one of the wildest booze-ups ever. My parents were going to Cheltenham to the races for the week, and they were so relieved that I was home in one piece that they told me to plough ahead. My local publican, Tommy Hanratty, sold me some kegs of beer and actually set up a bar in the kitchen of the house. The party started on Friday night and finished on Monday morning. I invited over 100 people and we rocked and rolled. At one stage the Gardaí actually set up a checkpoint outside my mother's front door to make sure none of us were drinking and driving. We invited them in for a beer when they were off-duty. I had to pay local cleaners to come in and clean up the house from top to bottom when the party was finally over. When my mother came back, she thought the house had never been tidier, thanks be to God.

Later that year the British Ministry of Defence decided to have a ceremony at Downing Street for all the Fleet Street war correspondents. Everyone was invited except me. Because I was Irish I wasn't officially recognized as a fully fledged MOD war reporter. Each of the lads was given a medal to commemorate their work and to thank them for their help during the campaign. I was left out of the loop but I didn't give a damn. I didn't become a journalist to win medals; if I wanted those I would have joined the cops or the army.

It's not a reporter's job to write propaganda for any state. It is our duty to differentiate between the facts and the fiction and to write what we see. I wasn't spoon fed by the British or American PR machine during the war and had gone my own way. The lads had a big piss-up in Vagabones later that night to celebrate their medals and I refused to pin one on my chest. I knew it meant a lot to some of them, and maybe if I was British it would have to me too. I was just happy knowing I had done a good job and had lived to tell the tale. And I was glad to be saying goodbye to the Middle East.

* * *

Being back was grand, and I was delighted to get back to some of the lighter stories in the job, this time chasing celebrities around the west coast of Ireland in search of a story.

If Rod Stewart couldn't resist a good Hollywood wedding, Julia Roberts did her damnedest to get out of one. The world of show business was shocked when she cancelled her impending wedding of the year to Kiefer Sutherland and fled to Ireland in June 1991 to escape the intense publicity, with her friend and new lover Jason Patric.

The *Pretty Woman* star was furious with wild man Sutherland, who had an alleged affair with a stripper behind her back, so all bets were off. I was back home for the weekend when the news desk called to say Julia Roberts' wedding was off, she was in Ireland and I'd better find her. The rumour was that she was staying in Dublin's plush Shelbourne Hotel, and within hours an army of reporters and photographers from all over Europe had descended on the capital.

I knew Jimmy Dixon, the head doorman at the Hotel, who confirmed to me that she was already gone, and that Dublin chauffeur Michael "Mick" Devine was driving her. As far as he knew she and Jason were gone west and were heading to Dingle, Co Kerry. I also had Mick's mobile number so was well ahead of the game.

The Fleet Street pack got together and decided to carve the story up. I'd go to Kerry with Andy Coulson, along with photographers Phil Hannaford and Charlie Collins, while Bill Akass of the *Mirror* and Baz Bamigboye of the *Daily Mail* would stay in Dublin along with Alan Lewis, the king of Belfast and former Photographer of the Year in Britain.

A towering handsome black man, Baz would call out with

a big bunch of flowers to Michael Devine's wife in Leixlip, Co Kildare, looking for information, but never got anywhere. I kept ringing Mick on his mobile, but he was playing a game of cat and mouse, and all he would say was that I wasn't too far away from Julia in Dingle.

We all booked into a lovely hotel in picturesque Dingle, right on the harbour, with some of the most breathtaking scenery in the world. We'd go on a daily hunt for the runaway bride all around the Dingle peninsula, and scout around the fabulous Blasket Islands, but there was no sign of her anywhere.

We also had to go on an extensive pub crawl around Dingle and Ventry, and despite loads of beers, we came no nearer to cracking the mystery. After five days on the lash relations became very strained with our colleagues in Dublin. Lewis in particular blew his top and claimed we were all too busy enjoying ourselves to be capable of finding Julia Roberts. He was partially right.

Twenty four hours later we discovered that Julia had left Ireland and gone back to the US, where she was filming the movie *Hook*. She had actually been staying in a £10 a night bed and breakfast on a hill about 100 yards away from our hotel. The star had sat outside in the sunshine watching every move we made, laughing her pants off. In fact, we also learned she was in the same seafood restaurant as us one night, but we were all so drunk we didn't notice her.

It took about a year before Alan Lewis forgave me; he was livid we didn't get a picture. My bosses in London were happy though, as they had a great page one story and a spread for Saturday on Julia's mad week in Ireland with her new lover.

Chasing a superstar was a tough job but someone had to

do it. Mick Devine and I had a great laugh about it all afterwards. It later transpired that he and Julia Roberts became very close friends, and that friendship lasts to this very day. He and his wife regularly visit her in America, and she comes over to see them. She never forgot all the loyalty he gave her in her hour of need.

* * *

For hundreds of years, the Catholic Church in Ireland ruled the land with an iron fist. Although the country was governed for over 800 years from England, the real power lay with the men and the women of the cloth, who guided the nation in its day to day life. Following independence from British rule in the early 1920s, the church's grip on the country got even tighter.

The Church ran the schools, directed the faithful, helped the poor, and looked after the orphans. Government did what the church told it, rather than the other way around. The Bishops and Parish Priests had phenomenal influence in every corner of Ireland. Nobody dared question the decisions of the Catholic Hierarchy, and nobody even dared question the wisdom of the Parish Priest. Equally the Christian Brothers and the nuns who ran the schools were all held in high public esteem. Religious leaders like Archbishop John Charles McQuaid of Dublin, in the 1950s, were unelected tyrants in their own right, who would beat down Ministers at every turn, if they didn't like what they were doing.

These church leaders laid down the law on contraception, abortion, divorce, sex outside of marriage, the school curriculum and even children born out of wedlock. Those kids born out of wedlock were often taken from their "shamed" mothers at birth and put into orphanages run by nuns, before being passed on to rich, childless couples, for a donation, of course.

The Catholic Church itself was a dictatorship, but just like the Berlin Wall in the late 1980s, its power would soon come tumbling down. Three different episodes would destroy the moral authority of the church in Ireland – those of Bishop Eamon Casey, Fr Michael Cleary, and the child sex abuse scandals in which hundreds of children were abused by those of the cloth, abuse then covered up by the church in the most sinful way. As we all know, new revelations continue to come out as to the widespread extent of these crimes against children.

Protecting the reputations of pervert priests and sadistic nuns and their church was deemed more important by the church leaders than helping the tragic children whose lives were so ruthlessly destroyed. In moving the sex brutes around the country after a sex abuse incident came to light, the church didn't solve the problem, they compounded it. Equally, some Gardaí were reluctant to investigate complaints against the clergy, in case it might affect their career prospects down the road.

The big issue for the church was and is celibacy. This church law banning priests from having sex and taking wives and girlfriends is lunacy. It is unnatural and unhealthy. But more importantly, it is not God's law, it is man's law. Celibacy was brought in by the Popes to protect the wealth of the church.

Most of Jesus' disciples were married or had women in their lives.

Today, our priests are left to die as lonely old men, unwanted and unloved, with little or no family to care for them. The issue of celibacy will come to a head over the next

20 years as the number of priests continues to dwindle. Vocations to the church are way down because fewer people believe in a life of celibacy.

Tabloid newspapers aren't afraid of the church. In fact, we like nothing better than a good old fashioned kiss and tell sex scandal, and we got one in the case of Bishop Eamonn Casey.

In the summer of 1992 I was considering returning to Ireland to live for good when the story broke, rocking the whole Irish Catholic Church from top to bottom. An American woman, Annie Murphy, claimed that the Bishop of Galway was the father of her 17 year old son Peter, and that she had been involved in a legal dispute with him over child maintenance.

The story was initially broken in the upmarket *Irish Times*, by its widely respected Washington correspondent, Conor O'Clery, and within 24 hours it was all over every paper in Britain and Ireland.

A reformed alcoholic, Annie lived with her partner Arthur Pennell and her teenage son in Ridgefield, Connecticut. She had first met the Bishop, a friend of her father, a New York doctor, on the set of the Marlon Brando film *On the Waterfront,* when she was seven, during a family trip to Ireland. In an amazing interview with RTÉ radio the day after the scandal came out in the open, Annie said that they met again in April, 1973 when her dad sent her back to the Emerald Isle after she had gone through a painful divorce

Bishop Casey, who was then Bishop of Kerry, met her on arrival at Shannon airport and it was "love at first sight". She was 24 at the time while he was 46. The American revealed how the randy Bishop used to call her his "temptress" and how he behaved like a teenager in love during their year long affair.

"He was like a scoundrel, like a teenager, like a man set free and I was like his mistress," she said. The couple use to have sex on a regular basis in a 19th century cliff-top stone house he used as his presbytery, overlooking Inch Strand, Co Kerry.

She stated: "My relationship with him was the most magical thing in my life. The moment I laid eyes on him, it was a spontaneous kind of love; it was out of this world. I often used to wonder why Cole Porter wrote those beautiful songs and what they meant. For the first nine months with Eamonn it was like I was on 'gossamer wings'. I don't mean to sound corny but I idolised him.

"We had a lot of fun together; we were very close. We never argued and we just had a lot of fun; we were like two little children. I would wait for him at night; we held hands at dinner, and then the physical relationship started three weeks after we met. We talked about the possibility of a child and he said he would do his best to avoid it. I said that if it happened I wouldn't care."

Miss Murphy recalled that the Bishop's late cousin, Joan Brown, often told them that their love was obvious and that Eamonn should leave the church and marry her. Joan felt he was madly in love with Annie.

She became pregnant by November of that year, and when she broke the news to him their relationship changed and descended into hell. Annie believed that the pregnancy and its threat to Dr Casey's position as a bishop soured their affair. He told her "it was God's will" that the baby, born in a Dublin hospital, should be put up for adoption.

She fumed: "What he led me into was brainwashing; that I was an immoral person and had to be cleansed; that I had to give up the baby and then I would be reborn as a good Catholic, Christian person."

Initially, she was put into a home for unmarried mothers in Dublin where the nuns tried to persuade her to give baby Peter away. When she gave him Peter to hold soon after he was born, the Bishop flipped. When the baby was put in his arms he flinched and said: "What's he doing here? It has to be adopted. Here are the papers, you must sign them."

Annie said: "I loved Eamonn very much. I would have been prepared to live in Dublin and have him see his son, but he didn't want anything to do with him." The Bishop would visit her once a fortnight in a flat she rented with her father, who knew their secret. She added: "Eamonn had a terrible fear of his son; he touched him like he was on fire."

Annie then decided to return to America. Her relationship with Casey became extremely bitter, and she negotiated a monthly cash settlement with him to help pay for their child.

She stated: "He had belligerently and begrudgingly offered me $100 a month. I thought it was chickenfeed and I said I would go to Rome and make our son a ward of the church. Within 48 hours he said he would pay me $175 a month and I said ok. Eventually the payment went up to $260."

As the child grew up she decided she would not keep the secret from Peter. When he was nine years old she showed him a picture of Eamonn and explained that this was his father. The child replied: "Oh, he's bald; I don't want to look like him."

At one point during those years she returned to Ireland and the romance resumed. "There was a chemistry there, but it was a case of fatal attraction. But then I came back to America and it was over," she said.

By this stage Dr Casey was Bishop of Galway and Annie had taken up with Mr Pennell, a native of Kinsale, Co Cork.

When Peter was 14 years old she returned again to Ireland to see Pennell's family, but the youngster became infuriated that his father would not recognise him. The Bishop would regularly ring them in America, but when Peter answered the phone, he refused to talk to him and this angered the child.

In 1990 he paid Annie £65,000. Then, in August 1991, the Bishop came to see her and agreed to meet Peter for four minutes and shook his hand. Soon after that she signed a document relinquishing personal claims against the Bishop. The Bishop got the money to help Annie over the years from various benefactors. There were discussions about more cash payments to keep the scandal quiet but it came to nothing.

The fallout from the scandal in Ireland was huge. Bishop Casey was one of the most high-profile and liberal within the Irish Catholic hierarchy. It genuinely shocked people that he had broken his celibacy vow, but typically, there was also a wave of public sympathy for him, as many felt Annie Murphy was manipulating the situation.

Originally from Tralee, Co Kerry, Casey was one of ten children, and made his name working as a curate in Slough in London with Irish immigrants in the 1960s. In 1973 he headed the Irish Church's Third World agency Trócaire, and did fantastic work, making it one of the most effective agencies of its kind. He also had a huge connection with young people and stood beside Pope John Paul II during the Pontiff's historic visit to the Republic in 1979, at an open air youth mass for 250,000 in Galway.

He flew to Rome and tendered his resignation as Bishop to the Vatican as soon as Annie went public. The church issued a statement saying he would continue working as a priest on missions abroad.

I went to the West in the hope of tracking down Dr Casey,

but he was nowhere to be seen. The story ran and ran for several days, much to the dismay of the Catholic hierarchy.

It really opened up the whole debate on why celibacy is unnatural and whether priests should have the right to marry and have children. Just because he had sex with a woman didn't make Bishop Casey a bad man. Nobody could fault his work in the religious community.

The story demonstrated the sheer hypocrisy of what was going on behind the scenes in the church. Bishops were lecturing people about contraception and the need for young women not to have sex until they marry, while one of their own was breaking all the rules himself.

It would be several months before Bishop Casey turned up. Author Gordon Thomas, who lived in Co Wicklow and had written extensively on religious affairs, contacted literally thousands of people before getting a tip-off that Eamonn Casey was in Mexico. He came across a woman who was a friend of both the Bishop and Annie. This lady had a number for Casey in Mexico, so Thomas was able to track him down. He and photographer Charlie Collins flew to Mexico, where they found him living inconspicuously in a tiny village. Dr Casey was staying with nuns in a convent that even had its own swimming pool.

Gordon and Charlie found him walking down the street and confronted the Bishop, who had never said a word publicly on the scandal. He gave Gordon a few quotes and fled. Charlie got a picture of him, and it was published in the *Sunday Independent* before going around the world. It was a great hit at the time because every news organisation was looking for the Bishop.

Casey flew back to New York and lay low for a few more months before going public. He gave an exclusive interview to reporter Veronica Guerin, who would be shot dead for her crime stories a couple of years later. The interview, published in the *Sunday Tribune*, was Veronica's first big break.

As we now know this was just the tip of the iceberg of revelations about the Church in Ireland that were to come out in the years ahead.

I had a great time and learned so much during my time working in England, but I missed Ireland and I was longing to be home again. I knew there were plenty of juicy stories right in my own back yard, and I had the feeling that the tabloid business in Ireland was going to continue to grow and prosper, and I wanted to be there to see it.

The Daily Mirror
1992-1996

Part 1

I had never come face to face with soccer hooligans until the night English soccer fans went on the rampage at Lansdowne Road in Dublin in February 1995. I was watching the match in a pub not far from the ground when it all kicked off.

Ireland were leading 1-0 when the England supporters decided to explode and start a full scale riot in the top tier of the stands, causing the "friendly" match with the old enemy to be abandoned. Dozens of people, including many young children, were injured in a night of shame.

As I made my way from the pub to the outside of the ground, rampaging animals in gangs of 20-30 were fighting battles with innocent spectators as people fled the area in droves. There must have been 2-300 of the marauding thugs in all. Ambulances were racing to the scene to treat the wounded. I couldn't believe what I was seeing.

In a matter of minutes Gardaí were on the scene. Nothing, however, had prepared the thugs for the hiding they got from the Gardaí as they tried to create havoc across the city. The rules of law and order went out the window, as the police gave them a hiding they'd never forget, armed with their batons, their boots and their fists. All rights went out the window as the brave men and women of the Gardaí put manners on the right wing National Front thugs. They even rounded up a 100 or so of the thugs and put them on a boat and launched them out to sea!

Ironically, when scores of those same thugs appeared in court the next day, they were like frightened mice, battered and bruised after a night in the Dublin cells. Many were rich, posh boys who decided to become scum for the game. They couldn't believe their ears when they were remanded into custody in the city's tough Mountjoy prison, where our criminals were waiting to dish out their own brand of justice.

I was to become involved in a bust-up with football's favourite hard man a couple of hours later, one Mr Vinnie Jones, the notorious captain of Wimbledon, and now a budding Hollywood actor. As the riots took off live on television, I was up to my eyes in the story, and London decided to send Ted Oliver over to help me as back-up.

I finished filing for the London editions around 2 a.m., when Ted landed and booked into Jury's Hotel, where I decided to stay over and join him for a drink. Four of us, including a senior official from the English Football Association, were sitting in a quiet corner of the bar chatting over a bottle of wine, when a drunken Vinnie crashed in with a pal and two pretty young women.

We got up to shake his hand as the introductions were made, when suddenly Vinnie, right out of the blue, clasped Ted's nose with his teeth and shook him like a dog with a dead rabbit. Blood gushed out of the fang holes on either side of Ted's nose and Vinnie burst out laughing like a child playing a silly prank in a school yard.

Ted already had a few bruises and scars on his face, the marks of war from the Troubles in the north, where both the IRA and the UVF had failed to intimidate him. He'd also received a few beatings while covering the Falklands war for the paper in Argentina.

The blood turned a white table napkin red as Ted tried desperately to stop the flow. Someone suggested Ted should leave, but he said no. Under no circumstances was he going to be frightened off by a stupid footballer after such a night of violence out on the streets.

Jones soon realized Ted was angry and came over to the table a second time to calm the situation. But my colleague was worried he was going to try and bite his nose off this time. Vinnie tried to make a joke of it. "It was only a bit of fun. I always do that to people I like," he said. Ted showed him the blood all over the napkin and said: "Some joke." Vinnie Jones went away for a while as I tried to dissuade Ted from decking him with a box.

An hour later the footballer had discovered that Ted was a reporter and came back, pleading with him not to do or say anything. "Please don't write anything about this," he begged, "think of my career, think of my wife and my young child. You could ruin it all."

Ted showed him the napkin and told him: "You should have thought about that before you bit me."

As it transpired, Jones had been on the lash all day long. He'd got involved in a nightclub row, was turned away by a taxi driver because he was drunk and obnoxious, threw toast at former English skipper Gary Lineker and called him "Big Ears", and got into a row at Jury's Hotel over a £300 drinks bill.

The next morning, after a few hours sleep, Ted decided to make a formal complaint of assault with the Dublin Gardaí against Jones. He went to the nearby station and made a full statement. I later made one as a witness to the incident. He went to a local doctor and got an anti-tetanus jab and a HIV test. He also asked for an anti-rabies injection when the medic laughingly told him: "I know – you've been bitten by a mad dog."

When Ted informed the office what had happened they couldn't believe it. The editor was rightly outraged and agreed to support Ted in his legal action against Jones. The next day we splashed the story with the famous headline: "Vinnie Jones Tried to Bite Off My Nose".

Word of the incident had spread right across the media before we went to press. Although everyone was mopping up the fallout from the soccer riots, photographers from rival papers were ordered to doorstep the hotel to see if they could get a picture of Ted Oliver's nose. Ted had to stay in his room all day where he made a serious attack on the mini bar with a handful of colleagues. The world renowned Royal Photographer of *The Sun*, Arthur Edwards, had been sent over to Dublin to do the riots. He thought it hilarious that he finished up trying to get a snatch shot of his great friend Ted!

The case with Vinnie Jones never went to court. But Ted did receive compensation when the footballer settled a civil action.

I was to meet Jones several years later in a completely different environment. He is now extremely friendly with a pal of mine, Tommy Scanlon, a businessman from Co Westmeath. He has come over to support a number of charity events in Mullingar.

We had a long chat about the Ted incident but Vinnie said he was so drunk and didn't remember much. He was very embarrassed by it and said his wife gave him a serious bollocking when he got home.

The Vinnie Jones today is a completely different man than the Vinnie we met that night. He has concentrated on his acting career and quietened down a hell of a lot. In fact, as I've now discovered, Vinnie sober is a real gentleman who would go out of his way to help anyone.

My great friend Ted Oliver passed away from cancer two years ago. We had many a laugh reminiscing about the night

Vinnie Jones bit his nose. It was the easiest splash he ever got, even if he did have to spill a bit of blood in the process!

* * *

By the summer of 1992 I decided to come home for good and get married. The plan was to start up a freelance news agency in Dublin serving all the London tabloids with stories coming out of Ireland.

I covered the general election for the *Daily Star* for a month and then started working from my new office in an upstairs bedroom of our house in Drogheda. I had two phone lines, a fax and a small Tandy computer, which allowed me to write copy and send it wherever I wanted.

Working from home was a new challenge. It meant being up at 7 a.m.; listening to the first news bulletin of the day; sniffing out stories around the country; building up contacts; renewing old ones; but most important of all, being disciplined. You just had to shut the door of your office and enter your own little world. If you didn't get stories, you didn't make money; you needed the hunger and desire to survive as a freelancer.

Within days I was flogging stories to the *Daily Mirror*, via the paper's Manchester office, which looked after Ireland. I already had good contacts on the paper from my London days, so I had my foot in the door.

As a kid I always loved the *Daily Mirror* – the lay out; the writing style; the working class values it stood for. You could also always rely on the *Daily Mirror* to tell you the truth; to stand up for the underdog; to shout for the underprivileged and to expose the corrupt and those who abused their positions of power.

The paper had survived the Bob Maxwell era, when the greedy tycoon robbed the pension fund to prop up his financially stricken empire, before falling off his yacht, the Lady Giselle, and drowning in the Mediterranean.

I always remember how reporter Gordon Hay was dispatched to the morgue in the Canary Islands by Editor Richard Stott to make sure the body was Maxwell and he was dead. Hay rang the London desk to inform them they were just cutting up the "fat C***" with a chainsaw to fit him into the coffin! There was no love lost for Maxwell.

* * *

Within weeks I got lucky. Paul Smith, a friend of mine who worked briefly on the *Daily Star* news desk, was appointed the *Daily Mirror's* new regional news editor in London, under Editor Colin Myler. Paul was to take charge of the Irish, Scottish and Welsh editions, which was great news for me. Smithy was an excellent newshound and a joy to work with, even if he was occasionally distracted by his love of horses and Tottenham Hotspurs! He began calling me every day, looking for stories and I kept delivering the goods.

Within a couple of months he flew over to Dublin and offered me a contract as Ireland correspondent for the *Daily Mirror*, covering Ireland for the London editions but equally, providing content for the Irish editions. I was absolutely over the moon. I was also to work closely with our legendary Belfast correspondent Joe Gorrod.

Joe came over to the North for the *Daily Express* before the start of the Troubles in the mid-sixties, just for a couple of months. He fell in love with his wife Eileen and ended up staying for the rest of his life. A gruff son of Sunderland, Joe didn't tolerate fools and was always straight as a die. He had many hairy moments during the Troubles, falling out with IRA men and Loyalists alike. Joe despised the terrorists with a passion but he never lost his sense of humour, even in the darkest days.

Joe would work six days a week including Sundays. The only day he'd take off was Wednesday. This was Joe's anointed day out on the beer, when he would do his tour of the pubs in Belfast, meeting contacts, sipping with the cops, lawyers and other hacks. He would start early and finish late. Smithy soon discovered asking Joe to do a story on a Wednesday was looking for trouble. He was only to be called upon in an emergency, when Smithy would phone various pubs in Belfast trying to track down Gorrod. Often photographer Alan Lewis was sent to find him as a last resort. Joe also didn't drive, so his wife or colleagues would ferry him from place to place on various assignments.

As a former soldier who did his national service in the British Army, Joe had a great love of war board games. One evening the night news desk rang him up and asked Joe: "How are things?" "How are things? Not good kid," said Gorrod in his Geordie accent, "Hitler has just won the fuckin' war!"

On another occasion Joe telephoned Paul Smith to ask him if he ever heard of Seamus Heaney

Smithy: "Is he a jockey?"

Joe: "No."

Smithy: "Does he play for Spurs."

Joe: "No."

Smithy: "Then I wouldn't know him."

Joe: "He's a famous poet who's just won the Nobel Prize for Literature."

Smithy: "What did he write?"

Joe: "He penned the epic Irish soccer anthem: Here We Go, Here We Go, Here We Go."

Gasped Smithy: "Did he really?"

* * *

My first big job with Joe was the Shankill Road bombing, in October 1993, in which nine innocent people and one of the IRA bombers, Thomas Begley, were killed. Fifty others were injured. Two Provos dumped a bomb in Frizzell's fish shop and it exploded as they fled. Their target was loyalist leader Johnny "Mad Dog" Adair, who had attended a paramilitary meeting upstairs shortly before the bomb attack, but had left the building. The second bomber, John James Kelly, was pulled alive from the rubble. He was later convicted of mass murder but freed under the Good Friday Agreement.

Gorrod and I covered the story along with Ted Oliver, who was sent over from London. Originally from Bangor, Ted had covered the North for the *Daily Mail* before going to Fleet Street. He was one of the senior reporters on the paper. We based ourselves in the Europa Hotel, the most bombed hotel in Europe, and at The Crown Bar, which is just 20 yards across the road.

Gorrod decided I'd go up to the Shankill and get all the eyewitness stuff; Ted would do the colour, while he would pull together all the political reaction. Ted found it highly amusing that I was running around the Shankill with my Dublin accent, considering the anger and resentment towards nationalists over the bombing.

The tradition on the *Daily Mirror* was that you earned your stripes, and I was being blooded at the deep end. The only stupid thing I did was drive a southern registered car up the Shankill. I got a red card and a warning from the cops that I was asking for trouble, and to get the car out of there before I got lynched. I drove it back to the hotel and got a lift up with another colleague. We got all the quotes and pictures we needed and no one threatened me.

By Friday night I headed back home to Drogheda for a rest. Shortly after midnight on Saturday night the News Editor in London, Eugene Duffy, called to say five people had been shot dead by a Loyalist gang at the Rising Sun pub in Greysteel, Co Derry. Wearing Halloween masks, they sprayed the bar with bullets shouting "trick or treat" in revenge for the Shankill road massacre.

Eugene asked me to get on the road at 4 a.m. and to pick Gorrod up on route. Joe and I arrived in Greysteel at 6 a.m. By lunchtime the pair of us and Alan Lewis had every word and picture we needed on the atrocity. Joe was a master wordsmith and by 3 p.m. we had filed every last cough and spit, filling the first seven pages of the *Daily Mirror*.

I had done some big stories in my time but this was an eye opener for me. It was one thing reporting on the hatred in the Middle East, but it was heartbreaking to witness such tribalism at close hand, not far from your own home. The North in those days was poisoned by an eye for an eye, tit for tat philosophy, with no respect for human life on either side. Nobody cared who they killed so long as they hurt the other.

The police soon arrested three known gunmen in Derry over the shooting. I will never forget the hatred of one of them, Torrens Knight, as they were brought into Limavaddy court several days later to be charged with the murders. He was ranting and raving at relatives of the victims who

gathered outside. He had no remorse, no regrets, and no
sympathy for those he killed or their loved ones. The same
attitude prevailed during the trial. Knight got life but was later
freed under the Good Friday Agreement, like the rest of the
Republican and Loyalist killers.

* * *

It was around the same time that I got to meet the party
leaders in the North, including John Hume and Dr Ian Paisley.
I was always a great admirer of Hume, and had met one of his
sons at the Gaeltacht in Donegal, where you go on a three
week holiday to learn our native tongue. John Hume and I
had a mutual friend, Michael "Mixer" Hand, the former
Editor of the *Sunday Independent*. Hume and Hand went
back a long way and would often have a drink together
anytime John was down in Dublin.

I found Hume to be an extremely courteous, polite, and
passionate man who engaged in the politics of sensibility. He
never reached for the stars; he just tried to land on the moon
first. The role he played behind the scenes in the peace process, when he persuaded the IRA to pursue the political
road and to renounce violence, should never be under-
estimated.

As a Catholic Southern boy, I had a love/hate relationship
with Paisley. His hatred of our church, our bishops and our
Popes always alarmed me growing up. The only word he
seemed to know was "No". He seemed to despise everything
Irish, and was scarred by tunnel vision rinsed in the colours
of the Union Jack flag; red, white and blue. But I had also
heard on the grapevine that Paisley was very good to his
Catholic constituents and had a wonderful sense of humour. I
also sensed that there had to be some very simple reason why

so many Protestants voted for him – maybe he's actually a nice man.

The first time I met Dr Paisley was at a meeting of the party leaders with the then British Prime Minister John Major at Hillsborough Castle, in Co Down. After their individual meeting each party leader came out to give a press briefing to the assembled media. One of Paisley's favourite journalists is the broadcaster Eamon Malley, a Catholic from Crossmaglen. When he came out he started chatting to us, and I went to ask him a question. Dr Paisley looked at me suspiciously and said; "I don't think I know you?"

I said my name was John Kierans and I worked for the *Daily Mirror*. Eamon intervened and explained that I was a friend of his and a decent bloke.

Paisley looked me up and down with a big smiling face and put his arm out to shake my hand. "You seem a nice young fella," he said, "but I don't think your one of us!"

The whole press pack fell around the place laughing.

It was in those few seconds that I got Paisley; it was his charisma. He is an extremely charming and jovial man. That's why I always knew he and Martin McGuinness would get on so well when eventually they became First and Deputy First Minister of Northern Ireland. It's not easy for arch enemies to become friends but they did it. Paisley and the Sinn Féin President Gerry Adams, however, would not have lasted in a room together for more than a few minutes.

Gorrod also tells a similar story about Paisley. On another occasion he went to Rome to annoy the Pope. He flew back to Belfast in triumph, having delivered his message to the Vatican and attracted all the media attention he could wish for. In a press conference at the airport he boasted of how he had denounced his holiness as the anti-Christ, and that all

Catholics were deluded fools on their way to the eternal fires of hell. Then Paisley spotted Ted Scallan, a reporter from the *Daily Mail*, who had been an altar boy in the Ardoyne, in north Belfast. Paisley looked at Ted with a benign smile and said: "Present company excluded Mr Scallan."

* * *

Fr Michael Cleary was, for years, the working class face of the Catholic Church in Ireland. An out and out Dubliner, he was known as the singing priest, and was instantly recognizable everywhere he went, with his trademark beard and glasses. He was repeatedly used by the Church to get its message across to young people, but he was also extremely conservative, and took the hard line stance on a variety of issues, especially contraception and divorce.

Fr Cleary was a personal friend to the stars in Ireland, and he regularly appeared on TV and radio shows. He had his own five nights a week, hour-long programme on Dublin's 98 FM radio station, as well as regular newspaper columns over the years.

He loved his weekly round of golf and had a reputation for being game for a laugh, and would constantly laugh and joke with people. I'd met Fr Mick on a handful of occasions; he was very friendly with the late Dublin bookie Terry Rodgers, and he officiated at the wedding of Terry's son Bill and his wife Helen, friends of ours.

He struck me as very pleasant; a down-to-earth man of God who had real conviction in his religious beliefs. His Mass was also good natured, humorous and never boring. But the truth was that Fr Cleary was preaching one thing, but living a lie for most of his life.

Just like Bishop Casey he fell in love, had children, and

covered it all up. The story broke on January 14, 1994 in
Phoenix Magazine, thirteen days after Fr Cleary's death from
terminal cancer at the age of 60. It claimed he had fathered a
love child but didn't name the woman or the child.

The cleric's three sisters issued a denial and claimed the
allegation was "despicable" and just not true. Top broadcaster
Gay Byrne, a friend of Fr Mick, went on the air and said:
"The man is barely in his grave and they are starting at him.
This will cause outrage and disgust." But friends later
revealed that the rumours about his private life had caused the
singing priest much distress before he passed away. It would
be almost a year later before the truth came out.

Fr Cleary's housekeeper Phyllis Hamilton decided to go
public and spill the beans. She and Mick had lived together
as, effectively, man and wife, for 27 years, sleeping in the
same bed every night. They also had two children, Ross who
they kept, and an older son Douglas, who they gave up for
adoption. She also had a daughter Felicia, who was born and
adopted in America. She became pregnant with this child
after she was raped by a trainee priest who discovered that
she and Cleary were lovers and Ross was their baby.

Phyllis told how Fr Mick first seduced her when she was
a 17 year old trainee nurse and she adored the ground he
walked on. She said he carried out his family life in secret
because he was following the church's "rules".

She stated: "He was everything – everything he appeared
to be. When he was ad-libbing with people he was the best
person on the planet, and that was the person I loved. He
loved the three areas of his life – the priest, the performer and
the man at home. I fulfilled the last part of his life and
organized the other two. I was the housekeeper, the wife and
the mother."

Although they couldn't marry, she and Cleary carried out their own private wedding ceremony, where they took their vows and pledged to live as "husband and wife". Legally it was a sham, but for them, in their circumstances, it worked. Ross lived with them, and although he couldn't call Michael "daddy", he just simply referred to him as Father. The public regarded the child as Phyllis's illegitimate baby, but Ross knew Fr Mick was his dad. He bathed him every night, helped him with his homework, and taught him to play football like any normal dad.

Phyllis recalled: "I think that if he had just been an anonymous parish priest he would have given up the Church for us. He loved Ross and me so much, he couldn't live without us, of that I have no doubt. But he was so well known that if he had told the truth, the damage to the church would have been immeasurable. What we did for all those years was illegal in the eyes of the church. But Michael and I will leave it to God to decide if it was immoral.

"I was fated to love Michael. He was my man, my mate, my companion. And there was more love and happiness amid the turmoil than there is in a good deal of ordinary family homes. The hardest part was the lack of dignity and respect for me. Because I lived with Michael for so long, people assumed that he kept me and my illegitimate son under his roof because he was such a kindly man.

"I wanted to celebrate our love and glory in our family, yet it could only be done when the curtains were closed and the door locked. He was tormented. He could never face the truth – he couldn't have both things he needed most, his family and the Church. He made me feel important and special. We always believed that in the eyes of God we were married."

It was in the summer of 1969 that she first realized she was pregnant. "For the first time it dawned on him that what he was doing was wrong, but he simply said he would deal with it."

She was sent to London and returned to Dublin for the birth of Michael Ivor, now known as Douglas Boyd Barrett, in March 1970. Parishioners assumed she had an affair in England, and the baby was adopted by an Irish couple. Fr Mick's name was never mentioned.

A year later Phyllis moved in full time with Cleary after his housekeeper retired, and they got the chance to live under the same roof. She said: "This was officially the start of our life as a married couple and it felt like the most natural thing in the world. We were together in every sense until someone knocked on the door, then Michael was the priest and I was the housekeeper. I would make coffee, provide biscuits and disappear. Once the visitors were gone it was back to the little love notes and all those affectionate things which make a relationship tick."

She became pregnant again in 1976 and spent time with her sister in England for a couple of months before giving birth to Ross in November. Yet again local people didn't become suspicious and assumed she'd had another fling abroad.

Phyllis stated: "When Michael first saw his son, he was as amazed as any new father. But there was no way we could take him home with us. My anger and resentment was growing, but I loved Michael so much I did not dare bring the whole world crashing down on him. Ross was fostered, although I was determined to make a life where he could grow up with me."

She went to America for a year in 1977 to continue her

training as a nurse, but Michael came out to bring her home. She added: "I fell into his arms like a child. I knew we were going to pick up where we had left off. He was so charming he could have talked God out of an argument, and I adored him."

Phyllis claimed she only ever went public for recognition from the church and Michael's family. She was left living on social welfare handouts after his death, as the tap of the church was turned off. But Fr Michael left both of them a house in his will.

Now 32 years of age, Ross said at the time: "My mum told me when I was ten that Michael was my dad. I had never guessed, but I understood instantly and my whole life fell into place. My parents fell in love and remained that way despite the odds. Can that be so completely wrong? If there is one thing that my father taught me, it is that unless you have human love, you have nothing at all."

Ironically, even Bishop Casey knew about the love child Phyllis had with his friend Fr Cleary. She revealed: "Eamonn Casey knew about Ross and our affair, but Michael didn't know about him, although we stayed at his house in Co Kerry."

The Archbishop of Dublin, Dr Desmond Connell, a close friend of Fr Mick's, also knew in the months before the priest's death, but decided to keep silent.

Sadly, Phyllis Hamilton didn't have much luck after Fr Cleary's passing. She published a book, *Secret Love*, on the scandal, but subsequently died, like her lover, of cancer. Ross went to court and proved to Cleary's family that he was his son, and inherited his €100,000 estate.

I always had huge sympathy for Fr Cleary. He was a decent man of the cloth, and it wasn't his fault that church law forbade him having a wife and children. I've always believed priests should be allowed marry, and in the fullness of time, I'm convinced it will happen. Fr Mick probably should have left the priesthood and married Phyllis. I suspect he would have if he hadn't been so high profile. Instead, he lived a lie the best he could, and was ultimately faithful to all in his life.

* * *

One of the great joys of being Ireland correspondent for a paper like the *Daily Mirror* is that you get to travel to every corner of our beautiful country in the line of duty.

I remember one week when Smithy ordered myself and Alan Lewis to do a tour of the country and see what we could come up with, as the News Editor Eugene Duffy was looking for something off beat for the London edition. Alan and I first went to Connemara, Co Galway after a tip-off, and we discovered that U2 had a secret recording studio, not far from Cong, where the legendary movie, *The Quiet Man*, was filmed. We did the pictures and got the story and then decided to go down to Cork and Kerry to see what else we could come up with.

While driving through the small town of Mallow, Alan spotted a newspaper billboard outside a newsagent which said *Ollie Reed Buys House!* We got the local paper and found that the great British actor and his new young wife had indeed bought a fabulous new home between Mallow and Charleville. We got the address and went up to interview the owner on the off chance we could catch her before she moved out.

She was a real chatty country woman who was thrilled not only that she had a buyer, but that someone as famous as Oliver Reed was moving in after her. She gave us a personal tour of the property and allowed us to photograph every room, including the matrimonial bed! We asked her if the house was haunted, and she gave us the classic quote that there would be no shortage of spirits around with notorious boozer Ollie living in the house!

The story made a super spread and the editors in London were over the moon. We soon made contact with Ollie and found him boozing in a local pub in an adjoining village. Although he had a reputation as a wild man, Ollie Reed was one of the nicest people you could ever meet. He enjoyed his benders and the craic, but also he was very kind, gentlemanly and considerate. He also adored children and would tell stories to them for hours on end. Ollie fell into life in Cork like a duck to water. The local people treated him as one of their own. He enjoyed the outdoor life and, like his wife, he loved horses.

Alan and I spent several hours drinking with him and his missus. They told us over games of pool how happy they were moving to Ireland from Jersey, and that they had found their dream home. Over the next few years, Ollie gave us great copy, whether it was going on the beer for a few days in Cork city and posing with every tourist, or arriving in off a plane drunk on the baggage carousel. He lived life to the full and was never boring, unlike so many of the so-called celebrities we have today.

* * *

If Ollie was one of the brighter sides of this job, then Brendan O'Donnell was one of the darkest. When you come face to face with a killer, it is something you never forget. I can still see the madness in the eyes of O'Donnell, the evil teenager who kidnapped a mother, her three year old son and a priest, and shot them all dead.

The disappearance of Imelda Riney, age 29, her little 3 year old son Liam and Fr Joe Walsh, age 37, caused deep shock and anger across the country in early May, 1994. Imelda was a new age hippie who lived in a hideaway cottage on the shores of Lough Derg in Whitegate, Co Clare. She was missing for a number of days before the local Gardaí took her disappearance seriously. I got involved when her estranged husband, Val Balance, went public, and I was contacted by a freelance, Declan White, in nearby Mountshannon. White had worked for many years with Independent Newspapers in Dublin, but had got out of the rat race and was living the good life with his beautiful Dutch wife and children down the West.

Declan got me a picture of Imelda and her son and we splashed it. Within 24 hours all the rest of the national press were on to the story and everyone headed for Co Clare.

Brendan O'Donnell was an out of control local delinquent who became badly traumatised at nine years of age when his mother died, and he descended into a life of crime. His drunken father used to regularly beat him up with a poker or a hurley stick, in what was an extremely violent home. By the time he was 13, O'Donnell was constantly in trouble, and was often found lying on his mother's grave crying. He became an angry young man who was ready to vent his fury and get revenge on society.

Imelda was last seen alive driving out of Whitegate at 1:30 p.m. on Friday April, 29 with Liam in the front seat and O'Donnell in the back. It transpired that O'Donnell was obsessed with Imelda and he used to call to her home regularly in the weeks before the murders, and she would give him food. The teenager claimed he and Imelda became lovers, and he would call two or three times a week and they would have sex upstairs, while Liam played below.

Within a week of their disappearance, a full scale search was launched for O'Donnell, who was named Ireland's most wanted man. Imelda's burnt out car was found near Clegg Wood and hundreds of Gardaí were drafted in to try and find the missing trio.

O'Donnell was armed and dangerous. There was an alarming sense of fear in Co Clare as he roamed the countryside like some untouchable. People were literally sleeping with their shotguns by their side. The Gardaí seemed helpless as they tried to catch him in a 10,000 sq ft area of woodland, on very difficult terrain that he knew extremely well.

On the morning of Saturday, May 7, the Garda helicopter was up and I decided to go scouring the countryside with reporters Cathal O'Shea from the *Sunday World* and Liam Collins of the *Sunday Independent*. We had heard reports that O'Donnell was spotted that morning, and that another girl, Fiona Sampson, age 18, had been abducted.

We followed the helicopter for as long as we could, until we lost them, but we continued on in the vicinity of the last sighting. About an hour later, in a moment of sheer coincidence, we came around a bend and straight into a gunfight. Detectives had intercepted O'Donnell as he tried to highjack another car from local farmer Eddie Cleary. The Garda patrol car was pulled across the road. We got out and hid behind our car as we heard two or three shots going off. We could see O'Donnell fighting in the car. We hoped and prayed we wouldn't get caught in the crossfire.

The young killer had pointed a gun at Eddie and said: "Stop or I'll blow your fucking head off." He had a hold of

Fiona in her nightdress. As O'Donnell opened the car door, the elderly farmer could see the Gardaí and officers coming out of a ditch.

One shouted: "Give up O'Donnell, you're surrounded, you can't get away."

The police fired a warning shot, but then O'Donnell put the rifle to the girl's head and said: "Back off now or I'll blow her fucking head off."

He pushed Fiona into Eddie's car, sat beside her, and ordered the pensioner to turn. But brave Eddie fumbled the move to give detectives the chance to storm the car. O'Donnell fired a shot through the roof and Eddie grappled with him and wrestled the weapon off him. Gardaí reached O'Donnell and grabbed him by the scruff of the neck out of the car. They immediately threw him to the ground and handcuffed his arms behind his back.

Fiona was crying, relieved that she was rescued. Mr Cleary was still in a state of shock and told detectives he had expected to die at any moment. He knew that if O'Donnell got away in the car, he and Fiona were dead.

O'Donnell was ranting like a lunatic and verbally abusing the cops. One of the Gardaí kept hitting O'Donnell with his cap, screaming at him: "Where are they? Did you kill them?"

His capture was all over in seconds, and the Gardaí were extremely relieved to have their hands on him. Two of the detectives had been extremely brave, way above the call of duty. And boy were we relieved it was over too!

I couldn't get over how young and innocent O'Donnell looked. He was only a small fellow, about five feet four inches, but he obviously had a massive chip on his shoulder. Before he was taken away into custody, we asked him again where were Imelda, Liam and the priest, but he told us to "fuck off", saying he didn't know. His eyes, however, were wild with hatred like some demented soul.

Later that night Fr Walsh's body was found in the woods, and soon after Imelda and Liam's bodies were discovered 150 yards away, buried together in a shallow grave.

O'Donnell claimed at his trial: "I was in love with her and she with me." He said he didn't see as much of Imelda when her ex-husband Val came back from England, and he wouldn't call if his car was there.

O'Donnell was totally deluded on the morning of the killings. He stole a rifle from a neighbour's house, and was planning to rob Whitegate Post Office, so he could get the money to emigrate for a new life in France with Imelda. When he called to her cottage she told him to put the gun away. They went upstairs to have sex, but when they came back down a voice in his head told him to kill Imelda, that she was the devil's daughter.

He stated: "I told her I was going to kill her and that she was the devil's daughter. She said 'Don't be raving Brendan.' I got the gun and pointed it at her and she started taking me seriously. I ordered her to come with me and to bring Liam with us. The child was very frightened. She got the car keys and I told her to drive to Cregg Wood, because I decided I wanted to kill her there. Imelda drove to the woods and I sat with Liam in the back. I don't remember any conversation between us. I just felt very happy because I knew I was going to kill the devil's daughter."

O'Donnell said that when they got to the wood he made them walk through the trees. He stated: "Imelda was very nervous and frightened. Liam was afraid and he was crying. I went into the trees and told Imelda 'lie down on the ground; I'm going to shoot you'. She tried to pull the gun off me. She had the barrel in her fist but it was facing directly at her face. She pulled the gun, I pulled the trigger and she was shot in the eye.

"I felt very happy when I killed her. I saw the blood coming out of her face – I liked it. I had killed the devil's daughter. That was what the devil told me to do."

Heartless O'Donnell showed little or no emotion as he recalled how he executed little Liam. The child hadn't seen the killing of his mother because he was hiding behind some trees.

He said: "Liam asked me where's mammy and I told him I'd shot her. I felt very happy at the time. I decided not to leave Liam without his mother, like me, so I put him down beside his mother. I couldn't look at his innocent face so I shot him in the side of the head. I felt happy he was with his mother."

Over the next few days he slept rough and he kept hearing voices in his head telling him he was the devil's son. When he was passing Fr Joe Walsh's house in Eyrecourt, Co Galway, on his way to visit his granny, another voice told him: "Kill Fr Joe – he's trying to christen the devil's baby son."

He broke into Fr Joe's and kidnapped him at gunpoint and ordered him to drive to Clegg Wood. He said he told the priest he was going to kill him but Fr Joe said he was sick and begged him to let him go. He brought the priest to the spot where he had killed Imelda and Liam, and ordered him to kneel down. He shot him twice, in the side of the head and then the back of the head.

O'Donnell said: "I felt happy. I'd killed a man who'd been trying to christen the devil's baby son."

The triple killer claimed he was possessed by the devil and believed Satan gave him special powers, including the ability to walk on water, and to kill cats just by looking at them. He had regularly prayed to Satan since he was a child, and his amazing powers were the devil's answer to his devotion.

Top psychiatrist Dr Charles Smith said O'Donnell didn't have a major mental illness, just a personality disorder. The jury didn't buy O'Donnell's madness and found him guilty of murder. He was given the mandatory life sentence, but ordered for treatment in the Central Mental Hospital, in Dundrum, Dublin. Before and after his trial he tried to kill himself on a number of occasions.

The man who appeared in court looked totally different to the one cornered by the Gardaí that day in East Clare. Whatever medication he was on had caused him to balloon in weight by about four stone, and he seemed to be spaced out most of the time, with no real idea of what was going on.

O'Donnell died 16 months later in his cell of a suspected heart attack, at only 23 years old. Relatives said that all he wanted to do was die in the weeks before he passed away. He couldn't live with the shame of being such a callous killer, who shot a child like a dog.

There was very little sympathy for O'Donnell on his death. Personally I thought he deserved a bullet in the back of the head. Others, like Declan White, felt society and the system had failed him. He wasn't born bad, but events had created a monster.

Neither the country nor I shed any tears for O'Donnell, and as the *Daily Mirror's* page one said, he can rot in hell. It was a headline that upset some of our politically correct friends in RTÉ, but then they never saw the madness in Brendan O'Donnell's eyes like I did. He was a man who wouldn't think twice about killing again. He had no respect for life whatsoever.

* * *

In those days murders in Ireland were very rare. We could have three or four a year and they would make front page headlines every time. We lived in a society where people in rural areas liked to think they were safe and could leave their doors unlocked.

I was only home from Clare a few days when another murder occurred that caused great worry and anxiety. Philomena Gillane, age 41, was seven months pregnant and had been missing for a week. Her body was found in the boot of her car at Athlone train station, Co Westmeath. She had been shot in the back and stabbed six times in the back with a steak knife.

My wife Karen was expecting our daughter Katie within days, but I was dispatched down to Mountbellew, Co Galway where the Gillanes lived in a big old farmhouse.

Philomena was a cook in a Dublin hospital, and she would work on a one week on, one week off basis. She had a nine month old son John. Her husband Pat raised the alarm when she failed to return home from work. Four different neighbours reported hearing a gunshot at the house, which the couple shared with Philomena's mother, brother and sister. Pat, a farmer, went public and made a passionate public appeal to try and find her. A man heard a description of her car and spotted it at the train station, 25 miles from her home.

The idea of a pregnant mother being shot in such a cruel and barbaric way caused national outrage. The peaceful Ireland we all knew and loved was changing, and very fast.

The Gardaí made it clear from day one that there was no connection with Brendan O'Donnell's killing spree. The finger of suspicion was pointed at the husband, with detectives working around the clock to get hard evidence.

We all booked into Hayden's Hotel in Ballinasloe for a couple of days, as the murder hunt got underway and Philomena's funeral took place. Even in the middle of such pain and grief reporters have to have some light relief to try to keep their sense of humour.

Senan Maloney was with us from *The Irish Star*; Paddy Clancy was there for *The Sun*; Ann Marie McEnaney from the *Irish Independent*; the *Sunday World* sent Mick McNiffe and a young cub reporter, Neil Leslie; and finally, there was photographer Charlie Collins, who was working with me. We started boozing in the hotel bar and all got pissed. We heard all this great music coming from the function room and decided to gate-crash it. At first we thought it was a wedding but didn't pay much attention. The room was full of all these older people laughing and joking and dancing the night away. We told a few people we were journalists up from Dublin on the Gillane story, and did they mind if we had a drink. The more beer we had the more the hacks got into the dancing.

Then we discovered it was the local Alcoholics Anonymous annual dinner dance! And two of the journalists were voted best dancers of the night and presented with specially inscribed AT Cross pens as their prize. We were the only ones boozing in the place. The next day we laughed our heads off thinking about what happened. It was the only light relief in a very grim week.

Philomena's husband Pat was later arrested for the murder. It transpired that he was having an affair with her sister Bridie, having sex with her while his wife was away working in Dublin. He also took her away on passionate weekends to festivals down the country.

Gillane had tried to hire two homeless men, Christopher Bolger and Mick Doyle, to kill her while he was up visiting the capital. He bluntly asked them: "Will you do a job for me." He then offered to pay them a substantial amount of money for the hit.

He had been seeing both women before Philomena became pregnant with his son. He then had to choose between them, and decided to marry Philomena. But the romance with Bridie continued after the wedding, and they would regularly have sex while his wife was working in Dublin.

His trial heard how he had married Philomena but was more attracted to Bridie, who had a sexual hold over him. He was also angry with his wife for getting pregnant in the first place, forcing him to pick one or the other sister. The bizarre love triangle was destroying the family. He claimed Bridie came on to him very strongly, but he rejected suggestions that he would lose everything if he split with Philomena, as she was threatening to withdraw financial support.

He came clean to his wife about his affair at Christmas time in 1993, and even claimed that he begged his wife to help him end it. He wanted to move out of the house but Philomena wouldn't leave with him. Gillane said he told Bridie their affair couldn't continue but it was no use. Bridie admitted cheating on her sister but claimed Gillane forced himself on her. She claimed he became very angry when Philomena got pregnant a second time, and that he didn't want the child.

The former truck driver was found guilty of trying to hire two men to murder his wife and sentenced to eight years jail. He became the first person in Ireland to be convicted of the offense of soliciting murder. No one, however, has ever been charged with Philomena's murder, and to this day the case remains unsolved. The Gardaí have their own theory, but no evidence to prove it.

* * *

The men who did the most damage to the Catholic Church were the perverts within its ranks who abused children across Ireland for decades. But worse still are the powers that be - the Catholic hierarchy, who knew about it and did little or nothing, preferring to cover the sex scandals up, at all costs. Their failure to call in the Gardaí and take action against these paedophiles has left a bitter taste in the country that will take years to wash away. The Church has repeatedly apologised for these beasts, but words are little comfort to the tragic victims, whose lives were destroyed by these men, devils in black suits who saw children as sex toys.

The worst bastard I came across was Fr Brendan Smyth, a member of the Norbertine Order, who was based at Kilmacrott Abbey, Co Cavan, before his arrest. He abused at least 80 different children, and likely many more, on a 40 year reign of terror on both sides of the border. His Abbot and a Bishop knew about it but little or nothing was done to stop him. Every time a new case of abuse emerged, he was moved on by his church bosses to another parish.

Smyth used the same modus operandi everywhere he went. He was like a pied piper who arrived with a car full of sweets for the children; one minute a kindly man, the next minute the bogeyman. He would gain access by first befriending the mums and dads, and then offering to take the kids off their hands. Parents looked upon him as an "uncle" who would sit the children on his knee, tickle and hug them, while slipping them sweets and pocket money. The unsuspecting victims would be treated to weekends away in guest houses, seaside visits, and trips to the pantomime and the cinema. And then, when their guard was down, he would pounce.

During one of the two trials against him, two boys and three girls told how Smyth took them to a Wombles concert in Dublin. He organised it so he shared a bed with the two boys in a guest house, and he encouraged them to play sex games with each other.

Many of his victims were altar boys, and the priest reckoned he could get away with abusing them because they would be too confused and scared to tell their parents. He deliberately preyed on youngsters wherever he could, in churches, schools and hospitals. He used God and the Church as a cover to induce children to do his sexual bidding, wrecking the innocence of youth, and leaving broken lives behind.

A true picture of the hurt and pain he caused came during one trial, when six of his victims chose to face him down in court and testify against him, even though he'd pleaded guilty. They each wept as they told how Smyth betrayed the trust of their families and destroyed their childhood.

One woman said: "He ruined my life. I was afraid of him until today, but now I am afraid no longer."

A middle aged woman recalled how she first met him as an 11 year old in hospital. The priest wormed his way into her home, and then on a visit to the movies, he interfered with her clothing and fondled her. He even had the audacity to follow her to boarding school, where the unwitting nuns would send her to meet "Fr Brendan in the parlour". There he would paw at her and indecently assault her. The poor girl became so desperate she tried to commit suicide several times as a result of his perverted actions.

Two sisters told a similar story of how Smyth visited their boarding school and groped them when they were put into a private room to see him, against their will. Another victim at the same school said Smyth's behaviour damaged her adult love life, which culminated in a long series of one night stands and no permanent relationship.

The pervert would stoop to anything for sex. On one occasion he tried to rape an 11 year old girl who was off school with a painful kidney infection. He confessed he cited any reason as an excuse to abuse a child. He would punish kids for laughing at Mass or failing to choose quickly enough from a restaurant menu. One 37 year old woman told how she has had sex problems and depression since she was 14, after Smyth spanked her for laughing in church.

The predator loved to touch his victims and have them caress him. He paid money to a teenage girl to "cooperate with him". He liked to kiss and fondle the breasts of young girls by bribing them with chocolates, holy crosses, statues and even a bible, to buy their silence.

When he was led off to jail one of his victims roared: "Rot in hell Smyth."

It later emerged that the Church's policy at all times in dealing with Smyth was to keep him one step ahead of the law. Anytime there was a complaint, he was simply moved on to another part of the country, free to prey on new victims. His Abbot in Cavan knew about it but did nothing.

Bishop Francis McKiernan was informed by another former priest, Fr Bruno Mulvihill, that Smyth was a paedophile in 1975, but also did nothing. He deliberately chose not to tell the guards. Fr Mulvihill had accidently come across two children Smyth had abused.

What makes me so angry is that if the church had dealt with him immediately, when the first complaint was made all those years ago, and called in the guards, the majority of his victims would have been spared all their pain and suffering.

The cover-up was a virus that spread through the whole of the Irish Church when it came to dealing with its perverts. Other brutes, like Fr Sean Fortune and Fr Ivan Payne, equally got away with it for years before they were caught, and named and shamed.

Smyth himself died from a heart attack in the Curragh prison in 1997 at 70 years of age. He'd only spent two years and ten months behind bars for his awful crimes. He did say sorry for what he'd done in the months before he passed away, but that was little comfort to the children whose lives he destroyed.

His behaviour was so damaging that even Cardinal Cathal Daly, the Catholic Primate of all Ireland at the time, privately admitted that the Smyth scandal was the biggest disaster the church had ever experienced. The problem was that the cover-up was worse than the crime, and Smyth even brought down a Government.

Albert Reynolds was forced to resign as Taoiseach in 1994, after it was revealed that extradition warrants to take Smyth to the North had been left gathering dust for nine months. Unknown to Albert, who had no hand, act or part in it, officials in the Attorney General's office and the Dept of Justice didn't act on the warrants. The revelation caused national outrage.

The head of the Norbertine Order, Abbot General Marcel Van de Ven, claimed the Abbot in Cavan neglected his duties in not telling him Smyth was a pervert. He stated: "I've said to people that the Abbot was more guilty than Brendan Smyth. It's terrible what Brendan Smyth did, he was a sick man."

I went back up to the Abbey in Cavan for Smyth's funeral. In an unprecedented move he was buried in the middle of the night, to avoid all publicity. I was desperate to have a picture of the coffin going into the ground so we could do the headline, "Gone to Hell".

In the end the church was ashamed of him, but sadly, the remorse was much too late. The victims who were robbed of their childhoods will remember Brendan Smyth until the day they die.

The fallout from the abuse scandals was phenomenal. The numbers attending mass reduced rapidly, the priests' role as the moral guardians of society was badly undermined, and everyone was afraid to let any of their children near a priest.

While the vast majority of the clergy are decent and honourable men, they were, sadly, all tarnished with the same brush because of the actions of a tiny minority. It had taken at least a decade for the people to start trusting their priests again, and the healing process was underway, but recent revelations from the Ryan Report about the extent of the abuses have reopened this issue and the wounds they have caused, so healing is still a long way off.

The Daily Mirror
1992-1996

Part 2

CHAPTER 6

The arrival of Piers Morgan as Editor in early 1995 heralded a new era on the *Daily Mirror*. Vocal, brash, full of energy and desire, he wanted to drastically change the *Daily Mirror* and bring it back to the glory days.

I had known Piers on the road and around the town as the writer of *The Sun's* pop column *Bizarre*. But then Rupert Murdoch shocked the whole of Fleet Street in 1994 when he appointed him the youngest Editor of the *News of the World* at 28 years of age.

Pier's appointment, thankfully, didn't mean too many changes of the top brass, and Eugene Duffy continued to news edit the *Mirror*. But Ireland became more important, as Piers wanted to increase sales here, and the pressure was on to keep coming up with the stories. He wasn't to be disappointed.

In September, 1995 a priest in Dungarvan, Co Waterford, Fr Michael Kennedy, got up on the pulpit and claimed a local girl who was HIV positive had been sleeping around on a revenge campaign, and had put up to 80 local men at risk of infection. The story was broken by a local reporter, Johnny Murphy, in the *Cork Examiner*, and soon all the other nationals and broadcasters picked up on it.

The fact that Fr Kennedy was a cousin of the former US President John F. Kennedy and Senator Edward Kennedy added more spice. The priest actually used to holiday with his famous American relatives every summer in Cape Cod, the playground for Boston's wealthy. Eugene was excited about it and saw it as a potential splash.

We all invaded Dungarvan and East Cork looking for this mystery woman and some of her victims. Fr Kennedy claimed he had contacted at least 25 men in the area who were worried sick after having sex with this woman.

She had been born locally but was brought up in London. She came from a comfortable background and had a posh accent. He told us all she had full blown AIDS, had only "weeks to live" and was being treated in a London hospital. The priest claimed she got the virus from an ex-boyfriend, an experience that left her with a burning sense of grievance against the male sex. Unfortunately after several days trying, none of us could manage to get the name of the girl, or track down any of the victims.

The story was wall to wall news but Fr Kennedy was hiding behind the church's confidentiality rules and refusing to identify anyone. He claimed: "People came to me in absolute fear and asked me to help. They refused to go to the health board and it is not my fault if I have created a scare."

The Gardaí were brought in but they couldn't find any evidence either, and even if they had, there was no legal offense in Ireland for an AIDS victim deliberately giving someone the killer disease in an act of sexual revenge.

Irish AIDS specialists and health officials expressed serious doubts about the authenticity of Fr Kennedy's story, and had severe reservations about the number of so-called casual sexual relationships. He, however, stood by his story and claimed he was telling the truth. The local people backed their priest, claiming many local men would think twice about sleeping around in case they picked up the disease. It truly was one of the most bizarre stories I was ever involved with.

I think Fr Kennedy was given some information and meant well. But he didn't realize the seriousness and implications of what he was saying, and the whole episode got totally out of control. Did the girl ever exist? Maybe. Did she deliberately sleep around and attempt to infect 80 men with HIV? I very much doubt it.

After a week of running around and getting nowhere the story just ran out of steam. Fr Kennedy kept a low profile after that.

* * *

The President of the United States is the most powerful man in the world. But little did I know the election of Bill Clinton would have a huge impact on my life, resulting in three different visits to the White House.

In late 1995, the IRA ceasefire was holding and the Northern Irish peace process was moving along at a hundred miles an hour. During the Troubles, Belfast city centre used to shut up shop at 7 pm every night, but now, like the rest of the province, it was dramatically coming back to life, free from the vicious cycle of killing and bloodshed. People embraced the new peace like a breath of fresh air. You could get out of bed every day without worrying whether you or your children where going to be shot or blown to bits, or if you were in the wrong place at the wrong time.

The visit of Bill Clinton and the First Lady Hillary to Ireland at the beginning of December of that year was a milestone in history. Presidential visits to Ireland are few and far between. JFK came to Dublin and his native Wexford after he became the first Irish and Catholic President of the US in the early sixties, while President Ronald Reagan came home to Ballyporeen, Co Tipperary to trace his roots in the eighties. But no President had ever crossed the border into Northern Ireland.

The Clintons came to Belfast on December 1, 1995 on what was to be an extremely emotional and life changing experience. There are days when you say you are proud to be a journalist and for me this was one of them.

As a reporter you write about some terrible things, but you rarely get to know or understand the real impact on the families left behind. For the Presidential visit, the organisers invited the children of Belfast to write a letter to the President, and the winners would welcome the Clintons to the city. Two children, Catherine Hamill, age 9, and David Sterritt, age 13, changed both of our lives, mine and President Clinton's. They lived on the opposite end of Belfast's Springfield road, one a Catholic, the other a Protestant.

Catherine wrote: "My name is Catherine Hamill. My daddy works as an assistant at Stewards Warehouse. I live in Belfast. I love where I live. My first daddy died in the Troubles. It was the saddest day of my life. I still think of him. Now it is nice and peaceful. I like having peace and quiet for a change, instead of people shooting and killing. My Christmas wish is that peace and love will last in Ireland forever. Please have a safe journey back to America. I hope you have enjoyed your visit to Ireland."

Catherine read out her letter in front of the world's cameras and hundreds of invited dignitaries at Mackey's factory, on the peace line between the Catholic Falls Road and the Protestant Shankill Road. The President and the First Lady were visibly moved to tears as they listened to her words. Mr Clinton embraced the youngster and wrote a little personal note on the back of her letter.

Catherine's real dad Patrick was killed by two Loyalist gunmen eight years previously when she was only 11 months old. They burst into the Hamill home and shot him dead at point blank range in front of her mum Laura, as her then two year old older sister Kelly ran around the kitchen screaming.

Catherine told the Clintons afterwards: "I can't remember my dad but I love him dearly. I know he was killed because of the Troubles. We all want this peace to last. I really wish my dad had seen me."

Laura found happiness with new partner, Emanuel Donaghy, but the brutality of what happened that day will never be forgotten. As she said: "The horrific memory of that day will live with me until the day I die. Patrick was a wonderful father who loved his children. During our darkest days I made a vow that his name will never be forgotten. The children grew up without a father but they knew everything about him. We all talked about him all the time and he was with them spiritually every day of their lives.

"Every night for years Catherine and Kelly would pray for peace. When the ceasefire was called all our prayers were answered. The most important thing in the world is, as Catherine said, the peace must last forever. Everyone was moved by what she had to say. I just kept thinking of everything we'd suffered when the President gave her a hug. Mrs Clinton even told her she was a 'cute little kid'. It's a great tragedy her daddy isn't alive so he could see her today."

David Sterritt told the President that he lived in a mixed area of Catholics and Protestants. "We play football and races together. I want to thank you for coming to Northern Ireland to help the peace process. I think peace is great because there is no shooting or bombing. It means I can play in the park without worrying about getting shot."

The words of the two kids made a huge impact on the President, and he kept referring to them during his keynote speech before over 100,000 people in the centre of Belfast. But more importantly, what Catherine and David had to say was echoed across the globe. Catherine's story in particular became the main line during the whole trip.

The Editor Piers Morgan and Regional News Editor Paul Smith were completely infatuated by her. The fact that Catherine was such a cute. kid also helped. Her story reinforced the need for a permanent peace in Ireland.

A couple of days after the Clintons returned home Paul rang and said he had an idea. In all her interviews Catherine had said she would love to visit America. He wondered if we could make her dream come true and fix it up. And if she could meet the President in the White House wouldn't it be even better! I contacted the Hamill family, and Laura and Emanuel said they would go if we could organise it.

First and foremost I needed to get Catherine an Irish passport, as she hadn't any, and also get the Irish Government on side to get her into the White House. I phoned then Taoiseach John Bruton's press officer Shane Kenny and he said to leave it with him. We also made contact with the American embassy in Dublin and London to tell them Catherine was going to the States. Piers said he had a vision of Catherine sitting on Bill Clinton's knee in the oval office wearing a *Daily Mirror* t-shirt! He didn't want much.

Smithy and I worked flat out to make it all work. Paul got the flights and hotel sorted, while I got the passport. John Bruton, and the Irish Ambassador to the United States, Dermot Hanrahan, paid an absolute blinder. Within 24 hours they came back with the remarkable news that the President wanted her to visit him in the White House. Not only that, he also wanted her to switch on the Christmas lights in Washington with him. Catherine's visit to the States was going to be a full blown media event.

The only thing the Government asked was that we bring the Hamill family into Government buildings in Dublin to meet the Taoiseach before they flew off. It was a lovely photo opportunity and it made a great opening story for the trip. John Bruton is an extremely charming man and he praised Catherine for her tenacity and courage. He said she was a brilliant ambassador for the country and the whole peace process and wished her well.

We flew to Washington where we were greeted by a team of camera crews on landing. This was a *Daily Mirror* exclusive so we had to control the amount of exposure the Hamills were getting. Photographer Mike Moore came with us from London and our New York correspondent, Alan Hall, was flown down to Washington to help.

I had met Mike in the Gulf and we had no problem working together. He is a total professional and knew exactly what pictures he wanted. We stayed in a lovely five star hotel just down the road from the White House on Pennsylvania Avenue. We liaised with the White House press office, who told us they'd call when the Clintons were free to see us.

Exactly a week after he'd met Catherine for the first time in Belfast, the call came on behalf of the Clintons for the child to go to the White House. An aide rang her hotel room and told her: "The President saw you in your country – now you come and see him in his home."

Like a modern day Cinderella, a slate grey Continental limousine took her to the gates of the White House for her date with the world's most powerful man. She and her family were first given a VIP tour of the building; they walked

through the west lobby with its priceless oil paintings of all
the previous Presidents, and they were shown the Cabinet
Room where all the major decisions are taken. One after the
other, members of the White House staff were queuing up to
shake her hand.

She then came face to face with Bill Clinton again as she
and her family were shown into the Oval Office. She was
wearing her *Daily Mirror* t-shirt but nobody minded. An ITN
camera crew from London was on hand to film the whole
reunion for the ITV *News at Ten*, along with the American
networks. The President gave her a big hug and let her sit in
his chair.

He told her: "You have done more for peace in Ireland
than all the politicians put together. I'm so sorry your daddy
died, but I know his spirit will live with you every day, and if
he knew where you're sitting now, I know he'd be very proud
of you. It is my honour to have you in the White House as we
approach Christmas – and I hope that you and all the children
of Ireland have a very peaceful and merry Christmas. If all the
good in your heart was spread around the world I'm sure
there would be no more war."

Catherine and her family spent 15 minutes in the Oval
Office. The President told her he really enjoyed his visit to
Ireland and that it was truly one of the best trips of his life.
He added: "I couldn't believe so many young people turned
out to see me, and I will work night and day to ensure they
will enjoy peace forever. I am totally committed to the peace
process and making it work. It's children like you who make
adults like me realise how futile hatred and bigotry is in the
world."

He then brought her down to the South lawn and they lit
up the White House Christmas tree in a live television

broadcast. The family went back to the White House for a small party with the Clintons afterwards. The Hamills were over the moon. Laura said she couldn't thank the *Daily Mirror* enough for setting it all up.

Piers Morgan was equally thrilled. Catherine made the lead story on the *News at Ten*, and there she was, in the Oval Office in her *Daily Mirror* t-shirt. The boss sent me a "herogram" saying job well done. But the whole team had made it work.

The Hamills were a wonderful family to deal with. Honest, down-to-earth, ordinary people who never got dizzy from their day in the White House. We also sent them down to Disney World in Orlando, Florida, for a week, where I had a well earned rest. We did a spread of the family on holidays courtesy of the *Daily Mirror*.

Shortly after Christmas I was back in the White House again. The President decided that if he had Catherine over he wanted to see young David as well. The trick in the peace process was not to show favouritism to either side.

The Sterritts were also extremely grounded people and equally a pleasure to deal with. There wasn't as much publicity but the trip was a fantastic success.

I found the President to be an extremely charming and likeable man. I asked him a couple of questions about the peace process and he was more than happy to cooperate. He reiterated the need for the politicians to keep talking and stressed that the Unionists and Republicans must find common ground to secure a lasting peace. It was very clear to me that President Clinton had fallen in love with Ireland and he desperately wanted a permanent solution in the North as part of his Presidential legacy. The amount of time and effort he put in was phenomenal.

A couple of months later, in June 1996, I returned to Washington for the third time in several months, on President Mary Robinson's official state visit to the United States. Our President was very laid back and a pleasure to be with. Piers had absolutely no interest in the visit but it made good copy for the Irish edition.

Yet again I got to sit down with Clinton in the Oval Office, and also met Senator Ted Kennedy, one of my heroes. Later that night we went back to the White House for a ball in a marquee on the South Lawn, which was attended by nearly all of Irish-America.

Before you go down to the party everyone queues up inside the White House, in what is called "the line", to be personally introduced to each of the heads of state and their partners.

Gene McKenna, the widely respected Political Editor of the *Irish Independent*, and Paddy Clancy of *The Sun* were with me. Gene is a native of Drogheda and comes from a housing estate in the town called Yellowbatter. At one stage during the evening I went to light up a cigarette when I got a tap on the shoulder from one of the security guards informing me that the First Lady doesn't allow smoking in the White House. He politely suggested I go outside the main front door of the building if I fancied a puff. Gene, who neither smokes nor drinks, said he'd come outside with me.

We were standing there chatting and leaning up against one of the main pillars of the White House, the most famous symbol of power in the world. We could see all these tourists with their cameras outside taking pictures of us. Gene turned around to me in his dour Drogheda accent and said: "Hey John, I think we've come a long way from Yellowbatter."

In one quick witted second he captured the whole

wonderful occasion. From Drogheda to the White House, that
took some achieving!

* * *

I first met U2 when I was a cub reporter in 1982. The band
were playing support to Phil Lynott and Thin Lizzy at the
first ever Slane rock concert. I was introduced to Bono,
Larry, the Edge and Adam Clayton by my friend Lord Henry
Mountcharles, the intrepid owner of Slane Castle, who had
a vision of bringing the top music acts in the world to
Ireland.

I did an interview with them backstage in between
rehearsals, and they struck me, at that stage, as very down to
earth, ordinary lads with no delusions of grandeur. It was the
start of what was to be a long and fruitful relationship.

There has always been an unwritten rule among the Irish
tabloid hacks that we don't piss all over our own. This meant
we wouldn't put a team of reporters and snappers around the
clock following our home-grown stars morning, noon and
night to see what they were up to. It didn't mean they couldn't
be criticised, but generally, we left them and their families
alone.

I know for a fact that what U2 feared most was seeing
pictures of their children in the papers. They deliberately kept
them out of the limelight and protected them at all costs.
What U2 loved was the freedom of being able to walk around
Dublin without anybody annoying them. This would never
have happened in London or New York, because the
paparazzi photographers would have followed them
everywhere. And that's why, despite all their millions, they
decided to remain living at home, proud of their Irish roots

and heritage, and most importantly, it is where they get some peace. I don't know how many times I've walked into the Horseshoe bar in the Shelbourne Hotel, Dublin, to see Bono there with his mates having a drink. Nobody passes any remarks and he just lives like a normal citizen.

U2 were also blessed with two great public relations girls in Lindsey Holmes and Regine Moylett, who always kept us in the loop about what the band were doing, and kept us up to speed about every U2 story going.

Unlike many of the modern day PR spin doctors who fill you full of lies and rubbish, they always played with a straight bat, even if it didn't always suit them.

The on and off romance between Adam Clayton and supermodel Naomi Campbell kept us all busy. They met on a flight from London to New York and fell madly in love. Within weeks she was sporting this gigantic engagement ring and we all got into a spin about the forthcoming nuptials and the glittering prospect of a U2 wedding.

But Naomi, unfortunately, has a reputation as a hot tempered lady, while Adam is an extremely quiet, shy, placid type of man. So within months, her tantrums kicked off, fuelling speculation about their on and off romance. The story filled reams of newspaper columns, but the U2 machine, in fairness, always kept us on the right track. Eventually Adam had enough of Naomi, threw in the towel and the engagement was off.

The biggest scare we ever had with U2 occurred a few days after I met Bill Clinton in the White House with peace kid David Sterritt. We had decided to bring the family down to Orlando, Florida for a holiday after our trip to Washington.

Bono, his family and some friends flew into Jamaica on an old Albatross World War II sea plane for a holiday, and were landing on a beach when the authorities mistook them for drug smugglers. It was like a scene from a Jim Carrey movie, only it wasn't funny and you couldn't make it up. Trigger happy cops fired at least 100 rounds of bullets at them as they disembarked from the aircraft, hitting the plane at least seven times. The star and his wife Ali, and children Jordan, age 6, and Eve, age 3, dived for cover, fearing they were about to be killed, but miraculously, escaped unhurt.

It was all a case of mistaken identity, and when the Jamaicans discovered who they were, they were free to go. The story made front page news across the globe. Bono and his family were so shocked that they decided to get the hell out of Jamaica and fly straight to Miami.

The office rang me and told me to get the next flight from Orlando to Miami with photographer Arnie Slater and see if I could track Bono down. As I walked through the arrivals hall the first person I met was Graham Dudman, a colleague from London who was freelancing in Miami and was on the story for *The Sun*. He was doorstepping the airport for Bono but had to settle for another Irishman — me, instead.

We booked into a hotel on the beach front and I rang Regine Moylett, U2's PR girl, and I told her I was in Miami and needed to speak to Bono. I also informed her that Editor Piers Morgan was on my case big time, and I needed a full sit down chat with Bono and Ali as soon as possible. I pointed out that it was such a big story that they were going to be hounded everywhere they went until they went public and explained to their fans exactly what happened. I also argued the case that he might as well do it with one of his own who had always left him alone in Dublin, someone he could trust.

Regine accepted that if the interview got a big hit in the *Daily Mirror* it would be picked up by everyone else, taking the heat off. Within a couple of hours Regine phoned me back and said Bono would do it. The deal was simple – he and Ali would meet me down at the beach, pose for a picture and give us an interview, provided we kept the kids out of it. They were anxious that we wouldn't follow them around Miami trying to get family pictures of them and the children. I gave Regine my personal assurance that we would wrap it all up in 20 minutes, and then we would leave them alone to enjoy the rest of their holiday. I would also keep the name of the hotel where they were staying a secret, and not tell other journalists.

Bono and Ali were as good as gold and came out at the pre-arranged time to meet us outside their hotel. We went off and did a beautiful set of pictures of them on the beach. Ali Hewson is a lovely woman. She was extremely charming and polite, and knew we were only doing our jobs and helped us get on with it. They were both in extremely good form considering their ordeal, and very thankful to be alive.

Standing in the sunshine and holding Ali's hand, Bono told me straight up how lucky they were to be alive. He said: "I don't know how we came through it. These boys were shooting all over the place. I felt as if we were in the middle of a James Bond movie – only this was real. It was absolutely terrifying and I honestly thought we were all going to die. Thank God we are safe and sound."

Bono recalled how he dived on Ali and the kids on the ground to try and shield them as the bullets were flying everywhere. "My only concern was for their safety. It was very scary. You can't believe the relief I felt when I saw the kids were ok. They normally see gunfire on the telly and have been writing about it at school. This time the bullets were hopping around them. The whole episode was very scary and it is something I never want to experience again. But we've all taken it in our stride. The kids are now over the shock of their ordeal and getting back to normal," he said.

The star explained how the Jamaican police had made one horrendous mistake but that he didn't hold anything against them. He was particularly embarrassed that he and his friends, including the millionaire owner of Island Records Chris Blackwell and singer Jimmy Buffett, could be mistaken for drug barons.

Bono stated: "We were travelling in a real old plane and how the police thought criminals would use this type of aircraft for drugs is beyond me. The whole shooting match was a total cock-up. Still, we got out of it alive and that's all that matters. It won't stop me going back to Jamaica. I love the place and always will."

The singer also told me how the first time he ever heard real gunfire in his life was on a New Year's Eve in Sarajevo, Croatia, during the Balkans conflict, when Muslim soldiers fired into the air in celebration. He added: "The Caribbean incident was a bit different in that the gunfire was aimed at us. But thank goodness we can celebrate our escape."

The Jamaican cops apologised to Bono and his friends for the incident. They were acting on information that the plane was carrying drugs to the United States, an allegation that was totally wrong. Piers was delighted with the piece and it made the page one splash in all editions of the *Daily Mirror*.

I've met Bono on a number of occasions over the years but we've never spoken about it. The U2 star has taken a lot of flack in recent years for his political role in trying to help the poor in the Third World and highlighting the need for more money and help from the West. Pundits tend to sneer at him for being a do-gooder, but I think much of it is extremely unfair. Bono is a decent guy whose heart is in the right place.

You don't last for 30 years in show business unless you have something between the ears. He is not a drunk, he is not a junkie, he is a good father so what is the problem? I'll tell you, it's the usual bitchiness and begrudgery that scars almost all of western society today. I'd have Bono and U2 any day before most of the dickheads in celebrityland.

* * *

Chris de Burgh had a squeaky clean image for years before he was caught cheating on his wife Diane with their nanny Maresa Morgan.

I have always loved the singer's music, and two of his hits, *Spanish Train* and *A Spaceman Came Travelling*, are among my favourite songs. He's always kept a pretty low profile in Ireland, living in a lovely house in Dalkey village, and would only do a handful of TV and radio interviews here in any year.

His number one hit *Lady in Red*, which was dedicated to Diane, really raised his profile across the UK and Europe. And it was nearly everyone's favourite love song around that time. When Diane broke her neck and almost lost her life in a horse riding accident there was huge public sympathy for the couple.

The blonde, 19 year old nanny was employed by de Burgh to look after their three young children, including the future Miss World 2003 and top model Rosanna Davison, while bed-ridden Diane recuperated from her injuries. But Chris fell head over heels in love with the university student and they soon started a sexual relationship. It was only by chance that the tabloids got wind of it.

De Burgh flew Maresa over for a concert in Birmingham, and the couple were caught kissing in a hotel bar. Someone rang *The Sun* news desk in London and tipped them off. A reporter was sent to Dublin and worked on the story for three months, following de Burgh and his lover. They eventually brought in a team of photographers and caught them together.

The London news desk was on it at a hundred miles an hour and I was ordered to go and find Chris. Photographer Charlie Collins and I headed for Dalkey, where we doorstepped the de Burgh residence along with the rest of the pack. The singer was obviously in a deep state of shock and was hiding indoors. We soon discovered his lover Maresa was living around the corner, five minutes away, but there was no sign of her either.

For five days we played cat and mouse trying to track down de Burgh. We eventually got a tip off that he was hiding out in his brother-in-law's house in Annamoe, Co Wicklow, 20 minutes away. We got a shot of him but he didn't say anything.

Eventually, the media pressure got so great that Chris decided to do a radio interview and spill the beans. He confessed that he had been "stupid" and Maresa had become a crutch for him in his hour of need. He relied on her heavily from both an emotional and family point of view.

Chris said: "On more than one occasion I needed to express my grief at Diane's accident and I wept in Maresa's arms. For a time we were lovers but it became clear this relationship was going nowhere. I was wrong to become so close to her and deeply regret my actions. My wife is my dearest and closest friend and I love her very much. Our marriage is rock solid and I pray she will forgive me for my stupidity.

"I am deeply sorry for the pain I have caused my wife and children. I should never have cheated on her. When I stood up in church and said for better or worse, for richer or poorer,

God help me I meant it. Why I got involved in something away from the marriage bond is still baffling.

"My apologies go not just to my family but to those who believed in me as the perfect family man. My wife and I have been held up as moral icons and this is something neither of us wanted, because marriage isn't like that. It comes and goes, ebbs and flows. I don't want to lose my family. I don't want my wife to leave me and I love my children."

Chris compared his affair with Maresa to a train ride. "When I got on board the train it was stationary and it started moving a little faster, and a little faster again, and by the time we were going 80 mph I realised that I couldn't jump off without getting badly hurt. I am in a business which is full of temptations and people who are performers need love and approval."

The story did serious damage to Chris's image. And to be quite honest, I did feel sorry for him, because he was caught bang to rights with his pants down, but worse still, no one expected it from him. If he had been some serial sex cheat it wouldn't have received a fraction of the coverage.

Maresa of course took it all in her stride, keeping mum and going about her studies at University College Dublin like a stunning princess. Pictures of her made the front pages. Being a traditional, middle-class girl, she didn't sell her story for cash, even though she was offered hundreds of thousands of pounds by various newspapers.

The story died a death after few months and Chris was left to pick up the pieces. But then, right out of the blue, he was spotted with his young lover at an exclusive London hotel. He had taken her from Dublin to the Conrad Hotel on his private jet. When he finally got back home Chris was kicked out of the family house. He and Diane then lived apart for a year before eventually getting back together.

Chris had made one mistake in his life and she had the good sense and the heart to forgive him. Their marriage is now extremely strong, although they keep a low profile on the Dublin social circuit.

In later interviews the singer acknowledged he was probably going though a mid-life crisis. He was 45 years old at the time of his affair with Maresa. He added: "At the end of the day no one died. Everybody makes an error once in a while. I'm a survivor and I'm proud of the fact that I went through a public mauling on behalf of me, my family and friends and emerged stronger at the other end. It's not something I wanted to go through but here I am. What happened to me is, I became two different people, and thank God I now have control of both of them. There is the famous guy who I take out into the public arena, and when I go home I am not the famous guy anymore. I walk into a room full of yelling children and it's like the famous guy doesn't exist."

The one lesson he learned from the whole episode was men take women too easily for granted. "Men are no good at saying they're sorry, but I've got really good at it," he said.

Maresa got fed up with the affair constantly being dragged up in Ireland and moved to France a couple of years ago.

We now hear more of Chris's daughter Rosanna than the singer, and she is constantly in the public eye in Dublin. Her Miss World victory in 2003 was a moment of great joy for her family.

* * *

One of the most remarkable people I've met was Brian Keenan, the former Beirut hostage who spent over four years – 1,574 days – in captivity. The university scholar had taken up a teaching post in the Middle East four months earlier when he was abducted by Islamic Jihad on April 11, 1986. A Belfast Protestant, Keenan was, in my book, the bravest of men, who faced up to his ordeal with the greatest of courage.

He initially spent two months in isolation before being moved into a cell that he shared with the British journalist John McCarthy. He was kept blindfolded throughout most of his time as a hostage, and was chained hands and feet for all but a few minutes every day, when they were allowed to exercise their wasting muscles.

The plight of the two men and the other hostages, including the Archbishop of Canterbury's special envoy, Terry Waite, touched the heart of the world. However, neither the British nor the American governments would negotiate with terrorists so all three were, from a diplomatic point of view, largely ignored.

Keenan's plight was taken up by his two sisters, Elaine Spence and Brenda Gillham, who campaigned vigorously to publicly highlight his case. John McCarthy's cause was equally promoted by his long time girlfriend Jill Morrell, and she ensured his name was never forgotten.

Since Brian was travelling on both British and Irish passports, the Irish Government fought tooth and nail to secure his freedom. Irish diplomats worked extremely closely with Iran, and constantly pressed for his release. The lobbying eventually paid off when Brian was freed on August 24, 1990.

I was privileged to be at Dublin airport in the early hours of the morning when he flew home on the Government's private jet to be reunited with his family. The then Taoiseach, Charles Haughey, who played a pivotal role in getting him out, was there to greet him in a fanfare of publicity. It was a huge media event, and TV cameras from around the world were present to hear Brian speak for the first time about his horrendous time in captivity.

Brian looked extremely pale and drawn, and behind all the smiles for the cameras, we could see he was still carrying the severe scars of his nightmare ordeal. He came out with the line "I want to make love to all the women in the world", but his main concern was for his friend John McCarthy and the need to secure his release. He wouldn't feel free until John was home as well.

Brian told how they were kept chained to a radiator, stripped to their underpants, blindfolded and regularly beaten. The long conversations between him and John helped keep each of their minds alive in the most atrocious conditions. He was extremely worried that John wouldn't be able to cope isolated and alone. It was almost a year later before John McCarthy was freed and both men were reunited.

Brian sought the sanctuary of the West of Ireland to recuperate from his kidnapping and to get back to some sort of normal life. He bought a cottage on the outskirts of beautiful Westport, Co Mayo, where he was warmly welcomed by the locals. He also met and fell in love with his wife Audrey Doyle, the physiotherapist who helped nurse him back to full health, and the couple had two children, Jack and Cal.

One of my big regrets was having to do stories on Brian's new life. He hated the media spotlight and just wanted to be left alone. The public, of course, were interested in the Beirut hostage and how he was adapting. After a couple of months the story became a bore and all the papers rightly gave him the space he needed.

Brian's wedding in May, 1993 in the Wicklow Mountains, was also fun and games. We got pictures of the couple coming out of the church and the shot made page one headlines. We had all been led to believe that the reception was at a hideaway hotel about 20 minutes from Dublin, but it turned out to be in a completely different place, so Brian got his revenge!

In the summer of 1995 John McCarthy and Jill Morrell split up. Their romance and her very public love for the TV reporter had caught the imagination of the British public and everyone assumed that after John's release it would end in a fairytale wedding. But life sometimes doesn't work out according to plan.

After a few years back together John and Jill discovered, like any couple who had been apart for a long period of time, that they had both changed, and were not the same people who had fallen in love with one another. Jill admitted she was actually very jealous of the five years Brian spent with John in captivity, years that she had lost out on spending with John. It was time they went their separate ways.

John decided to fly to the West of Ireland to get away from it all.

A team of reporters descended on Co Mayo to try and find him. We spent a week trying to track him down to speak to him about the split with Jill, but it was like looking for a needle in a haystack. He wasn't in the Keenan cottage or at any hotel in the county.

John got married a couple of years later in England to Anna Ottewill, and both Brian and Terry Waite were present.

Brian Keenan now lives a very happy life out of the public eye in Dublin. In March of 2008, he returned to Beirut with his family for the first time since his release. It was for him a very personal journey, and the final step in putting the whole ordeal behind him. The BBC made a documentary of it.

Brian said: "I was terrified on the flight. I remember looking out the window down on the city as the plane came in to land not knowing what to expect."

He went back to the street where he was abducted and to the buildings in which he thought he had been held captive. He wanted his kids to see Lebanon as a country other than a land of imprisonment and hate.

Brian added: "I always had a sense that I'd return to Lebanon. I wanted to see the country I never got to see. And I wanted to take my kids to the place where they knew bad things happened to their dad, to see it's not bad."

When he arrived in Beirut airport he thought the plane had missed a turn somewhere. He was struck by how different it looked, compared to the menacing, gun-filled terminal that greeted him all those years ago. "There was a sea of people with colourful clothes, balloons, flowers and chocolates. But of course it is still a city in turmoil. It's still a beautiful flower but you soon learn there is poison in its petals," he said.

He took his wife and kids swimming on the beach, to St Mema's Monastery and to the caves in Jeita, and out of the city to the Bekaa Valley – one of the places he was driven in a coffin sized box during his imprisonment.

They only got nervous when Hezbollah spotted camera equipment and stopped to check their passports. He and Audrey got very protective of the children and expected the worst, but this time, it was totally different, and they were allowed carry on.

Brian added: "The kids had a ball and now they'll associate Lebanon with fun times. It's a country that has been constantly invaded, but it has always survived. Lebanon's greatest attribute is its ability to survive."

It's down to Brian's own pure survival instincts that he is alive today.

* * *

The barbaric murder of Veronica Guerin was the lowest point in the history of Irish journalism.   It was the first time one of our colleagues lost their lives in the line of duty, killed by a low-life gang of scum who fought like cornered rats to protect their multi-million pound drug empire.

I wasn't a friend of Veronica's but I'd met her on a number of occasions during murder trials down in Dublin's Four Courts, and always found her to be pleasant and courteous. She wasn't one of the tabloid gang around the city like her great rival Paul Williams and Mick McNiffe, and she always worked alone.

Unlike the rest of us, Veronica didn't come up through the ranks in newspapers, where you served your apprenticeship on a local paper before you moved up the ladder to the nationals. She was a late comer to the industry and she certainly made an immediate impact.

During the late eighties and early nineties criminals were running amok in Dublin in the battle to supply drugs on the streets. Indeed, many observers would rightly say that things haven't really changed and that Irish society has exactly the same problem today.

Veronica moved over from the *Sunday Tribune* to the *Sunday Independent* and began making her name writing about the different crimelords operating in our society. She quickly built up a big following penning pieces about The Monk, Gerry Hutch; The Coach, John Traynor; The Penquin, George Mitchel; The Viper, Martin Foley and Factory John Gilligan. Their respective nicknames were given to each of them by either Paul Williams in the *Sunday World* or by Veronica since, for legal reasons at that stage, they couldn't name them.

Veronica chronicled the various criminal activities of each of the gangs with leaks from her Garda sources about what they were up to. In addition, she began approaching the Godfathers directly, and some of them, like Hutch, agreed to talk to her. The interviews made riveting copy, giving readers a fascinating insight into how these guys thought and lived.

Gerry Hutch himself was a bit like the General, Martin Cahill, who saw himself as a good old-fashioned criminal. He didn't drink, smoke or do drugs. He and his cohorts were blamed for numerous armed robberies, including the £2.9 million Brinks-Allied Security depot heist near Dublin airport. Hutch has since gone straight and repaid millions in unpaid taxes to the Criminal Assets Bureau, which was set up after the reporter's death.

Thanks to Williams' dogged determination, the real names of all the crimelords eventually all came out into the open. He was under 24 hour Garda protection after numerous death threats, and also had to flee the country when the Psycho, Dublin gangster PJ Judge, threatened to kill him.

Because of the intense competition and rivalry with Williams, Veronica began pushing herself to come up with bigger and better stories. She took numerous personal risks and made acquaintance with John "The Coach" Traynor, a small time crook whom I had written about in the *Sunday World* in the late eighties, after he was jailed in England for several years for trying to cash stolen bonds worth a couple of million. He fled back to Ireland when he was given a weekend release in 1993. He got the nickname The Coach as

a result of teaching karate to kids. Veronica's association with
Traynor would ultimately lead to her death.

They would regularly meet for chats and she would
question him about the activities of various criminals. He was
extremely close to the John Gilligan gang, which was making
a fortune at the time smuggling in ecstasy and cannabis from
Amsterdam and selling it across Dublin. Gilligan had made
his name robbing warehouses and factories, hence his
nickname Factory John. But he moved up into the big league
with his drug empire, and was living a life of luxury with his
family in his country retreat, Jessbrook, a luxurious house
complete with stables and an indoor horse riding arena
outside Enfield, Co Meath. He was also believed to have had
£10 million cash in the bank and was laundering £30,000 a
week in drug money via bookie shops across the country.

Veronica, by this stage, had heard numerous stories on the
grapevine about the power and the wealth of the Gilligan
gang, and was pushing Traynor for more information on
them. She even threatened to name and shame Traynor as a
drug dealer if he didn't come up with the goods, resulting in
him taking a High Court injunction against the *Sunday
Independent* to stop her. He claimed in a sworn affidavit that
his life was in danger if his name was published.

Veronica was first shot, in the leg, in January 1995 by a
lone gunman who called to her North Dublin home, where
she lived with her husband Graham Turley and their son
Cathal. The incident made national headlines, but it didn't
deter her from her mission to expose the bad guys.

She recalled: "The door was pushed in on top of me and I
fell back. There was a figure standing in front of me. He was
carrying a long grey steel handgun. I looked up into his eyes
to appeal to him not to shoot me, and then there was a

Bill Clinton told Catherine Hamill: "You have done more for peace than all the politicians put together." © *Irish Daily Mirror*

A moment of great relief, as Brian Keenan is reunited with his family in Dublin Airport after being released from five years of captivity in Beirut. Charlie Haughey played a key role behind the scenes to secure his freedom.
© *Collins, Dublin*

The happiest day of Brian Keenan's life, when he wed his beautiful bride Audrey. © *Collins, Dublin*

The darkest day in Irish journalism, when Veronica Guerin was shot dead on the Naas dual carriageway. Gardaí and colleagues gather at the scene in total shock. © *Collins, Dublin*

The man with Veronica's blood on his hands, John Gilligan, the gangland boss who allegedly ordered the hit. © *Collins, Dublin*

The happiest couple in Irish showbiz, Bono & Ali Hewson, who escaped from a frightening ordeal in the Caribbean. © *Collins, Dublin*

Tabloid maestro Craig MacKenzie, who ruled the *Mirror* with an iron fist, and took no prisoners. © *Collins, Dublin*

Love birds Van "the Man" Morrison and Michelle Rocca. © *Collins, Dublin*

Bertie meets Jumbo at the zoo.
© Collins, Dublin

Bertie meets the real "Jumbo" at Government Buildings before the last election. © Collins, Dublin

Sinead O'Connor, who had a habit of falling for *Mirror* men, namely
Neil Michael and Nick Sommerlad, who she later married and divorced.
© *Collins, Dublin*

stinging sensation. I couldn't believe I hadn't been killed, but I did feel a sense of relief. I don't feel a target; they are not going to kill me."

Veronica publicly vowed to carry on her work because she believed that someone had to tell the people how the crimelords were taking over Dublin. Her husband Graham gave her his full backing vowing "Veronica will not be intimidated by any group or individual". He was absolutely right and she was back at work within days.

However, later that September she bravely decided to go and confront Gilligan at his home about his criminal activities. Normally in these circumstances a news desk would send at least a second reporter and a photographer when confronting a gangster like this, as witnesses and for protection. But the *Sunday Independent* didn't even know she was doing it. She worked most of the time on her own, away from the office, and arrived in with her copy for publication at the weekend. She kept in touch with her bosses at the paper by telephone. Veronica was one of those strong minded people who, if you tried to keep a tight reign on her, would just leave and move to another title.

When she called to Gilligan's home he went ballistic. She asked him – was he the country's crime Mr Big? Was he a multi-millionaire? Where did all his cash come from? How could he have all the cars, the race horses, the properties, the exotic holidays in St Lucia? He got extremely agitated; he didn't like the questions and he didn't like her.

Like the boot boy he is, he beat up Veronica, punching and kicking her, and leaving her body black and blue while ripping off some of her clothes. He told all his gang: "This little bitch isn't going to get in our way."

Gilligan later rang her up and again threatened: "If you do

one thing on me, or write about me, I will kidnap your son and ride him. I will shoot you. Do you understand what I'm saying? I will fucking shoot you, I will kill you." She came away in a deep state of shock, extremely frightened, and made a formal complaint of assault to the Gardaí

The heat was starting to be turned up on Gilligan and he became extremely concerned. If he was convicted of beating up the reporter he would be going back to prison for a couple of year's stretch, the last thing he needed when his drug business was booming.

Gilligan had begun bringing in cannabis in late 1993 after he was freed from prison. He initially started off with shipments of cannabis from Morocco via his base in Amsterdam, but then it spread out to ecstasy and cocaine. He had good contacts in Holland and Spain and the turnover was around £34 million a year. The gangster soon organised the distribution of the drugs all over Ireland, selling it to other gang members. He had an army of up to 150 dealers selling on the streets, each making £500 a week for themselves. Gardaí reckoned the Gilligan gang had smuggled in drugs with a street value of £180 million in just a couple of years. Gilligan was the muscle but Traynor was the brains.

Gilligan was also living the life of a squire in Co Meath, and none of his new rich neighbours had any idea about his criminal background. He and his wife Geraldine were living the dream and had an awful lot to lose. They also believed they were untouchable.

Veronica was warned two weeks before her death by The Monk that there was a gangland hit out on her. She also believed she had identified the gunman who had previously shot her, and got a freelance photographer to get a picture of him. She was planning to run this story soon and also asked the Gardaí to stop giving her protection because it was starting to interfere with her work.

Gilligan had gathered his cohorts Dutchy Holland, Brian Meehan, Paul Ward and Traynor, and told them he wanted her executed. He told them: "No journalist is going to destroy my empire." Meehan, in particular, was worried they would all be named and shamed in the *Sunday Independent*.

Gilligan loved money; it was the most important thing to him in the world. If he couldn't lead the gang because he was in prison, he would effectively lose everything. He told Traynor he was going to sort Veronica out once and for all, but Traynor claims he never for once thought Gilligan would kill her.

On June 26, 1996 Veronica went to Naas district court where she was up before the judge and she was fined £150 for speeding. She was delighted she had not been banned, and drove down the Naas dual carriageway towards the city. John Traynor had told the gang where she would be that day and they tailed her from the court.

As she was stopped in traffic at the Green Isle Hotel, two men on a motorbike rode up beside her red Opel Calibra sports car and opened fire. She was shot five times through the driver's window, twice in the head and three times in the chest. She died instantly.

Brian Meehan drove the bike and Dutchy Holland was the alleged hit man. The assassins escaped towards Tallaght and Paul Ward dumped the bike and the weapon in the Grand Canal.

I was sitting in a restaurant in Temple Bar with my friend Dave Curtin when my mobile phone rang five minutes later. It was a shocked Garda contact telling me what had happened, and that Veronica was dead. He said he was almost certain the Gilligan gang had carried out the hit and Traynor was up to his eyes in it.

I was extremely angry and dismayed. The lunatics were now running the asylum, and if reporters were being executed at random what chance had Ireland as a free and democratic society. This wasn't just an attack on all journalists; it was an attack on every citizen in our country. And it bluntly meant that no one was safe from these drug lords, and that Ireland was going down the road of Columbia, where criminals ruled with ruthless fear and intimidation.

One of the first on the scene was Paul Williams, a man who had lived under the constant pressure of death threats. Although Veronica was his rival, he knew it could easily have been him lying dead in the car. He was stricken with grief for his slain colleague, and like the Gardaí, he vowed to do everything in his power to ensure the culprits responsible were captured and brought to justice.

The public backlash was phenomenal. Everybody admired Veronica, and everyone took her murder personally. All our hearts went out to her husband and her little son Cathal. Although she was a fearless journalist, Veronica Guerin was firstly a loving and caring mother who lived for her family, and her beloved Manchester United.

The Government, under Taoiseach John Bruton, acted swiftly and brought in new anti-crime legislation, setting up the Criminal Assets Bureau to go after the money and to put these hoods behind bars. The theory was if you went after the cash, you'd nail the criminals.

Gilligan fled the country but was subsequently arrested in England and sent home to face the music after a couple of years fighting extradition.

Justice did eventually prevail before three judges at

Dublin's Special Criminal Court. Thanks to the evidence of two gang members who turned supergrasses, Charlie Bowden and Warren Russell, the state got its convictions. Bowden had actually prepared the Magnum gun used to kill the young mother.

Brian Meehan got life for the murder of Veronica; Dutchy Holland was given 20 years for drug dealing, while Gilligan got 28 years [reduced to 20 years on appeal] for drug offenses. I was there when both Meehan and Dutchy were convicted. They showed little or no emotion as the Judges delivered their sentences. Holland was overheard remarking: "It was just another job". His words were cold, cruel and callous. He had no remorse whatsoever for his actions. Although he wasn't convicted of pulling the trigger, it is generally accepted that he did. In the world Dutchy Holland lived in, shooting a mother like Veronica Guerin was just like shooting a dog.

The Guerin family and her husband Graham Turley were all relieved they were off the streets and no danger to anyone else in society. There was a great air of relief around the courts that day, and a feeling among all the journalists that some semblance of justice had prevailed. But I think we all kept thinking how it could easily have been any of us.

This gang had no respect for life in any shape or form. Veronica's death was just a shocking waste. She had so much to live for and so much to offer.

As a family, journalists are constantly bickering and back-biting with each other. However, when the chips are down and there is an attack on the fourth estate, we all collectively stand together. We are all extremely proud of our jobs and what we do, and the majority of the time the good far outweighs the bad.

Gilligan got his comeuppance in March, 2001. It was a

long wait, but it was well worth waiting for. He had done everything in his legal power to avoid coming back to Ireland to face the music. The Brits picked him up at Heathrow Airport with £300,000 in his suitcase, on his way from Spain to Holland. He was held in the maximum security Belmarsh prison in London, where he battled to avoid extradition but eventually lost.

On the day he went down, the Judge, Diarmuid O'Donovan, told Gilligan he had "grave suspicions" that he had been involved in the reporter's murder, but that his guilt had not been proved beyond doubt. He still received a 28 year jail sentence for running his drug empire.

I think everyone in our business felt an overwhelming feeling of triumph that good had prevailed over evil. Gilligan's conviction meant that no matter how much gangsters bullied, intimidated and even killed people to protect themselves, nobody is untouchable. And I think in Gilligan's case we would all love to just throw away the key. He who lives by the sword should die by it. Society should have no place for the drug lords destroying our kids.

Meehan and Gilligan are still behind bars in Portlaoise prison and long may they stay there. Holland was released but later convicted in England for his involvement in an attempted kidnapping. He was found dead in his prison cell at Parkhurst Prison on June 19, 2009, having died of natural causes.

John Traynor was the only member of the gang to get away with it. Unfortunately, the Gardaí didn't have sufficient evidence to charge him. He is still out on the streets and living a new life in the south of Spain. He has repeatedly protested his innocence, but I for one definitely don't believe him. Anyone who knows Traynor would tell you he would say Mass or sell his mother to get off the hook.

Charlie Bowden and Warren Russell were given new identities under the Witness Protection Programme, and both are believed to be living in Australia.

Veronica Guerin is gone but she will never be forgotten, and it is up to each and every one of us to ensure that her death was not in vain. New drug dealers are on the streets and the sooner we get rid of them the better.

* * *

Catherine Zeta Jones is one of my favourite actresses. Beautiful and intelligent, she shot to fame in the smash-hit British TV series *The Darling Buds of May*. In the mid-nineties, in the days before she became a Hollywood A-list celebrity and married Michael Douglas, the whole of Fleet Street was infatuated by her.

A simple kiss with her good friend Liverpool actor Paul McGann in the front seat of his car in London was enough to spark off a media frenzy that culminated in the whole press pack spending a week running around the hills of Donegal.

Paul and his wife Annie were happily married and had two young children. They became friendly with Catherine and her family during filming of the movie *Catherine the Great*, in which she had the lead role. And then by chance, Catherine and Annie had found themselves on the same flight back to London together, and Catherine confided in her about her personal problems, cementing their friendship.

In May of 1996, Paul and his three brothers Joe, Mark and Stephen began working on a new BBC series about the Irish famine, *The Hanging Gale*. The actors and their families were all staying around the picturesque villages of Ramelton and Rathmullen in Co Donegal, where the bulk of the historical drama was being shot.

A week into filming Paul had to fly to London to do a voice over, telling Annie he would be meeting Catherine and picking up some pictures taken of them and their families on the *Catherine the Great* set. He agreed to meet Catherine outside the office of a film industry insurance doctor in Sloane Square. Catherine spotted Paul in his car, got in and gave him a traditional "luvvy" kiss. The pair got out and went for a walk when Catherine spotted a freelance photographer following her. She got upset and said she was after having a horrible day, and started crying and Paul put his arm around her. The pictures of the kiss and the hug appeared in a Sunday paper, fuelling speculation that Paul's marriage was over and he was having a relationship with Catherine.

I was immediately dispatched to Donegal with photographer Alan Lewis to find Paul and Annie to see if they would talk about it. Unknown to us, Paul had told Annie he had given Catherine a kiss and somebody had photographed it. Annie had also spoken to Catherine on the phone, who assured her there was absolutely nothing going on.

The whole week up in Ramelton was just totally mad. We set up base in the Bridge Pub in the village, and so began a game of cat and mouse with the McGann brothers, as they plotted and planned to keep Paul away from the tabloid hacks. They were ferried to and from the set in different vans with no windows. Extra bouncers were brought in to keep the photographers at bay and stop them from getting shots of Paul with their long lenses.

On one or two occasions it got a bit hairy with the security men trying to use their muscle and the Gardaí were called. Joe McGann, who was obviously extremely protective of his younger brother, wasn't too shy about telling us what he thought of us. The brothers were itching for a scrap, but the BBC, terrified of a public relations disaster, did everything in their power to keep the McGanns under control.

We received numerous tip-offs from locals as to where the boys were staying, but they were sending us on a wild goose chase. It later transpired that Annie had actually moved from where she was originally staying to a house in the middle of Ramelton, where she could stare right out the window at us. After fruitless searches we had no idea where the couple were staying. Then rumours started doing the rounds that Catherine had secretly flown over to be with Paul.

By the end of the week the news desk got bored with the stories and so did I. I also got sick and tired of the constant rain; the weather was crap. Hearsay filed in some other papers that Paul and Annie had split up turned out to be totally rubbish. I ended up getting a story from a very good source on the set that the Zeta story was bullshit and Paul and Annie were together and extremely happy. It turned out to be right on the money.

The TV series *The Hanging Gale* was absolutely brilliant, and one of the best period dramas the BBC had filmed for years. It was an extremely accurate reflection of Irish history, which saw over one million people die in the famine. Many of those deaths occurred in Donegal, where the barren but beautiful landscape is very difficult for any farmer to make a living off, even in modern times. Thousands also fled Donegal on coffin ships to America and to Scotland to avoid death and to start a new life.

Years later I met Joe McGann in Dublin and we had a good laugh over it. I would have loved to have had a few drinks with the four McGann brothers because I suspect they are very good company, but it wasn't the time or the place.

Catherine Zeta eventually found happiness and true love with Michael Douglas. Good luck to her.

* * *

Christmas to most people should be a time of peace and tranquillity. But the problem with our business is that you never know what's going to happen next. It's also what makes our job so refreshing and exciting. And that's why you go to work with your passport in your pocket and an overnight bag packed in the boot of the car.

When the body of a beautiful young French woman was found near her holiday home in Skull, West Cork, on December 23, 1996, a massive murder probe was launched. Sophie Tuscan du Plantier was battered to death in a brutal murder, which once again shocked the nation. Her body was left lying at the entrance to a lane 100 yards from her house, and was found by a neighbour, Shirley Foster. She had been beaten several times with a blunt instrument, and then a concrete block had been dropped on her.

Sophie had made a phone call at 11 p.m. the previous night, and detectives could not determine whether the killer had tackled her at the crime scene and then gone to her house and turned off the lights, or whether she was murdered after daybreak. The immediate investigation was hampered because the state pathologist couldn't get to the scene from Dublin until 24 hours after the body was discovered, and the Irish Dept of Justice had no cover for him. He therefore, was unable to establish at precisely what time she was killed. There was also no sign of a break-in at the house and nothing was stolen. Her bed was also unmade and she was lightly dressed, so there was no indication of whether she went to bed on the night of December 22.

The Gardaí could track all of the blonde, 38 year old TV scriptwriter's movements from the moment she arrived in Cork airport, but they had no idea if she was alone on the night of her death.

What was to follow was one of the most bizarre incidents I have ever come across. A local reporter, Ian Bailey, who originally moved over to West Cork from England, and did the odd bit of freelancing in the area, began filing on the story. By St Stephen's Day I decided I better get down to Cork, as the story was really taking off.

Our Regional News Editor, Paul Smith, had known Bailey from doing some Saturday shifts on the *Mail on Sunday* in Fleet Street, and felt he knew his stuff. Within hours of getting down there I quickly discovered Ian was one of the prime suspects in the case. He had apparently been seen by a local woman washing blood off his boots not far from the murder scene in the early hours of the morning – evidence that, years later, would turn out to be a total lie.

He had also personally known Sophie and had been known to have the very occasional drink with her in the local pub or at her house. The Gardaí were extremely suspicious of Ian and began leaking stories he was in the frame. It was also all the gossip around the Mizen peninsula where Ian Bailey had made his fair share of enemies.

Sophie, ironically, was no angel. She and her millionaire husband Daniel, who was 55 at the time, had an open marriage. She had previously had an affair with a French artist, who had beaten her up in a jealous rage when they split up a year before. That relationship had been rekindled in the

12 weeks before her death, and they were due to work together on a new French TV programme.

It was later discovered that she was involved in a love triangle, and had been having sex with her first husband, Pierre Baudey, the father of her then 15 year old son, her husband Daniel, and her secret lover, the French artist. She had confided to friends that she was seriously thinking of divorcing Daniel to be with her lover, and she had planned to go to Senegal with him on Christmas Eve to sort out their lives. But the artist could prove to detectives he wasn't in Ireland at the time off her murder.

Sophie would visit Ireland several times a year to get away from the jet set lifestyle she lived with her well connected husband, a personal friend of former French President Jacques Chirac. She enjoyed the peace of West Cork, where she could write undisturbed to her heart's content.

Police became convinced that the murder wasn't a crime of passion but more of a fatal attraction by somebody local who was infatuated by her; someone she knew. There were also rumours that Ian had a history of beating up his partner, Jules Thomas, and this again helped fuel the local gossip.

Paddy Clancy of *The Sun,* Senan Maloney of *The Irish Star* and I decided to go and front up Ian Bailey. In one of the tensest interviews I'd ever do, we confronted him on every allegation, in the sun room of his home, with Jules by his side. He seemed distant and strange, but then who wouldn't be given the pressure he was under. He didn't shirk any of the questions and vehemently denied killing Sophie, dismissed any innuendo that they had a secret sexual relationship, and categorically denied washing his boots anywhere near the scene on the night of the murder. He admitted he was a suspect but vowed to clear his name. We had a page one story and the reporter who was reporting the news was suddenly making it.

Several weeks later Ian and Jules were brought in for questioning by the Gardaí but he was never charged. As soon as he was released he again proclaimed his innocence and fumed: "They told me they'd prove I did it. I know I didn't. I believe I'm being set up. I had nothing to do with it, I didn't kill her. I've nothing on my conscience." He had also given the Gardaí his DNA, but there was no connection to any evidence found at the crime.

Jules stood by her man and said she was bewildered and amazed at their double arrest. She stated: "Ian is innocent, he is not the killer. Why would he write so much about the murder if he was involved in it? We've been together for seven years and I don't suspect for one moment he had anything to do with Sophie's death. I feel sorry for Sophie but my life has been a misery since her death. The Gardaí haven't left us alone. I am totally stressed out."

Bailey's life was ruined by the allegations. The harsh truth is that there was never any real hard evidence against him. Whoever killed the French woman is still at large and may never be convicted. The file on the case is still open. I suspect either a prowler or someone from France with a grudge against her did it. I don't think we will ever really know.

Murders in West Cork are very rare indeed. They just don't happen out of the blue and Sophie, for whatever reason, was a very easy target.

* * *

By this time, I was Irish News Editor of the *Daily Mirror*, and we were now publishing an Irish edition of the newspaper. To add to the fun I became a father again in April 1997 when my son JP arrived on the scene. Over the next couple of years we would continue to build the Irish edition to the point where, by 1998, the powers that be decided to set up in Belfast and produce and publish the paper in Ireland.

The Irish Daily Mirror
1996-1998

Part 1

CHAPTER 7

He came onto the *Daily Mirror* like a hurricane, shouting and roaring at a hundred miles an hour. Loud, confident, brash Craig Mackenzie was a Fleet Street hack to his fingertips. The younger brother of the former Editor of *The Sun* Kelvin, Craig was brought up in all the traditions of tabloid newspapers, and didn't take any prisoners. Come what may he wanted the perfect paper for his readers every day.

Both his parents were journalists and he cut his teeth learning the trade on the streets of South London. He had made his name as a sub-editor on *The Sun* and the *News of the World*, became Features Editor of the *Daily Express*, before being appointed Deputy Editor of the *Sunday Express*.

We first met in the bar of *Express Newspapers* when he would come down for a few well earned scoops between editions, and we would trade insults about our rival papers to a chorus of laughter. Initially, I thought he was a cocky, noisy fucker who was a bit of a prick. But when I got to know him I discovered he could talk the talk and walk the walk, even if he was living in the shadow of his famous brother.

Kelvin, in a four letter rant, would eat you alive for breakfast and fire you in a flash. His bollockings in *The Sun's* newsroom were the stuff of legend, but he was also blessed with a fantastic sense of humour. If Kelvin got scooped on a story everybody got it in the neck, everyone shared the pain. He once decided to sack his astrologer and sent her a note: "As you have already seen in the stars… you're fired".

Craig, despite his temper, had a big heart, even if he didn't show it to many people. He was extremely vain, and always very conscious of his appearance and image. He was also super fit, going to the gym almost every day.

Craig's energy was phenomenal and earned him the nickname the "bouncing bogbrush", largely due to his failure to sit still for more than three seconds, and to his trademark grey flicked-back hairstyle. He also much preferred the company of women to men, finding them far more entertaining, but he is a totally devoted family man who adores his wife Pippa and their children.

It was Kelvin who gave Piers Morgan his big break in journalism, and trained him like a treasured son. He recognised Piers' intelligence and talent at a very early stage, and promoted him up through the ranks of *The Sun* newsroom. By 1996, as Piers got stuck into his new job as Editor of the *Daily Mirror,* he decided to bring Craig on board.

The boss wanted to shake up his regional editions and Craig was the man. They both felt that there were big sales to be gained in Ireland, Scotland and Wales, and the company, under then Managing Director Roger Eastoe and Chief Executive David Montgomery, was prepared to invest millions in the process. Soon after, Kelvin arrived over from News International as Monty's number two, much to the horror of the London hacks, who were terrified of what impact he would have on their lives.

Within weeks, Ireland went from being a token edition of two or three page changes being produced in London, to at least ten pages of Irish news and sport.

Craig was on the phone from early morning til late at night looking for stories, demanding to know what was going on. I rarely had time to catch my breath, as he was pushing and pushing for more and more. As the sales began increasing and we consistently produced an Irish page one every day, the company decided it was time to open an office in Dublin and hire more reporters.

We already had veteran reporter Joe Gorrod and his protégé Conor Hanna in Belfast, so I went and hired Neil Leslie and two unknown young reporters, Nicola Tallant and Lynn Kelleher.

Leslie, the proud son of a Dublin bus driver, was as clever as they come and we soon christened him "brains". He quickly became my right hand man, and his news sense was outstanding, which is why he is Deputy Editor of the *Sunday World* today. Pat Flanagan and Caoimhe Young, along with Karl Brophy and Neil Michael, were quickly added to the team as we battled to take on *The Irish Sun* and *The Irish Star*.

Craig was in his element; Piers let him do what he wanted and didn't interfere. I effectively became News Editor in Dublin which meant I was on the road less and less. As soon as Craig woke up, he was on his mobile asking what each of our rivals had splashed with, demanding answers. He was also trying to get into the Irish mindset and quickly learn why the other papers handled a specific story in a certain way. His hunger and desire were relentless, and he was extremely proud and passionate about everything we did. He also had a great ability to laugh both at himself and at some of the decisions he'd made.

Any time we missed a story I would have to break the bad news to him, a job that would leave the best of people quaking in their boots. He would descend into a 60 second rant with some of the finest expletives you ever heard, and then finish with the line "at least that's over then". He hated surprises in any shape or form and if we fucked it up he wanted to know straight away. But he was also blessed with an ability to move on and would immediately focus on the next day's edition. In newspapers you have to forgive and forget very quickly and, most of all, never take things personally. "It's just business, nothing personal Johnny", Craig would say as he laid down the law.

We quickly built up a terrific understanding. I wasn't afraid to stand up to him and take him on, and far more importantly, he was willing to listen to me and respected my judgement. If I felt a decision was wrong, seven times out of ten he would eventually come round to my way of thinking. It wasn't a battle of wills; I was just trying to keep him and the paper right. The last thing Piers needed was Craig and me dropping him in it over some story we mishandled in Ireland.

As Piers would often remark over a pint: "Imagine Kierans, my future could be in your hands…frightening thought really!" It was, however, a thought Craig and I both took very seriously.

* * *

It wasn't long before Craig and I delivered a big exclusive for the new look *Irish Daily Mirror*. I had met a top notch private investigator from Dublin while on holiday playing golf in Spain. In June 1996 he rang me right out of the blue asking to meet me, with the carrot that he had a cracking story for us.

One of the big celebrity romances at the time was between Van Morrison and his now wife Michelle Rocca, a former top model and Miss Ireland beauty queen. Michelle is a stunning woman and was always in the Dublin papers and Irish magazines. She was also 16 years younger than Van, which made their relationship all the more interesting, from a public point of view.

Van is a music legend on both sides of the Atlantic, and has always been very low key and reclusive, especially when it comes to his private life.

In those days Van and Michelle had a very stormy relationship, constantly falling in and out of love. She clearly wasn't in it for the money because she came from an extremely wealthy background herself. She had also been married previously to John Devine, an Arsenal soccer star who played for Ireland during his career.

The tabloids were obsessed with their three year romance and the *Mirror* was no different. Van and Michelle had got engaged and we were all speculating about their wedding.

I met my contact in a Dublin hotel and he told me Michelle was cheating on Van the Man, but more importantly, he had the evidence to prove it. He handed me a file with all the details, and not only that, he also had a video taken at another hotel in the city which showed Michelle with her secret lover.

It transpired Michelle was two timing Van with Angus Gold, who at the time was racing manager in Newmarket for Sheikh Hamdan Al Maktoum, one of the world's richest men. She had been meeting her married lover for regular nights of passion in the Dublin hotel while Van was away from the Dublin home they shared, working on his music.

My contact wouldn't tell me who had hired him, but he had been instructed to get the story out in the papers. Michelle had been followed, unknown to herself, for a number of weeks. I rang Craig and told him the story and he couldn't believe what we had.

Van was extremely litigious so we had to ensure the story stood up and we had Michelle banged to rights. I checked through all the evidence and the private investigators had done their homework. There was absolutely no way Michelle could wriggle out of this one.

I sat down that night and began writing the story. Craig ordered me over to London on the first plane the next morning so we could go through every last detail with our lawyers. He was so excited, so full of energy, and he was determined to give this story the full Mackenzie treatment. This meant wiping out page one and doing the first five pages on it. We would also do a massive follow up on day two, when the rest of the opposition would be trying to play catch up with us.

The story came as a huge shock, especially to Michelle Rocca, and was followed up everywhere. The world and its mother were camped outside the couple's home in Dalkey, Dublin looking for quotes from her. Van was obviously nowhere to be seen, and was believed to be in England.

The problem for her was that she couldn't deny the story; it was true and she knew I had all the hard evidence to prove it. She was literally caught with her knickers down.

Thanks to a very good friend I managed to get a mobile number for Van and phoned him. He was angry, annoyed and amazingly, he agreed to talk to me. He told me the engagement was off, their relationship was over and he didn't want to see Michelle again.

He said: "It's all over, I've been betrayed, we're finished. I'm completely disgusted by the behaviour of everyone involved. I have no plans to go back to Dublin; we won't be getting back together. It's over and that's that."

Angus Gold had to go back and face his wife, and was later fired by Sheikh Maktoum. We tried to doorstep him at his home but he wouldn't speak to us.

The next day Michelle phoned Van and pleaded for

forgiveness. She apologised, said she'd made a big mistake, and didn't deliberately set out to embarrass him.

The whole story was run by Craig like a military operation, and sold brilliantly. Sales were way up and everyone was happy. We had landed a cracking scoop and remarkably, it didn't cost us a penny, in what was the heyday of cheque book journalism.

It didn't take long for Van and Michelle to make up. A couple of weeks later she checked into the Rutland Centre, Dublin, the country's top rehab clinic, for treatment for a booze problem. When she sorted herself out Van took her back. He was always head over heels in love with her, and found it in his heart to forgive her.

The following year, the couple married and are still as happy as ever today, living near Bath in England. The sceptics didn't expect their marriage to survive but it did. They keep a very low profile and stay out of the public eye completely. The only time you ever see Van Morrison publicly these days is on the stage.

* * *

Piers Morgan himself is a very decent guy. Forget his loud-mouthed public image and ego. He is an extremely kind, caring and considerate person. He is also extremely loyal to his friends and colleagues, has the most fantastic sense of humour and a great ability to laugh at himself.

I first met Piers when we were on the road in London, and we hit it off straight away. I didn't buy into any of his celebrity bullshit and could see right through it, which is one of the reasons I believe we got on so well.

Piers is first and foremost a reporter who has the natural ability to see a story from a million miles away. This is a skill you can't really teach – you either have it or you don't. He was writing the *Bizarre* showbiz column for *The Sun* and was regularly doing the big set piece interviews featuring pictures of him with each of the stars.

Kelvin loved all the hype, and kept pressuring Piers to deliver more and more, and the young gun didn't let his highly demanding boss down. Slowly but surely he was starting to become a celebrity himself, regularly appearing on TV and radio, and he was well able to talk the talk.

We often bumped into each other at Vagabones or the Wine Press at the bottom of Fleet Street on a Friday night, where there would be laughs and jokes galore. I wrote very few showbiz stories but fully realised how important they are to a tabloid newspaper. Piers had built up great contacts and they would stand him for years to come.

He also had extensive Irish roots which gave him a keen interest in things over here. His relations came from Co. Offaly and his mother ensured he never forgot his roots, and he got to know all of his cousins over in the Emerald Isle. Piers loved visiting Dublin and would try and pop over every chance he got.

He particularly enjoyed a dance in Lillie's Bordello, or a game of pool upstairs in Renards nightclub, where we'd bet a fiver a man. Piers hated losing and every game was like a World Championship final, with great pride and passion at stake.

During his time as Editor he held a number of think tanks in Ireland at the K-Club and the Morrison Hotel near Temple Bar. Up to 20 of us would spend the whole day locked behind doors in conference, coming up with new ideas for the paper, and then that night he would lead us on a tour of the city from pub to pub.

One thing about Piers – he had an open mind and

everything was up for discussion. He might not always agree with you, but he liked people who had opinions, rather than those who would sit there and sneer like silent puppets. Being a "Yes" man around Piers Morgan was a recipe for disaster. You wouldn't last very long.

He was also extremely good at making quick decisions, a trick he learned off Kelvin. He didn't hang around mulling over things, and if he decided he was going a certain route, off he went at a hundred miles an hour.

Another great trait he had was that he would give people a chance. Numerous people got a leg up the ladder, including myself, thanks to him. He was a great believer in the work hard, play hard mantra. And like each and every one of us he would go to the ends of the earth for a story.

I remembered being at one think tank in England that Piers had to adjourn after George Michael rang him. Piers interviewed him in 20 minutes and within an hour had filed a page one splash and a 4-5 spread. He didn't pass it on to one of his minions to write like some editors would. He did it himself; it's what journalism is all about.

But the thing I probably love most about Piers is that he is great craic. He has absolutely no airs or graces and would fit in anywhere. I always remember the first time he came over to meet all of our new young reporters, and he just mixed with them as if he was one of the lads. He had tremendous respect for their drive and enthusiasm, and recognised the built-in hunger they had for stories. Indeed, he was so impressed at one stage that he wanted to bring Neil Leslie and Nicola Tallant over to work in London. I, of course, was selfishly horrified at the thought of losing two of our best reporters, but thankfully, they decided they wanted to stay put and didn't fancy living in London.

Piers had a great passion for politics and was deeply committed to the paper's left wing Labour roots. He had very strong opinions and wasn't intimidated in any way by the British Government or aristocracy. He passionately despised the war in Iraq; he thought it was morally wrong, ill conceived, and that Britain was only pandering to the idiotic George W. Bush in the White House. He decided, much to the horror of the Tony Blair government, to totally oppose the war at every corner and every turn, and take the *Daily Mirror* right back to its working class roots.

Piers was absolutely right. What was the point in sending young lads from Liverpool, Glasgow or Brighton out to the Middle East to die trying to get rid of Saddam Hussein, when there was no evidence whatsoever of any nuclear threat from Baghdad to the world? The West went into Iraq on the basis it had weapons of mass destruction, an allegation that was totally false and supported by CIA misinformation and lies.

Bush, of course, painted this ideological picture of young American and British men and women saving the West after 9/11, hunting down the enemies of the United States across the globe. Unfortunately for him, 19 of the 20 bombers who perpetrated the attack on the World Trade Centre in New York came from Saudi Arabia, a close ally of America. The US is hugely dependent on Saudi for its oil supply, so naturally enough, it didn't bomb Dhahran or Riyadh in retaliation. Instead, they went after Saddam, their former ally against Iran, and Afghanistan, where the mastermind of 9/11, Osama Bin Laden, was supposedly hiding.

I was in Iraq in 1991 and the Americans could easily have gone all the way and toppled Saddam but Bush's father bottled it. The son felt he had some sort of unfinished business with the Iraqi dictator. Piers held the view that it wasn't a cause worth dying for, and he has been proven right. Unfortunately for him, he took some stick over it.

The *Mirror's* anti-war stance was interpreted by our enemies, both politically and commercially, as being anti British Armed Forces, an accusation that was totally false and without foundation. After the outrage of 9/11 many people wanted revenge at any price. But now, in the cold light of day, I think that the families of most British servicemen will agree with Piers' view, that the current war is a waste of time and is going nowhere. Thankfully, most of the British soldiers have now finally come home from Iraq.

I remember being at Atlanta airport last summer and seeing a plane full of 300 troops heading to Shannon on their way to Baghdad. I went and had a cigarette with some of the soldiers in the smoking room. They were all young kids, extremely polite and mannerly. Many were in the National Guard to earn a few extra quid and got called up for service. They were nervous and scared despite all the gung ho bullshit drilled into them. I kept thinking that five or ten of them on that plane would come home in coffins. And just imagine the worry if it was your son or daughter. You can also bet your life that there are no rich American kids going to fight the good fight for the love of their country.

The war was to cause Piers his job. He made a mistake running pictures showing British soldiers beating up Iraqi prisoners. The pictures proved to be fakes. Piers had upset some extremely powerful people within the British establishment, and they were over the moon when he got fired. The staff were devastated.

I remember phoning him that night and he was very down; his enemies were pissing all over him and lining up to kick

him in the nuts. But as always he has had the last laugh. Ten
years editing the *Daily Mirror* was a long stint and he
probably needed a break. His book *The Insider* was a best
seller and now he has hit the jackpot as a judge on *Britain's
Got Talent* and *America's Got Talent*. He always got on well
with Simon Cowell and the entertainment guru got him his
TV break.

He has also now done his own show on Channel Four and
it won't be too long before he becomes the new Michael
Parkinson. He'll go back to where he started, interviewing the
big stars, only this time on the box in prime time.

* * *

Of all the people I've met over the years, the former
Taoiseach Bertie Ahern is one of my favourites. We first met
through a mutual friend, Dublin PR David Curtin, after Bertie
became leader of Fianna Fáil on November 19, 1994, and
maintained close contact throughout his whole tenure as
Taoiseach. From the first time I interviewed him we hit it off,
as we both shared the same dreams for our country. Like me,
Ahern was working class. He wasn't born with a silver spoon
in his mouth, and he never forgot where he came from.

We also both passionately believed that the troubles in the
North had to be sorted out once and for all for Ireland to
develop her potential economically, on both sides of the
border. Having seen the effects of 30 years of murder and
mayhem, and the tribal hatred between Catholics and
Protestants, we both felt it was imperative that both sides
came to their senses and reached a full and lasting settlement.

Bertie also had a very warm, approachable personality and
had proved over the years, as Minister for Labour and

Minister for Finance, to be a brilliant negotiator. I knew right away that if anyone could get both Republicans and Unionists over the finishing line it was Bertie Ahern.

I was also very aware that, unlike Charlie Haughey, who lived the millionaire lifestyle with his big mansion out in Kinsealy, North Dublin, thanks to the millions he received from big business associates, Bertie Ahern wasn't in it for the money. He lived a very humble lifestyle, in a modest four bedroom house in Drumcondra, and enjoyed his few pints of Bass every Saturday in his local pub, Fagan's, right across the road from his constituency office, There are no airs or graces with Bertie Ahern, what you see is what you get. He is a gentleman to the last, a complete workaholic and the ordinary people loved him.

The only black mark Bertie had against him was the break up of his marriage to his wife Miriam and the fact that he was now living with his long time lover Celia Larkin. This was used by his enemies within his own party, Fianna Fáil, and by some members of Fine Gael and Labour, to stir up trouble and try to damage his credibility. At the time, we as a paper had no issue with it. One of the sad facts of life is that marriages do break up for various reasons, and it shouldn't stop a person becoming Taoiseach.

The Catholic Church wasn't happy about it, even though Bertie had great personal faith and went to Mass once a week. The Church's influence was on the slide but this didn't stop the then Archbishop of Dublin, Desmond Connell, who is now a Cardinal, from having a go at the nature of Bertie's public relationship with Celia. The voters took little or no notice.

On the day Bertie was elected leader of Fianna Fáil, my colleague Paddy Clancy, who was working as a fixer for Sky

News, decided to confront him about his love life. Celia was sitting at the press conference with Bertie's two daughters, Georgina and Cecelia, and Paddy got the TV cameraman to deliberately film them.

The country was due to have a referendum on divorce so Paddy asked him what his attitude would be towards it if he was elected Taoiseach, as a separated man with a girlfriend. All of Bertie's supporters in the audience went ballistic and if looks could kill Paddy would have been stone dead; they wanted to rip his head off.

Paddy recalled: "All the rednecks at the back of the room started booing and howling. They were extremely angry with me. I had nothing personal against Bertie. Everyone in politics knew he was separated from the wife and was living with Celia, but the greater public, however, had the right to know. Bertie, in fairness, took it all on the chin. He was ready for the question; his advisers had warned him he would be asked about his personal life, and he answered it."

He also confirmed Celia was his girl and that she would be accompanying him on all official engagements if he were elected to the highest office in the land. The story about him being quizzed about his love life actually became the main story in all the Sunday papers the next day, rather than his election as party leader.

Bertie replaced Albert Reynolds, who had to resign over a cover up in the Attorney General's office relating to pervert priest Fr Brendan Smyth, something which he had no control over but paid the price politically. It resulted in the Labour party walking out of Government with Fianna Fáil and forming a new rainbow coalition with Fine Gael and the Democratic Left under the leadership of John Bruton. Bertie went into opposition and over the next three years he began rebuilding Fianna Fáil from top to bottom in readiness for the 1997 general election.

Charlie Haughey once described Ahern, as "the cutest, most cunning of them all". He was dead right. Bertie surrounded himself with some very clever advisers, notably Gerry Hickey, Paddy Duffy, Joe Lennon and Mandy Johnson. They were all extremely sharp and knew how to play the game. He also brought Charlie's former Press Officer, PJ Mara, back to co-ordinate the election campaign.

On my recommendation, the *Irish Daily Mirror* decided as a newspaper to support Ahern and Fianna Fáil in the election. Both Craig and I felt that the Northern peace process was the number one issue, and that if Bertie got into office, he could finish the deal once and for all. I worked extremely closely with Bertie's team during the whole campaign, and was constantly briefed on policies and stories as they developed on the election trail.

It was the first time in the history of Irish general elections that one of the main political parties, Fianna Fáil, realised that tabloid newspapers had a huge audience and could make or break elections. Up until then all of their media focus had been directed at coverage in the country's three broadsheets, the *Irish Independent*, *The Irish Times*, and the *Irish Examiner* plus RTÉ, the national broadcaster, and all the independent local radio networks. Bertie had the brains to see that the majority of voters – the working class – read the tabloids and he used them fully to his advantage. He also made it his business to speak in ordinary language that the ordinary people, those who had their dinners in the middle of the day, understood.

I touched base with Gerry, Mandy and Paddy most evenings to see what was going down. The Fianna Fáil campaign was highly motivated and energetic, with a desperate desire to get back into Government. The pundits felt the outgoing rainbow Government held all the aces and that Bertie would find it difficult to win. With a few days to go until polling day, he asked me to accompany him on a helicopter tour of the country, and it proved to be a real eye-opener.

We left Dublin in the early morning and flew down to counties Carlow, Kilkenny, Waterford and Wexford, canvassing all the way. Bertie was a brilliant campaigner. He loved being out on the streets meeting and greeting the people. Everywhere he went he was treated like a long lost son with hugs, kisses and warm handshakes from everyone he met. And they weren't just your usual gang of rounded-up party supporters, these were the real people coming out to meet a man they were about to put tremendous trust and faith in. I just knew from the reaction I saw everywhere I went with Bertie Ahern that day that he was going to win the election.

On the journey back to the capital that night he asked me what I thought of the reaction. He wasn't being over confident or cocky; he just wanted feedback from an outsider looking in. I told him straight up that judging from the response I saw in every town and village we called to, he was definitely going to be our next Taoiseach.

There was a huge goodwill towards him and there was a swing on the streets toward Fianna Fáil. For the next few days, right up to polling day, Ahern worked around the clock, surviving on only three hours sleep a night, hitting every last corner of the country. He was driven like a man possessed and took absolutely nothing for granted. He wanted every last vote he could get his hands on, and was personally enjoying every minute of the campaign.

We ran a page one leader urging *Mirror* readers to vote for Ahern. Both Craig and I honestly believed he could deliver, and in fairness to him he did. As the people went to the polls and campaigning stopped, he personally thanked me for all our help. And he genuinely hoped that if he was elected Taoiseach he would not let the people down.

Election night was one of the most exciting ever. We had the whole team watching the television as the votes came rolling in. Because of our electoral system, which is based on proportional representation, it can take up to two days before the final results are known. This applies particularly to the large, five seat constituencies, where the battle for the final seat, based largely on the transfer of preferential votes, can often go right to the wire, with only a handful of votes dividing candidates.

It was clear, however, from relatively early on, that the wind was with Bertie. He was winning most of the marginal battles. Everything that could go his way in the marginal constituencies he'd targeted did. But also, because he was a Dubliner, born and reared in the heart of the capital just around the corner from Croke Park, the people of the capital had rallied behind him and his candidates. All his hard work, criss-crossing the country for three solid years in opposition, paid off in spades.

Back at Fianna Fáil headquarters they were all over the moon. We called it that Bertie had won the election.

The way the numbers stacked up, he was in a position to form a new coalition government with the smaller Progressive Democrats party, plus four independent Dáil deputies, most of whom, like the colourful Jackie Healy Rae from Kerry, had their original roots in the Fianna Fáil party.

I adjourned that night to Doheny and Nesbitts pub in the

heart of Dublin's political district, to celebrate with Mandy, PJ, Gerry and all their background team. I politely reminded them not to forget the *Mirror* when they got back into power, and to keep me in the loop.

On June 26, 1997, Bertie Ahern was elected by parliament as the country's youngest ever Taoiseach, at 45 years of age. He was extremely humbled and honoured by his appointment, in what would be the first of three historic election victories.

Bertie rolled up his sleeves and got stuck into office. The North, as I had hoped, was put at the top of the political agenda alongside trying to get the country on the track to full employment. Bertie was determined to see peace and prosperity for Ireland, and was prepared to compromise if necessary along the way.

Ahern immediately struck up an excellent personal relationship with the new British Prime Minister, Tony Blair, and quickly discovered they were singing from the same hymn sheet when it came to the six counties. Blair worked on the Unionists, particularly their leaders David Trimble and Dr Ian Paisley, while Ahern focused on Sinn Féin and its leaders, Gerry Adams and Martin McGuinness.

The Unionists were obsessed with decommissioning the IRA's weapons, while the IRA's Army Council didn't want to hand over any guns or Semtex. The IRA was on a ceasefire and many hardliners within the Republican movement viewed the giving up of guns as an admission of defeat. They believed that the only thing that mattered were the guns staying silent. Unionists, on the other hand, felt that Sinn Féin had no right to be in government in Northern Ireland while it had its own private army. Paisley, in particular, was beating the decommissioning drum as loudly as he could.

Both Ahern and Blair, backed up by President Bill Clinton in the White House, worked endlessly behind the scenes to get the two warring tribes to the table. Less than a year later, during Easter week 1998, they got both sides together at Stormont's Parliament buildings, to reach a final settlement once and for all. For two solid days, they negotiated around the clock, with little or no sleep for any of the players involved.

In the middle of all this, Bertie Ahern's beloved mother, Julia, was dying in a Dublin hospital. He had to leave the intense negotiations to say his final farewell. After his mum passed away, Bertie returned to Belfast. He wasn't going to let his mother's sad death stop the country from securing a lasting peace.

After endless rows and showdowns, all sides eventually reached a deal, in what was to become known as the Good Friday Agreement. In what was, in my view, Bertie's finest hour, the Irish and British Governments, and all the parties in the North, agreed a peaceful and democratic framework for power-sharing. Not only that, it was to be voted upon by all of the people on the island of Ireland, who later gave it a massive majority yes vote.

The new deal meant the Republic would ditch it's constitutional claim on Northern Ireland, while the British stated they would leave the North if the majority of people there wanted to be part of a 32 county Republic.

The truth is that the British people had no interest in being in Ireland, and all the province cost it was grief and money. The view was that you have to unite the people of Ireland on both sides of the religious and political divides before you unite the land. It also meant Republican and Loyalist paramilitaries were finally giving up their respective terror campaigns, a move that was welcomed across the globe.

Both Bertie and Blair received huge international praise for their efforts. There were many hiccups along the way, as various vested interests tried to torpedo the agreement, but it got there in the end.

One of the darkest moments of all was the Omagh bomb, carried out by Republican dissidents, the Real IRA, on August 15, 1998, which left 29 people dead and 220 injured. It was the single worst terrorist atrocity of the Troubles, but it didn't weaken Ahern and Blair's resolve. If anything, it reinforced the need to have a lasting, permanent peace on the island.

Ahern forced the Gardaí to wage a war on dissidents in the Republic, resulting in the arrest and jailing of the Real IRA leader Michael McKevitt. I know for a fact that Bertie was deeply disturbed by what happened that day in Omagh, and his heart went out to all the families of the victims.

Throughout his whole time in office we kept in contact. Anytime I needed clarification on the issues I got it. And peace slowly came to the North and the economy of the Republic boomed, resulting in what was to be known as the Celtic Tiger.

In the run up to the last general election he won, in 2007, I remember sitting down with Bertie in his office in Government buildings and asking him what he thought his greatest achievements were. He cited the North and virtual full employment in the Republic, an amazing achievement considering the mess the economy was in throughout the 1980s.

It was, in my view, one of the saddest days for Ireland when he was effectively hounded out of office. His good name was damaged by a bitter personal campaign against him over £39,000 in personal donations he received from businessmen in Manchester after his marriage broke up in 1993.

The revelation only came out during the Mahon Tribunal into the "payments to politicians" scandal in 2006. The lawyers at the Tribunal made millions from the enquiry and were gunning for a big name to justify their existence, and Bertie Ahern was in their sights.

The Tribunal was originally established over the behaviour of Charlie Haughey, who didn't think twice about accepting a fortune to fund his champagne lifestyle. One of Ireland's top businessmen, Ben Dunne, admitted giving Haughey £1.3 million after being informed Haughey was in financial trouble at the time. Dunne has always maintained that he never expected or received anything in return for the money; he did it because he thought Haughey was a good man.

I've known Bertie Ahern a long time, and the one thing I can tell you is that he isn't corrupt. In those days, our politicians didn't have to publicly record any donations they received, but now they do. And while he was very efficient in running the country, he was negligent, and at times naive about organizing his own personal affairs.

The other thing I know is that Bertie never made money, apart from his salary, out of politics. He was far more interested in helping people than in feathering his own nest. And to this very day I don't know of one single politician who worked as hard as he did. The history books will show he was one of the greatest leaders we ever had, and the country will look back at the Ahern era with wonderful memories.

* * *

By this stage we had created the *Irish Daily Mirror*, writing, producing and printing a full-blooded Irish tabloid newspaper here in Ireland. Craig Mackenzie moved over to Ireland and we set up a production unit in Belfast, bringing out our first edition in February 1998. I became Deputy Editor and was hands on copy tasting, driving the news agenda, writing headlines and getting the baby off stone on time every night. It involved a lot of hard work and mammoth days, often starting at 9 a.m. and finishing at 1 a.m. the following morning! But one thing about the Kierans and the Mackenzies was that we were never afraid of hard work and we both had an incredible passion for the job.

Craig, as ever, was a hard taskmaster, but he taught me many of the tricks of editing, lessons I am extremely grateful for to this day. I knew nothing about newspaper production and he knew nothing about Ireland, so we both learned from each other, with many rows along the way.

In the space of a few short years we had gone from having myself, Joe Gorrod and Conor Hanna in Ireland to a team of over 50 journalists, as we set about establishing a seriously profitable business.

Craig and I shared a flat in Belfast with our number three Ken Parker, a no-nonsense, good humoured son of Sunderland, for the first couple of months. Craig and Ken had worked together for Express Newspapers in London and were very close mates. Every time Craig moved up the ladder he brought Parker with him. Every morning Kelvin Mackenzie would ring at 8 a.m. to make sure there were no fuck-ups the night before, enquiring about what stories we splashed with north and south of the border. The Irish operation was a big investment and Kelvin, as Deputy Chief Executive, was ensuring we didn't fuck it up. I soon learned that it's great getting the good money but nothing prepares you for the pain that goes with it.

One Saturday morning Craig decided to come down to Drogheda to play golf with me. He went into the shop to buy the *Irish Daily Mirror* and came out ashen faced. Page one looked great – the only problem was there was no price on it. One of the backbench guys who was sending page one didn't put it in. We had both checked the front page but neither of us had spotted the missing price.

Craig was inconsolable and in a rage. I was an idiot, he was an idiot, we were all idiots. If any of us had brains we'd be fucking dangerous. He had to ring Kelvin and tell him the bad news and the mistake was going to cost the company thousands. The only saving grace was the bar code was in so if the newsagents scanned it the price would come up. Unfortunately, most shops would just think the paper was free.

Kelvin, in fairness, took the bad news sensibly. He didn't fire any of us and told Craig we were all dickheads and to make sure we didn't do it again. The mistake certainly spoiled our day, but then tell me the man who hasn't made a mistake in newspapers, then he is not a man at all. The last thing we do every night now is check the price and the date before the paper goes to bed.

For the first few years in Belfast we shared an office with the *News Letter*, the world's oldest newspaper, which was then owned by the Mirror Group. Craig being Craig put signs all over the wall saying "welcome to *Mirror* country". He had a small office where he would shout and roar like a sergeant major barking orders all over the place.

The peace process at the time was in full swing and our Chief Executive David Montgomery, a native of Bangor, Co Down had a very keen interest in it. Every week he would

ring up quizzing Craig and the *News Letter* Editor Geoff
Martin about what was going on behind the scenes.
Montgomery was extremely supportive of the whole process
and like almost every sane person on both sides of the Irish
Sea, wanted to see a permanent settlement. Both papers,
editorially, were fully behind both the Irish and British
Governments attempts to get all the political parties in the
North to agree a deal. Montgomery also had big Unionist
contacts and was pushing their leader David Trimble to reach
an agreement with Sinn Féin.

By the time the Good Friday negotiations got under way
we were all over the story. Hundreds of journalists from all
over the globe had descended on Belfast and the world was
literally watching the endgame being played out in Stormont.
When the deal came there was a great feeling of elation not
only in the office, but all over the North. The people of the Six
Counties were sick and tired of the murder and mayhem, and
wanted to live in a society where they could walk the streets
in peace at night. The Troubles had taken their toll, both
mentally and economically, on a society who didn't want
their sons and daughters going through what they went
through.

We had both Catholics and Protestants working for us and
they were equally delighted. We did a wipeout page one
recording the historic moment and it was one of the best
papers we ever produced. There are some days when it is
great to be a journalist, and the day the Good Friday
Agreement was signed was one of them. We all felt the hand
of history was with us.

The Irish Daily Mirror
1998-2002

Part 2

Sinéad O'Connor loves journalists like no other star I know, but also has a habit of falling in love with them. I first came across her when she got upset at a story I wrote in the *Mirror* and she bombarded my house with phone calls and sent me a ten page fax with her ramblings on life. I thought she was a looney bin, but over the years I soon learned that she was quite clever and extremely manipulative.

One of her first romances was with *The Irish Times* columnist John Waters, with whom she had a child. But she also had the *Mirror* on her radar big time, falling in love with one of our reporters Neil Michael, and then marrying a second, Nick Sommerlad, a cousin of the Swedish royal family, who is currently working for us as an investigative reporter in London.

I hired Neil Michael as our Dublin showbiz correspondent in late 1996. A son of Dun Laoghaire, he was quite eccentric, but an extremely down to earth, hard working reporter.

It was during Sinéad's obsession with religion that he became friends with the millionaire star. They met on the Dublin social scene and before I knew it he was on his way to London to interview her at her home in Hampstead. They got on extremely well and she gave him a world exclusive that she was going to become a priest. Sinéad had already hit the headlines worldwide in 1992 when she ripped up a picture of Pope John Paul II during an appearance on the *Saturday Night Live* show on American TV. She was openly condemned by leading Catholics at home and in America, who viewed her behaviour as deeply offensive and insulting. But Sinéad typically took it all in her stride, and it was great publicity.

She was angry and hurt, as she'd been abused as a child and felt the church had deserted her in her hour of need. She met up with the rebel Tridentine Bishop Michael Cox, an advocate of the old Latin mass, who had been kicked out of the church for his controversial views. We wiped out page one with the story that Sinéad was to become a priest and it sold out. Neil Michael was rightly chuffed with himself and Sinéad invited him to join her for her official ordination. It was to be carried out in secret and he would be the only reporter present.

The singer chose the holy shrine of Lourdes in France as the venue for the controversial ordination. It was here on a hillside that the Blessed Virgin Mary appeared in an apparition to Bernadette, the daughter of a shepherd. Millions of Catholics from across the world visit Lourdes every year, and there have been various reported miracles among the sick, many of which have been officially recognised by the Vatican.

Sinéad persuaded Bishop Cox to officially ordain her, and she gave him a £150,000 personal donation from her singing fortune to show her appreciation in return. Afterwards, she was to be known the world over as Mother Bernadette, and have the power to say mass, anoint the sick, conduct marriages and hear confessions as part of her new ministry.

Neil was to meet Sinéad in London and then they would travel to Lourdes by train via the Channel Tunnel. My News Editor, Neil Leslie, briefed him to get the exclusive pictures and no matter what, to obey the number one rule of tabloid newspapers – keep your mobile phone on and stay in touch with the office. However, unknown to us, after a day alone together Neil and Sinéad fell madly in love and so began a whirlwind nightmare romance. For the next three days his mobile was switched off and we couldn't get in touch with him.

The boss, Craig McKenzie, who liked to be kept right up to date on every major story, was going ballistic, and Leslie, a normally soft spoken, gentle individual, was furious. There was a lot of money, time and effort invested in the story, and the last thing we needed was the reporter going on the missing list. Every time we rang his mobile it was switched off.

As the day of Sinéad's life-changing ordination arrived, we hadn't a clue where our man was. Eventually he checked in and said he was in Sinéad's room at some hotel in Lourdes. Leslie got suspicious and asked him what he was doing in Sinéad's room. And while she was getting ready to say mass Neil started his confession.

He told Leslie that he and Sinéad were lovers; he was really sorry and would be filing later. We'd cleared the decks to splash the story and to do a 4-5 spread. We wanted every last cough and spit, but most of all we wanted a picture of Sinéad the priest in her robes. By teatime Neil had filed. The copy was great. Sinéad apparently couldn't control her emotions during the ceremony, grinning broadly and then appearing close to tears, dressed in her white ropes and veil.

She proudly boasted to the paper: "I'm overjoyed. I feel as if I've been waiting for this day all my life and that I've been reborn. I'm sorry I ripped up the Pope's picture; I accept it was wrong. I don't think I'm a bad devil for it and I'm entitled to make a mistake."

Neil definitely made a big mistake. We didn't get a picture of Mother Bernadette, as she was to be known, until the following Sunday, causing World War III in the newsroom. Craig was like a madman full of rage, effing and blinding, and bollocking Neil Leslie and me. He couldn't understand how we couldn't get Neil Michael back on the phone or why the hell there were no pictures. In newspapers a picture is worth a thousand words, and what the world wanted to see was the first picture of Sinéad O'Connor as a priest.

We were also terrified that we'd be scooped and someone else might already have a photo. We were worried Sinéad had done a secret side deal with one of the Sunday papers and was deliberately fucking us over. We had all the colour, all the words from Sinéad, but we didn't have the shot to prove it all happened. We naturally ran with the story, minus the picture, and the story went around the globe.

Bishop Cox was full of it, giving radio and TV interviews at every opportunity. He praised Sinéad's dedication, remarking: "I would not have ordained her If I did not believe she had a true vocation. It was the most beautiful ordination I've ever witnessed or taken part in. It was just beautiful. This will open the flood gates for women to become priests. The fact Sinéad is a rock star is important. She can bring a far wider audience of young people, some of whom have probably never set foot in a church. It is wonderful she is so prepared to take the abuse that she may get in order to help the church."

Neil witnessed her first mass and then bedded her afterwards. Despite intense efforts, we couldn't get hold of Neil on the Saturday. Luckily the Sunday papers didn't have any pictures. By Sunday, the news desk tracked him down on the phone and he advised: "Mother Bernadette isn't making any comment today."

When Craig heard this he blew his top again, eventually got Neil on the phone, and reminded him that he still worked for the *Mirror,* and that if he wanted to stay in a job he'd better get a picture over as soon as possible. Neil explained apologetically why he couldn't get the pictures over on Friday; that he and Sinéad had a furious row; she had taken his mobile, credit cards and clothes and kicked him out of the room. Thankfully, they had made up, and he would have the first picture of Sinéad the priest over shortly.

Craig was like a dog with a bone and he would not rest until he had the ordination picture in the office. I just felt a huge sense of relief. The story had been extremely hard work, you couldn't make up what had happened, and it was a classic case of "Carry On" newspapers.

It was nobody's fault. Sinéad O'Connor was just such a maverick that you couldn't predict what she'd do next. In fairness to Neil Michael, he did deliver, as he always does, even if there were blood, sweat and grief along the way. The ordination pictures were fantastic and nobody else had them.

However, for the *Mirror* team, the fun and games of Neil and Sinéad's romance was only starting. When they got back home to reality, and the dust settled, the real fun and games began. Sinéad was constantly on to the office looking for Neil, and trying to find out where he was and what he was doing, every time she couldn't get him.

The other Neil, Leslie, had a pain in his ass talking to Mother Bernadette, and two months later, in July, 1999, the shit really hit the fan.

We went to an awards night at Jury's Hotel where the *Mirror* had a table. Craig, Neil Leslie and some of the reporters, including Pat Flanagan, Nicola Tallant, Lynn Kelleher and I were standing at the bar when Neil Michael calmly walked in, announced he was going to become a daddy, and that Sinéad was expecting their baby.

We were all completely shell-shocked. It was one thing having a fling with Sinéad, but another thing to be fathering her child. Some of the crew shook Michael's hand and just burst out laughing. Neil Leslie, like any good news editor, said: "At least we have a splash Sunday for Monday."

I decided it was drinks all round and we'd better celebrate.

I asked Neil how long was Sinéad gone and he said several weeks. We all agreed we'd have to do a story on it because the word was bound to get out one way or the other; Dublin was too small a town to keep Sinéad's new baby quiet.

I woke up on Sunday morning with the hangover from hell wondering whether Sinéad and Neil's great love story was going to end in tears. He was genuinely in love with her and was all excited at the prospect of becoming a dad. It was a bank holiday weekend and on the Monday morning we ran the story that Sinéad was expecting a new baby and was two months pregnant and that Neil was the father. We deliberately didn't use a picture of him.

The next day the *Star* got their own back for being scooped, and ran with a big picture of Neil on page one. Neil got the shock of his life when he went into his local newsagent to buy the *Mirror* and saw his face splashed all over the *Star*. He rang the office in blind panic wondering what he was going to do. We got him to calm down, lie low and just stay away from the office. Like it or not he had now become the story, always a bad idea for reporters.

By the afternoon *The Sun* had got revved up and sent reporter Gary O'Shea and a photographer up to our office in Terenure, looking for an interview with Neil Michael. They tried to get photos through the windows, and at one stage,

attempted to barge their way in the front door. N
the roof and ended up grappling with O'Shea ou
car park, bluntly telling him to fuck off. Leslie's vi
wouldn't doorstep a hack from *The Sun* in ımılar
circumstances, so what were they doing trying to chase one
of our staff.

Within a few days it all died down in terms of newspaper
coverage, but Sinéad was ripping the story was out in public,
and she and Neil Michael had a series of furious rows. A
week later they had split up and he was extremely upset.

She told Neil she wasn't having the baby and several days
later, clearly upset and angry, he quit the *Mirror* and got into
his car and took the ferry to London. He stayed there for a
number of years before returning to Dublin when the *Daily
Mail* started its Irish operation a couple of years ago.

Sinéad never had the baby and I think the whole episode
was a false alarm. Unfortunately we lost a good reporter. But
Sinéad wasn't finished with the *Mirror* yet.

I got Nick Sommerlad to come over from the Press
Association in Dublin and to start working for us. Before I
knew it, he and Sinéad were dating, and she would turn up for
a drink in our local boozer, Hanlon's, near our new offices on
the North Circular Road. She even came to one of our
Christmas parties, where she just casually mixed in with the
troops like one of the staff. Craig thought it was all great sport
and loved the idea of a big star like Sinéad once again dating
one of the team.

Nick is a very cool customer and never spoke about his
love affair with Sinéad. He is the type of guy who is just
interested in stories and gets on with it. He and Sinéad had a
whirlwind romance, and got married in a private ceremony a
few months later. Sadly the marriage didn't last and they

broke up. I got Nick freelance shifts on the *Daily Mirror* in London, and he later got a staff job there. He is one of the real good guys in our business.

* * *

I've never had the pleasure of meeting Roy Keane and don't particularly want to. He is the spoiled child of Irish sport who throws his toys out of the pram every time he doesn't get his own way. If he was your son you'd want to give him a kick up the ass. And while he might have had great football skills, the two things he always lacked were class and manners.

I first saw him in action at close quarters as Jack Charlton prepared the Irish team for the 1994 World Cup. The big Geordie decided to bring the squad up to the Nuremore Hotel in Carrickmacross, Co Monaghan for a few days relaxation before heading off to America for the greatest show on earth. Expectations were high after the Italia 1990 odyssey, when the Republic reached the quarter finals only to be beaten 1-0 by the host nation.

Jack had also brought three young lads into the team; Jason McAteer, Phil Babb, and our very own Gary Kelly from Drogheda, a youngster with no airs or graces and as down to earth as they come. I went up to Carrick to see how the team was getting on and mingled with the sports boys.

Keane would swan around the place with his head up his arse, completely ignoring my colleagues and treating them with utter contempt. He would stare at them as if they were the scum of the earth like some lunatic about to explode.

I remember asking my friend Cathal Dervan, one of the best sports writers in the country, how they put up with all that crap. He said most of the players, especially Niall Quinn, Paul McGrath, Mick McCarthy and Steve Staunton were decent, and Keane was just one of those alter ego footballers. He felt the best way to handle him was to ignore him. If you don't have respect in life what do you have. And at the end of the day we are all just doing our job.

During his early Manchester United days, Keane would come home from time to time and go on the lash, leaving a trail of havoc behind. On one occasion he ended up in court following a bust up with a neighbour's daughter as a result of a row in a nightclub. Every time Roy went on the razz I ended up in Cork writing about it. He always made headlines and always sold newspapers.

One thing I have to say is that Keane's mother is a lovely woman and was always courteous and kind in dealing with the press over the years. If she had something to say she'd say it and that would be the end of it.

While I never had an issue with Keane's football skills, it was his lack of social skills that appalled me. And nothing would prepare us for Saipan, when he walked out on the national team as they prepared for the 2002 World Cup in Japan and South Korea, splitting the country down the middle but selling thousands and thousands of newspapers in the process.

Craig of course loved Roy Keane. He was a closet Manchester United supporter, especially since his local team in South London, Crystal Palace, hardly ever won a match never mind a trophy. I went to see the Palace once with my cousins who lived in Croydon and we didn't have much to cheer about.

World Cups have, over the years, sold a huge number of tabloid newspapers in Ireland, and the whole country was looking forward to the summer of 2002. Mick McCarthy was managing the Republic and over the years there hadn't been

much love lost between him and Keane. There was a feeling
we had a pretty decent squad and if we got a few lucky
breaks, we could go far in the competition.

McCarthy decided to bring his team to the Pacific island
of Saipan for some R&R and team bonding before flying on
to Japan to do some serious training in preparation for the
tournament. The tiny island is famous for being one of the
last Japanese strongholds during World War II, before the
Americans dropped atomic bombs on Hiroshima and
Nagasaki in 1945.

We sent Mick Scully, a brilliant young sports reporter who
we knew would do the business. He was so excited about
covering his first World Cup, but little did he know what was
about to unfold.

The first sign something was wrong came when Keane
didn't turn up for his international colleague Niall Quinn's
testimonial in Sunderland. He claimed he wasn't available
because he was getting "preventative treatment" in France.
By the time he arrived at Dublin airport the next day he was
in a right huff.

The Taoiseach Bertie Ahern went out to see the team off
along with hundreds of fans. He went over to shake the
captain's hand and Keane, like the ignorant sod that he is,
didn't even get up off his chair to greet him. He was annoyed
that there were supporters in the same area as the team as they
waited for the flight, a typical prima donna. Bertie, being the
decent gentleman that he is, diplomatically brushed the
incident off and just got on with it, wishing Mick and the
boys the best of luck. It was clear that Keane didn't want to
be there. He couldn't stand McCarthy and some of the other
players on the team, and his mood swings went from bad to
worse.

The team had a 17 hour flight to the other side of the world and some of their initial training gear didn't arrive on time. Soon after their arrival McCarthy arranged a barbeque for the team and the press. There had been a number of spats between some of the players and reporters during the qualifying campaign, and Mick wanted to clear the air and start afresh to ensure that the media were right behind the whole team for the World Cup.

Keane, of course was furious that journalists were at the barbeque. He started tackling some of them over public criticism of his failure to attend Quinn's testimonial. He quickly had a bite to eat, said his piece, and stormed off to his bedroom. The journalists and the players had a good old party and drank all night at a nearby English pub.

The next day at training the row rumbled on. The captain complained that the pitch near their hotel in Saipan was like concrete and wasn't suitable. The session was to be more of a warm up than anything else, allowing the players to acclimatise to the tropical climate.

Keane ended up having a huge row with goalkeeping coach Packie Bonner and keeper Alan Kelly, and was caught on camera throwing a plastic bottle in a rage. He walked off the pitch in a fury and went back to his room, and was soon informing McCarthy that he was quitting the team.

He telephoned the Manchester United manager Alex Ferguson and his own personal adviser, London solicitor Michael Kennedy, who both persuaded him to change his mind. As Saipan was several hours ahead of us the whole story was developing in the middle of the night our time. This meant that it was all too late for that night's edition and we were running with it 24 hours later.

Scully called me to tell me Keane was cracking up and

there were wild rumours going around he was leaving the team and going home. The picture of Roy throwing the bottle was superb and we wiped out most of page one with it. The depth of anger was written all over his face.

The captain decided to up the ante and gave an interview to Tom Humphries of *The Irish Times* in an attempt to explain to the Irish people why he was so annoyed. He slammed the FAI, which he claimed was uninterested in player welfare, and claimed they'd proved it by putting the team up in standard accommodations and on economy flights for their pre-World Cup trip to Cyprus, while the association's officials stayed in five star hotels and flew first-class. He also felt that the set up in Saipan wasn't up to scratch and was unprofessional, and that the team should be getting down to serious training, not having a party with the press.

His comments were an indirect attack on McCarthy's managerial and organizational skills. It was immediately seized upon by all the media and Roy was back on the front pages again. Almost simultaneously, his former friend and biographer Eamon Dunphy, the Irish soccer TV pundit, was stirring it up, severely criticising both Mick and the FAI on every radio and television bulletin.

Mick McCarthy decided to have a players meeting and, holding up a copy of *The Irish Times* piece, he confronted Keane and asked him: "What's this all about?" He also accused Roy of faking injuries when he failed to show up at some previous matches, specifically the away leg in the World Cup play off against Iran in Tehran.

Keane took great offense at being singled out and exploded in anger. He went into a tirade and told McCarthy: "Mick you're a liar; you're a fucking wanker. I didn't rate you as a player and I don't rate you as a manager. I don't rate you as a person; you're a fucking wanker and you can stick your

World Cup up your arse. The only reason I have dealings with you is that somehow you are the manager of my country. You can stick it up your bollocks."

Niall Quinn later recalled that Keane's rant was clinical, fierce and earth-shattering to the person on the receiving end of it. None of his teammates backed him up, although two, Gary Breen and David Connolly, did go to his room and express support for him privately afterwards. All of the senior players, and specifically Quinn and Steve Staunton, backed Mick. Keane had put McCarthy in a corner and left him with no choice but to kick him out of the team unless he received an apology.

Mick Scully was on to the office like a shot and said it was all blowing up. We cleared the front half of the paper, as it looked like Ireland's World Cup campaign was going down the tubes before a ball was even kicked.

The manager immediately called a press conference and publicly revealed what had occurred. He said: "This is serious because Roy Keane will be playing no part in the World Cup. He's going home. How do I feel? I know it's going to be huge, the biggest story of the World Cup, but I stand over it 100 percent.

"I held a team meeting and asked anyone to air comments in a rational and logical way, including Roy, and it didn't happen. Instead, it turned into a slagging match, and I can't tolerate the level of abuse thrown at me, so I sent Roy home. As a player of his stature, I am very sad to lose him – absolutely. But as a squad member I'm not bothered one bit that he's gone.

"This action has been taken and all 23 players were there when it happened. It was a very public, very open show of opinions and hostility. There are certain things that can be said by players but he crossed the line – and the players will back me up on that. Since the beginning of the week it has been about this public criticism of everything with Roy. All press conferences have been about this and I'm getting a little tired of it.

"We needed to resolve this issue, but unfortunately a resolution didn't happen, and when there is a feeling around the camp like that, you try to clear it up because there is a feeling of unease. I think, as someone who has always tried to do his best for the players – not me first, the players the staff, my country – as a player, a coach, as a person I will not tolerate someone saying something like that to me.

"I said to the players it is a huge decision but I am quite happy with it – it's done. It didn't rumble on long and no other players got involved, not at all. I am happier to go to Japan with one man down than go with someone who shows complete disregard and disrespect for me. An emotional thing happened but I think I'm keeping calm and keeping my head about it."

McCarthy felt Keane's comments in the newspaper were bang out of order. "We came to Saipan for some rest and relaxation and we've done that. The other night there was a band playing and 22 out of 23 of them were singing along. I want to be treated the way I treat people. I wanted it reciprocated and it wasn't. When someone like Roy says he is going home, it's big enough. When he turns around and says he is staying I accept it. He is fiery and when he plays for us he is excellent. I don't see many complaints from anyone else. Sometimes Roy sees the world through his own eyes, completely different to everyone else," he said.

The whole story split the country down the middle. It was like the civil war all over again and you were either with Keane or a Mick man. I was very much in the Mick McCarthy camp. To me the greatest honour is to play for your country, and the last thing you do, no matter what your complaint, is to walk out on the team as they are about to take part in the World Cup finals. And to walk out as captain made it even worse.

I felt Keane was just a selfish bastard and didn't care about anyone but himself. He certainly didn't give a damn about the thousands of Irish fans who had travelled across the globe to support the boys in green at huge personal expense. Their hopes and dreams didn't matter to him. He only cared about number one.

I never knew a story to sell so much. For a whole week it ran and ran. There were pictures of Roy all alone going to the airport to get a Manchester United private jet sent to bring him home. As the team began their serious training in Japan there were almost daily pictures of him out walking his dog.

Numerous attempts were made behind the scenes to get Roy to go back to the team. The Taoiseach Bertie Ahern got involved as did Keane's adviser Michael Kennedy. Mick McCarthy, in fairness, was prepared to have him back if he apologised, but Keane couldn't bring himself to do it. So the team just got on with their World Cup campaign without him.

Eamon Dunphy kept stirring it up on the television and championing Keane's cause. They both hid behind the well known administrative shortcomings of the Football Association of Ireland at that time to justify Roy's disgraceful actions. Dunphy also kept slagging McCarthy off which was bang out of order.

Having spoken at length to Mick Scully and Cathal Dervan, who were both present in Saipan, I honestly believe Roy never wanted to be there in the first place. He was going through his own personal trauma at the time, in that he had his own battles with the demon drink. He didn't want to be away from his wife and kids for such a long period of time, but equally, he didn't want to be in an environment where there was any boozing going on. While the idea of some R&R was good for team spirit and morale, it was temptation to the volatile Cork man. Any time he ever got in trouble as a young man it was always when there was alcohol involved. The idea of the players out on an all night drinking session was like a red rag to a bull. If a mistake was made, it was that the captain should have been allowed to join the team in Japan when the serious training began. At that stage in his life he was only off the drink a short period of time. And as he revealed later in his autobiography, the drink didn't agree with him.

Another Irish legend, Paul McGrath, couldn't handle the booze either. He would often go on a bender for days on end out of pure boredom. I once met McGrath in a pub and he didn't know his own name. It was sad and frightening. Although he was a colossus on the football pitch, off it he was quiet and extremely shy. His career ended at Manchester United over his drinking because Alex Ferguson wouldn't tolerate it.

The late great George Best, who I met on a handful of occasions over the years, was exactly the same. Alcohol was George's drug and no matter how hard he tried he couldn't give it up. Even after his liver transplant, when he got a second chance in life, he couldn't help himself and stay off the demon drink.

The worst part of being a professional footballer is the boredom. You spend half your life waiting around in hotels for big games or having the afternoons off after training. Some people can deal with it while others can't. They are paid a fortune for their talents, but some just can't mind themselves.

For most of his career at Man United Keane had kept himself right. And one of the best decisions he ever made was giving up the drink. As he begins another stage of his managerial career with Ipswich, the only thing he ever drinks these days is a cup of tea, and we all have to admire him for that. Keane is a character we all love to hate but the truth is everyone wants to read about him and he sells papers to beat the band.

One of the best spoilers we ever did happened a few months after the 2002 World Cup. Keane's book was coming out and *The Sunday Times* had paid a fortune to serialize it. Eamon Dunphy had written it and was flagging it up all over the place.

I had brought Mick McNiffe over from the *Sunday World* to news edit the *Irish Daily Mirror* in Dublin, after Neil Leslie left to become an Assistant Editor on *The Irish Star*. On the Friday morning at conference, Mick and I decided we needed to do a big piece for Saturday on the book. After several hours of trying, we managed to get our hands on the cover plus a press release of what was in it. We also knew someone who knew what was in it and he briefed us on the content.

We splashed with the line about how Roy had battled with the booze and was fighting his inner demons, using the cover of the book on page one, plus two spreads inside. Craig was absolutely cock-a-hoop. The wipeout page one was so effective the readers would think we were serializing it. The sale went up that Saturday by an amazing 20 percent, which just proved how much the readers were interested in Keane. The whole country was talking about our world exclusive because Roy had never spoken publicly about his battle with the drink before.

The truth was his problem with alcohol had nearly destroyed him both personally and professionally and we had the whole lot for free. All the Sunday papers followed it up the next day and we were over the moon. It had been another exciting day on our newspaper and the team had yet again come up trumps. Craig phoned to say we were all geniuses. And for the first time we started to understand why he did what he did in Saipan and flew home.

I only ever met Mick McCarthy once but he is a very nice and pleasant man. How anyone could fall out with him I'll never know. He has been a great servant for his country both as a player and a manager. He and Roy eventually sorted out their differences in 2006 when the two teams they were managing, Sunderland and Wolves, were due to meet in a match. Keane phoned him up the night before and they buried the hatchet. Then there was a public handshake in front of the TV cameras before the start of the match. I was glad both of them had moved on.

* * *

Showbiz is the lifeblood of any tabloid newspaper; the readers love the gossip and expect to get it every day. If you don't have the stories you are dead in the water. We were blessed that Louis Walsh came along just as we were developing the *Mirror* brand in Ireland.

Love him or hate him, the *X Factor* judge is the biggest gossip in the country and knows everything that's going on. He has more stories in his head than anyone I know. An hour with Louis is not only highly entertaining, it's hilarious. He has a fantastic sense of humour, loves slagging people off and has a great ability to laugh at himself.

I first met Louis in the eighties when he was booking

bands with Tommy Hayden, a promoter in Dublin. I remember meeting him at a Slane Castle concert, and he was dressed in leathers from head to toe, sweltering in the scorching heat. I said to myself: "what an idiot, he's definitely looking for attention."

He came to prominence nationally when, along with John Reynolds, the owner of the POD nightclub in Dublin, they formed Boyzone in an attempt to create an Irish version of Take That. He advertised the auditions and cleverly brought Ronan Keating, Keith Duffy, Shane Lynch, Stephen Gately and Mikey Graham together. Louis knew exactly what he was looking for – good looking lads who could sing but also had some personality.

They were launched on RTÉ's *Late Late Show*, where the girls went wild drooling over them. Soon Louis cracked Britain with them where they had six number one hits, 16 top three singles, and four number one albums selling 12 million copies worldwide.

As a paper, for some reason, we seemed to have a problem with our showbiz writers. Richie Taylor left to go to *The Sun*, Neil Michael ran to London after splitting up with Sinéad O'Connor, and Gavin Duff was fired after filing an interview he claimed to do with The Corrs when, in actual fact, he nicked it off the internet, causing us huge embarrassment.

We'd given The Corrs' story a big hit on page one, and then cringed when Andrea Corr went on radio and, to my shock, said she'd never spoken to the *Mirror*. Gavin was hauled in, and after intense interrogation eventually admitted he'd never met the band and had just pulled the interview off an American website. Young Gavin was quickly given his marching orders before I rung his neck. We all make mistakes but no one gets away with hoodwinking his or her editor.

I learned a very harsh lesson – never trust the Internet. If we don't speak to stars ourselves then we don't run with it.

A few weeks later this noisy young English lad caught my eye in the newsroom in Belfast. Paul Martin was working on the *News Letter* doing bits and pieces. But he also wrote a sho-biz column and it wasn't bad. He could talk the talk and was full of confidence, but what impressed me most was his enthusiasm.

It's very hard to bullshit a bullshitter, so I took Paul aside and asked him would he like a crack at doing showbiz in Ireland for the *Mirror*. I bluntly told him he was a load of shit at the moment but we were going to turn him into a superstar. I was pretty confident that with the right training and guidance he would become one of the country's top hacks.

I told him he'd have to build up his contacts in Dublin and to make Louis Walsh his new best friend. Louis, in fairness, took Paul under his wing and kept him in the loop. He didn't have to, but he liked Paul's style and his great ability not to take himself too seriously, and to take the piss out of himself. If anyone can have a laugh, Paul can, but he also loves the gossip just like Louis.

By 1999 the band were starting to individually go their separate ways after several years of living and touring together. We sent Paul to his first MTV awards show in Milan and he came up with what he thought was a great story on Madonna. Louis rang him to say Madonna was pregnant and expecting another child, as Ronan had learned when he spent the whole afternoon out shopping with her, going around children's shops looking for baby clothes.

When Madonna held her press conference in front of the world's media, Paul was straight in congratulating her and asking how long she was pregnant. Madonna looked at him with an ice cold stare and said she hadn't a clue what he was talking about, she wasn't pregnant. Paul told her he knew because she had been out shopping for baby clothes all afternoon with Ronan Keating, and if she wasn't expecting why would she be doing that? But Madonna just cut the feet from under him and asked who Ronan Keating was, she'd never heard of him!

Louis had planted the story to get some publicity for Boyzone and Paul was left looking like a gobshite. When confronted, Louis just laughed it off and promised to make it up to him. I was glad we hadn't run the Madonna story until Paul had put it to her, otherwise we would have looked like right idiots.

We also had a running battle with Louis over Stephen Gately's sexuality. The world and his mother knew Stephen was gay but no one could break it. Paul had been out partying with Boyzone on numerous occasions and he was convinced that Stephen wasn't straight. He'd also seen a number of other gay lads in his company. Louis went to great extremes to ensure that the story didn't get out. Stephen was the main heartthrob in the band and all the girls loved him with his cute baby looks. Ronan and Keith Duffy had married so they needed to keep some of the boys single. Louis believed that any revelations on Stephen's sexuality would be seriously damaging to Boyzone, and very bad for business.

At one stage he rang Paul and told him Stephen was secretly dating Baby Spice Emma Bunton from The Spice Girls. We ran with the story but it later transpired the two were good mates but there was nothing else to it. Paul suspected Stephen was gay but naturally he couldn't prove it. He also didn't want to fall out with Louis because we would lose a lot of stories that were coming out, right in the middle of a cutthroat tabloid war in Ireland.

Eventually an acquaintance of Stephen's went to a rival paper with a kiss and tell. Stephen and Louis were backed into a corner and the only way to take control of the story was for the young star to come clean himself. Paul got the whole story off Stephen and we were soon writing about how he fell for a young Dutch lover. It was a huge relief it was all out in the open and he didn't have to lie or hide who he really was anymore.

The problem was that image is everything with boy bands, especially when you have young girls across Britain and Ireland buying your records. Louis could see the writing was on the wall for Boyzone, and the band had run its course. About a year before they split up he decided to form another band to replace them, one that he predicted would be bigger than Boyzone and Take That.

Louis rang Paul and asked him to come and see a private audition of his new group in Dublin's POD nightclub. He was calling the group IOU but later decided to change their name to Westlife. Paul went to see them and thought they were brilliant. Shane Filan, Kian Egan, Nicky Byrne, Brian McFadden, and Mark Feehily could not only sing but they were also natural entertainers.

Craig and I decided we wanted to be on board with Westlife from day one. We had a magazine on a Friday at that time called the *A-list*, and we decided to make Louis's new band the cover, even though no one had ever heard of them. And Paul also built up a great personal relationship with Shane Filan, a friendship that lasts to this day. Paul found him to be an extremely down to earth lad with no ego, who just loved his music.

In a lot of ways Westlife was to change Louis' life. Within two months they were signed by Simon Cowell of RCA Records, a deal which was the start of Cowell and Louis working together, and later resulted in both of them being judges on the hugely successful *X Factor* television series. The show has made both Cowell and Walsh household names.

A month into their new record contract Westlife had their first number one hit in the UK with *Swear It Again*. The group would later emulate the Beatles and enjoy 14 British number one hits plus six number one albums.

Louis gave us the story that Boyzone were to split up and Ronan Keating, the band's lead singer, was going solo. He would be managing Ronan. Ronan had watched Robbie Williams leave Take That and establish himself as one of the top solo artists in the world, and wanted to do the same. He was also desperate to crack America, something Boyzone had failed to do.

But as Westlife rolled on from one hit to the next, relations between Ronan and Louis became strained. Louis did a radio interview in which he said Ronan could be the new Cliff Richard, and the star got the hump. Ronan summoned Louis to a lunch time meeting where he wanted to straighten things out. Louis had gotten him the song *When You Say Nothing At All,* which went to number one and became the theme song for the smash hit Julia Roberts and Hugh Grant movie, *Notting Hill*. He also had a hit with *Life is a Rollercoaster*.

Ronan asked Louis what his vision was for Ronan's career, as he saw himself more as a rock singer than the Cliff Richard role Louis envisaged. But more importantly, he asked Louis to drop his cut for managing him from 20 to 10 percent. Walsh refused and the pair had a massive bust up, with Louis refusing to manage him any more.

As Paul Martin says when you fall out with Louis you fall out with half of Dublin. Ronan's career nose dived after that and there was a lot of negative publicity about him, although the *Mirror* wasn't involved in any of that. Louis even did an interview in which he remarked: "Ronan wasn't the most talented one in Boyzone – he's not a great singer and he's got no personality."

Ronan hit back and said: "Louis absolutely tried to ruin me, and if he thinks we can ever hug and make up he can forget it. I haven't heard from him in three years and I wouldn't have a problem if I never saw him again. He's not a nice man."

Louis got the hump with Paul when we carried a story of Ronan knocking him. He texted Paul for hours on end telling him what a bastard he was and that he'd never work with him again. Paul tried to ring him but Louis wouldn't take his calls.

I decided enough was enough and I wasn't going to have Louis pissing all over my showbiz man. I also don't take shit from anyone no matter who they are. I eventually got Louis on the phone and let him have it with all guns blazing. I basically told him that if he was having a war with Paul, he'd be having a war with me, and unlike Paul, I was a nasty bastard who would piss all over him from here to kingdom come. I told him all bets were off and he couldn't expect all nicey nicey stories about him or his acts anymore and I wasn't putting up with his nonsense. I went into full rant mode and Louis very quickly took what I was saying on board. I didn't particularly care about Louis or Ronan Keating, but I wasn't having Louis abusing one of my staff.

Within hours Louis was back on the phone and we made the peace. It wasn't in either of our interests to have a falling out. I needed him and he needed me. And to be perfectly honest, there is a lot of bullshit in the murky world of show business, and Louis is truly one of the nice guys in the game. He has also, in fairness, been extremely helpful to many people over the years.

Just ask Johnny Logan and U2. It was Louis who suggested Johnny enter the song *What's Another Year* for the 1980 Eurovision Song Contest, after hearing him sing it, and Johnny went on to win it.

When U2 were starting out and no one had heard of them, they were sitting in Captain America's restaurant in Dublin one night, contemplating who they'd get to manage them. Louis, by pure coincidence, happened to be sitting at the table next to them. The band had been approached by a man named Paul McGuinness, and after an hour long conversation agreed to turn him down. But Louis intervened, introduced himself to Bono and the boys, and said he couldn't help overhearing their conversation. He knew the man concerned, Paul McGuinness, and told them they were making a big mistake. He said McGuinness was a good guy and they should go with him. U2 changed their mind, and the rest, as they say, is history. Paul McGuinness is effectively the fifth member of the group and transformed them into the biggest rock and roll band in the world. Only for McGuinness, they would never have gotten to where they are now, making millions along the way. I'd say Louis' biggest regret is that he didn't sign them up himself, although he was always more into pop than rock.

The first cracks in Westlife came when Brian McFadden married Kerry Katona. We always had a very uneasy relationship with Brian, and he'd get very hot under the collar if there were negative stories about him. He and Paul had a love/hate friendship. One week he'd be texting Paul, the next week he'd be the worst in the world.

The Katona-McFadden wedding was one of the first big Irish showbiz weddings. The couple did a one million pound deal with Richard Desmond's *OK* magazine and the biggest day of their lives, in January 2002, turned into a circus.

When you do a deal like this the magazine calls the shots. The photographs are everything and they go to extraordinary lengths to ensure that nobody else gets a shot of the happy couple – they protect their investment. The venue was Slane Castle, and *OK* brought in bouncers who physically searched guests to ensure that they didn't bring mobile phones or cameras into the church.

As a person, Louis liked Kerry, but he felt that she was a bit of a loose cannon and liable to do anything. He also didn't think that the marriage would last – and he was proved right.

We got a tip off that the ceremony itself would be held in the Church of the Immaculate Conception in the tiny village of Rathfeigh, Co Meath. We got pictures of the chapel and splashed it.

The McFaddens were trying to keep it a secret because they didn't want thousands of fans turning up on the day with cameras. Brian went ballistic and was on the phone to Paul, angrily calling him every name under the sun. I didn't give a damn as all is fair in love and war, and if Brian wasn't playing ball with us, why would we co-operate with him?

He also got very annoyed when Paul got a story that Brian had been cavorting with a stripper on his stag, and Kerry went ballistic. Brian didn't do any harm but Kerry didn't see it that way. The stripper had been especially hired for the stag by Brian's mates. He, in fairness to him, knew nothing about her.

Three years previously, in July 1999, we had another wedding circus when Posh and Becks, alias David and Victoria Beckham, tied the knot in Ireland. The rumours were flying around for months that the couple would hold their big day here. Various venues were mentioned, from Ashford Castle in Co Mayo to Dromoland Castle, Co Clare and the K Club in Kildare.

With only a week to go we got a tip off that Luttrellstown Castle on the outskirts of Dublin, the ancestral home of the Guinness family, was the venue. We ran stories all week about what was happening, who would be there, and we tried to give the readers an inside track on one of the most famous couples in the world.

The security around the Castle was massive. The Beckhams had also done a deal with *OK* magazine. It was going to be nearly impossible to get pictures. My colleague Chris McCashin, now Editor of the *Sunday Mirror* in Ireland, was then working for the *News of the World* in Dublin, and he got a bit smarter than the rest of us.

He knew a guy who was working in Luttrellstown and got him to smuggle a small camera in down his underpants. He managed to get some pictures of inside the marquee where the reception was being held, and took shots of the "his and her thrones" where the Beckhams would sit after they wed. It was like a setting at a royal wedding.

Within minutes of getting the pictures, the contact got cold feet. He decided to put the film down his underpants, but was terrified he'd be caught by security in possession of the camera. He quickly decided to hide the camera up a tree, and it is still there to this day.

On the Friday before the wedding, Chris hired a helicopter, and with photographer Tony Kelly aboard, they got a general view of the whole wedding marquee by air. And as a bonus, just as they were flying overhead, he spotted David and Victoria walking around the grounds of the castle hand in hand, so they swooped down and got a picture of them with a long range camera.

Chris said: "We just got lucky – we were in the right place at the right time. As it turned out we had the only picture of the couple from the whole wedding weekend, and the only inside photographs of the marquee."

The *News of the World* splashed the pictures on the Sunday and *OK* magazine were absolutely furious.

We thought about sending up a chopper but unfortunately we hadn't the money to do it. Some you win, some you lose and sometimes you just have to get on with it.

Most of the Manchester United players who came over for the wedding were knocking around the town with their wives and girlfriends. We did manage to get some pictures of them which spiced things up and softened the blow. The story was a huge seller for us as there was massive public interest in the wedding. We also got the inside story from some of the Castle's staff about what went on behind the scenes at the wedding ceremony, and this helped us no end in putting the coverage together for Monday morning's paper.

The McFaddens' wedding didn't have as many celebrities but all the Westlife boys were there. Some shots were taken outside the church and there was little or nothing they could do about that.

Their marriage lasted just three years in total, and when they split up it came as no surprise. During their last year together there were all sorts of rumours that the marriage was on the rocks. It was Kerry who persuaded Brian to leave Westlife. She felt he didn't have enough control in the band and that he was an extremely good songwriter. She honestly believed he would make a lot more money and be far happier if he went solo.

The couple were living in Malahide in Dublin and they had two young children. She found it very difficult that he was away so much touring, and preferred to have him at home more with her. There was intense speculation about them in the media.

At one stage I was lashed on the Gerry Ryan radio show because snatch pictures of their kids playing on the street had appeared in another newspaper. Punters were ringing in giving out hell about it, and Gerry's production team called me on the off chance that I would go on air and talk about it. I was walking straight into an ambush but said to hell with it.

I took on the complaints one by one. First of all, I felt that what the other paper had done was wrong. However, I pointed out that the McFaddens, unlike many other showbiz couples, had no problem doing photographic deals for large amounts of money with magazines for pictures of them and their children. Neither did they think twice about bringing their children out to public events where they knew they'd be photographed. Others, like Bono and Ali Hewson of U2, for instance, never brought their kids to any public events or manipulated them for commercial reasons.

The arguments on the radio went on for an hour. Gerry Ryan, as usual, was very fair with me and I felt I got my point across clearly. I also pointed out that most people had no problem reading stories about the McFaddens or looking at pictures of them with their children. People couldn't take the high moral ground and have it both ways.

Brian eventually took the plunge and left Westlife. He was extremely unhappy about his role in the band while the rest of the guys were getting fed up with him. It would turn out to be the worst decision Brian made. His solo career never really took off as he struggled to get back in the charts. Meanwhile,

Kerry's profile soared when she won *I'm A Celebrity Get Me Out of Here*, and Brian flew out to see her being crowned queen of the jungle.

But then the marriage broke up and he fell in love with Australian model Delta Goodrem. They met while he was helping the former *Neighbours* star record a single and they are still very happy together.

For some strange reason Kerry always sold papers for us. Every time Paul Martin did a story on her and Brian the sales soared. The public have this amazing infatuation with her, and the trials and tribulations in her life continue to make headlines. I think her bubby personality is a bit like Jade Goody's, who tragically died this year. They both just appeal to people. The public fell in and out of love with Jade and I think it's the same with Kerry. She has a frailty about her that makes people empathise with her. And then, at other times, they think she is a right bitch. Kerry has had her own troubles with her second husband Mark Croft, but their marriage has somehow survived through thick and thin.

Louis Walsh and Ronan Keating have since made up as Boyzone were reunited. These pop rows are a bit like family feuds – eventually everyone sees sense. But more importantly, money talks and bullshit walks. Boyzone, like Take That, are coining it in again while Robbie Williams profile has plummeted.

Sometimes you just get too much of the one thing and boredom sets in. Bands and singers need to give the market and newspapers a rest every few years, as overexposure can be extremely damaging.

The tabloids have a life of their own. Every day brings a new story and a new scandal. We never get bored as there is always someone to write about. While Louis Walsh looks for the next big talent we are looking for the next big exclusive. We just hope that we get it and don't read it elsewhere. Louis says he has the "X factor" and is the world's next big star. Stop the press – time will tell if he is right.

And you never know, the next time I'm in America I might call in to see Barack Obama in the White House. I know me way around there!

Epilogue

During this time I made the transition from reporter to management, taking on the role of Deputy Editor of Ireland. Coming off the road and becoming Deputy Editor was a massive sea-change for me. In a matter of weeks I went from running around the country to being stuck in an office and learning the day to day mechanics of getting a newspaper out on the streets. I had absolutely no experience of production but under Craig MacKenzie I quickly learned the art of headline writing and making snap decisions about what sells and what doesn't sell tabloid newspapers.

I soon learned this is a very simple business where content is king. You can have the greatest design and best copy in the world, but if you don't have the juicy stories and the great pictures you are on the road to nowhere at a hundred miles an hour. One of my great talents was spotting a story a million miles away and it was this gift I brought to the backbench – the command centre of the paper.

If you can write a good intro to a story – the first vital paragraph – you can quickly write a good headline. On our backbench in the Belfast office we had a great laugh every day between myself, Craig, Ken Parker and Geoff Fraser, now Editor of the *News of the World* in Ireland, vying with each other to come up with the best headlines.

I remember when the Irish triple gold medal Olympic swimming champion Michelle de Bruin was banned for refusing to give a drug test sample and we splashed with the headline "Michelle de Ruin". The best headlines come to you immediately and I wrote that one in three seconds as soon as the story broke. On another occasion, Russborough House in Blessington, Co Wicklow where the famous Beit art paintings were stored, was broken into by a gang of thieves and we led with the headline "Raiders of the Lost Art".

We all stuck to one golden rule that if you couldn't write a decent page one headline then the story wasn't a splash. A boring headline meant a boring story and the readers would have absolutely no interest in it.

Every day we would go through thousands of stories and pictures from across the world. I was always looking for the human interest, off beat story and I particularly loved the weird real life tales coming out of America.

* * *

One of the biggest selling stories we ever had was when John F Kennedy Jr died with his wife Carolyn Bessette and her sister Lauren after a tragic plane crash over Martha's vineyard, off the coast of Cape Cod. They were on their way to a family wedding when the small aircraft came down and crashed into the sea after he got disorientated in a heavy haze across the skyline. He was a rookie pilot with just 46 hours flying time under his belt.

I have always had a huge interest in anything to do with the Kennedys simply because they sold papers in Ireland to beat the band. They were the nearest both Ireland and America had to a royal family. I remember grabbing hold of Craig and telling him we had to go with the first seven pages and do a wipeout page one.

People all over Ireland adored John F Kennedy, and to this day my parents' generation always remember where they were when he was assassinated. I still think one of the greatest pictures ever taken is the shot of the young John Jr at three years of age, saluting his dad's coffin as he held his mother Jackie's hand at the President's state funeral. I'm not a softy in any way but the look on his little face would bring a tear to anyone's eye.

John Jr's death was a shocking waste of such a young life. He was good looking, wealthy heir to the Kennedy throne and women around the world loved him. Putting a newspaper story together for a story like that was extremely moving, but we were professional to the last. We got John Jr's life and times; we did a whole piece on the curse of the Kennedys; we told the story of what happened that ill-fated day in every last detail.

Although I wasn't reporting from the front line in the USA, I got some satisfaction from helping to put the tragedy together in a form of words and pictures that would appeal to our readers. We handled it with great care and dignity and tried to ensure we didn't upset anyone.

Our old friend Fr Michael Kennedy from Dungarvan was out there for the wedding and we managed to get hold of him. He gave us a very detailed insight into the whole family's reaction to the terrible accident.

The story ran for the whole week and we stuck with it all the way.

* * *

We have a saying in newspapers that when the journalists start getting bored with a story, that's when the readers start getting really interested. Part of my new duties as a Deputy Editor was driving the content of the paper. This meant I worked very closely with the news desk every day, telling them the stories the Editor and I were interested in and what we wanted. From early morning until late at night I was constantly in contact with the News Editor to see how each story was developing and how we were doing on pictures. I still brought in a lot of stories myself from my own contacts, but equally I had to ensure they didn't waste our limited resources chasing stories we didn't give a damn about.

I also kept a tight reign on the sports department which is just as important as the news desk. Sport in Ireland is one of the biggest sellers, and the country has an amazing appetite for premiership football, racing, Gaelic football and hurling.

When Sir Alex Ferguson and Manchester United won their second European Cup in the summer of 1999 it was massive for us. United were 1-0 down with a few minutes to go against Bayern Munich and came back from the dead with two goals from Teddy Sheringham and Ole Gunnar Solskjaer in injury time. We gave it a massive hit and we sold out for two days in a row.

The secret of newspapers is to give the public what they want and we have always endeavoured to do that. We are all human and some days we get it right and other days we get it wrong. I've learned a lot over my years in journalism but I'm still learning. I love the idea of starting each day at 8am with a blank sheet of paper and then by 11pm you have filled it.

Our job is to inform, enquire, ask the hard questions, comment, but also to entertain. There are many critics out there of tabloid newspapers but I personally feel the good outweighs the bad. There are many stories out there you would never have heard about were it not for my colleagues. Of course we've all made mistakes, but then again, who hasn't?

On many occasions the snobs in the broadsheets, television and radio look down their noses at the tabloids. Quite often they use the old trick of tabloid bashing to get a debate going so they can mention a story they wouldn't dare do themselves. But to be perfectly honest, most of them wouldn't be fit to lace the boots of the majority of the tabloid hacks I know. We are a rare breed ready to take it on the chin and when the going gets tough we have balls of steel. We don't run for cover when the flak is flying – we fight it head on.

In August 2004 I was made Editor in Chief of the *Mirror* in Ireland and got to play with the train set myself. Over the past five years I've had some fantastic fun putting my own stamp on the paper.

But then again, that's another story...